Sexual Violence

Sexual Violence

Policies, Practices, and Challenges in the United States and Canada

edited by
James F. Hodgson
and Debra S. Kelley

LYNNE
RIENNER
PUBLISHERS

BOULDER
LONDON

Published in the United States of America in 2010 by
Lynne Rienner Publishers, Inc.
1800 30th Street, Boulder, Colorado 80301
www.rienner.com

and in the United Kingdom by
Lynne Rienner Publishers, Inc.
3 Henrietta Street, Covent Garden, London WC2E 8LU

ISBN: 978-1-881798-54-5 (pb : alk. paper)

Paperback first published in 2004 by Criminal Justice Press.
Reprinted here from the Criminal Justice Press edition.

Printed and bound in the United States of America

∞ The paper used in this publication meets the requirements
of the American National Standard for Permanence of
Paper for Printed Library Materials Z39.48-1992.

5 4 3 2 1

To my daughter, Emma Kelley Niederbrock
—Debra S. Kelley

To my daughter, Katherine Garnett Hodgson,
for when she smiles, the creator smiles on me.
—James F. Hodgson

Contents

Acknowledgments

We wish to thank all of the contributors who wrote chapters for this book. It was truly a pleasure to work with such a patient and enthusiastic group of scholars.

Special thanks to Tammy Hines, librarian at Longwood College, for her expertise and timely delivery of much needed material.

We thank Praeger for agreeing to publish this text, especially Suzanne I. Staszak-Silva, Frank Saunders, and all other editors who assisted us with this publication.

Finally, we thank our families who supported this project in words and deeds. Debra Kelley thanks her parents, Thomas Kelley and Margaret Thornhill Kelley, her husband, Mark Niederbrock, and her daughter, Emma, to whom this book is dedicated.

1

Sexual Violence: Policies, Practices, and Challenges

James F. Hodgson and Debra S. Kelley

INTRODUCTION

Sexual violence is a significant social and cultural problem within both Canadian and American society. Within the United States in 1999, 89,107 rapes were reported to the police resulting in a rate of 32.7 rapes per 100,000 persons (FBI 2000). Statistics from the National Crime Victimization Survey (NCVS) within the United States reveal that 141,000 completed rapes and 60,000 attempted rapes occurred in 1999 for a total of 201, 000 rape case (BJS 2000). Survey data from the National Violence Against Women Survey (NVAW) supported that 1 in every six women within the United States has experienced either a completed or attempted rape at some point in their lifetime (Tjaden and Thoennes 1998). Based on data from the Canadian Violence Against Women Survey conducted in 1993 by Statistics Canada, 6 percent of women reported experiencing a sexual assault as defined by the criminal code (Johnson 1996; Bonta and Hanson 1994). Findings from the same survey revealed that more than one-third of women reported experiencing a sexual assault at some point during their lifetime. Within both American and Canadian society, rape constitutes an experience that touches the lives of many individuals, both at some point during a lifetime and during any given year.

The prevalence and incidence of sexual violence in the lives of women produces social, physical, and psychological effects that often persist for years after the rape has occurred. The likelihood of violence is greater among younger women than older women as evidenced by the fact that the National Survey of Adolescents found that 13 percent of adolescent women had experienced sexual violence at some point during their lives (Kilpatrick and Saunders 1997). Such experiences often follow individuals for years, and surveys of women in state prison have consistently revealed the high prevalence of prior sexual victimization across all stages of the life cycle. Findings from the National Women's Study (Kilpatrick, Edwards, and Seymour 1992) revealed that almost one-third of rape victims developed posttraumatic stress disorder (PSTD) at some point in their life following a rape, a figure that was six times the likelihood of women who had not been raped developing PSTD. The same study also found that female rape victims were more likely than non-crime victims to experience other psychological difficulties such as depression, substance abuse problems, and suicidal thoughts. The scope of sexual violence as well as the adverse effects of such victimization impact on large sectors of women and persist across time, further impacting the potential for women to pursue the routine activities of life such as work, leisure, and personal safety. Though these findings are recent, the enormous impact of sexual violence on women's lives has been the case historically. Another historical fact that has been well documented is the indifference of the criminal justice system and other institutional entities that were charged with the care of victims.

In 1967, the President's Commission on Law Enforcement and the Administration of Justice issued a report titled *The Challenge of Crime in a Free Society*. This report, considered a "landmark report on American crime and the legal institutions that respond to it" (Fagan 1997, 16) did not include a concern with violence against women, a topic that at the time did not fit within the agenda of identifiable and pressing crime issues. Even eight years after the Commission's report, when the Law Enforcement Assistance Administration (LEAA) released its report, *The Report of the LEAA Task Force on Women*, the limitations of statutory definitions, lack of programs and services, and need for national-level attention to victims of sexual violence continued to dominate the discourse. The early 1970s had been the beginnings of the anti-rape movement, as the first rape crisis centers were established, first in San Francisco and then in Washington, DC. These initiatives occurred in the context of a society and criminal justice system that placed enormous burdens on the victims of sexual violence to prove their worthiness for justice.

Within Canadian and American cultures, sexual violence pervades a "sexual mystique" that is rooted in traditional, historical, cultural, and legislative responses. Within a historical context, a male could not be charged with raping his wife as long as they were legally married. Within the patriarchal apparatus, women usually are relegated as the property of the husband. Traditionally, in order to secure a conviction for the charge of rape, legislation required that survivors of sexual violence must be of previously "chaste" character and much of a victim's testimony had to be corroborated by other independent evidence. These traditional legal responses clearly expressed that women could not be trusted to tell the truth without other evidence to corroborate their complaint. This "sexual mystique" presents a shroud of "rape myths" that are expressed within social, moral, and cultural notions. These rape myths portray that women secretly "like to be raped" and therefore they provoked the act, or that the victim was indirectly "asking for it" by her choice of attire or location, or that "no really means yes."

In the 1975 LEAA report on the status of female victims, a concern was expressed for the blame often attached to the victim with the report's acknowledgment that "the system's response tends to focus less on the injury and sensitive treatment of the victim, and more on evaluating the victim's credibility" (OJP 1998, 44). The traditional perspective, as articulated by the criminal justice systemic response, is that the victim cannot be trusted to tell the truth. There is no other crime, property or personal, in which the authenticity of the victim's complaint is continuously questioned by the criminal justice system. There is no other crime in which the actors within the criminal justice process will spend so much time trying to assess the credibility or the chasteness of the victim.

The criminal justice apparatus often responds to the level of physical injury to the complainant as possible signs of consent, or the lack thereof. The criminal justice system operates within an atmosphere of victim believability in which a complainant of sexual violence who has received significant physical injury is perceived to have not consented to the sexual assault. Other factors that are used within the criminal justice system to assess the believability of complainants of sexual violence include such elements as the complainant's appearance—i.e., dressing in a "provocative" manner; the complainant's age; marital status; occupation; alcohol use; complainant's "mental state" before and after the assault; the complainants' sexual history and practices; the location of the attack; and the length of time it took the complainant to report the assault to authorities (see Figure 1.1). The criminal justice apparatus often use these types of extralegal criteria to assess the believability of complainants of sexual violence. These criteria are utilized within the criminal justice system to assess "founded" and "unfounded" cases of sexual violence. This set of criteria itself presents a model of "women who cannot be raped," in that complainants who do not meet the believability criteria as set out by the criminal justice apparatus often cannot be and often are not classified by the criminal justice system as sexual violence survivors.

The criminal justice system, as an expression and representative of dominant cultural ideologies, is sexist in nature. The dominant cultural expression of white, male, middle-class, Christian, middle-aged, educated, heterosexual, and patriarchal characteristics has traditionally responded to gender crimes with in-

Figure 1.1   Criteria of Victim Believability Utilized within the Criminal Justice System

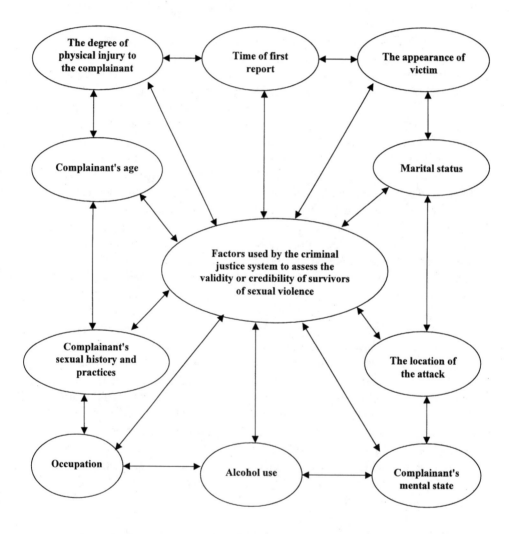

adequate laws, policies, procedures, and emphasis. The dominant cultural representations are projected from a distinctive value and belief system that obviously affects the services rendered by criminal justice agencies. This differential response by elements of the state apparatus to gender crime amounts to systemic discrimination. Typically and traditionally, the state apparatus has not treated gender issues and gender crimes with an equitable and appropriate level of importance, until such time as public or political pressure induce policy and procedural change. Moreover, it is important to recognize that although policies and procedures may have been altered within the institution, many of the prevailing ideologies, norms, values, and beliefs continue to be produced and reproduced by practitioners within the criminal justice system. Often the policies and procedures amount to little more than "impression management," masking the public face of the institution while the internal operations, for the most part, go unchanged and unchallenged. Impression management strategies within the criminal justice agency allow systemic discriminatory policies and practices to be operationalized with much anonymity.

Systemic discrimination occurs when the frequently inherent social, economic, political, or customs of an organization or culture have an impact on a historically disadvantaged group that prohibits or denies full societal participation and consideration. Systemic discrimination results in inequality of condition and opportunity that affects current societal groups and is produced through successive generations. Systemic discrimination is often difficult to detect because of its latent application and practice within our social, economic, and political apparatuses. Often an individual does not even know that he or she has been a victim of systemic discrimination. Systemic discrimination is very difficult to detect until the trained observer steps back to observe the macro picture, which often reveals the social, economic, and political barriers that may be in place to affect the micro social conditions or circumstances.

Systemic discrimination is the differential and unequal treatment of a group, deeply embedded in social, economic, and political institutions. This is discrimination that occurs as a result of the structure and functioning of public institutions and policies. Institutional, systemic discrimination includes the systemic exclusion of people from equal access to and participation in a particular institution because of their race, religion, class, ethnicity, or gender. Systemic exclusion can lead to another type of discrimination, which can be described as the interaction of the various spheres of social life to maintain an overall pattern of oppression.

Sexual violence provides for another unfortunate example of systemic discrimination against women in legal response and practice. A historical legal analysis discloses, for example, as indicated earlier, that a male could not be charged with raping his wife as long as they were legally married; a survivor of sexual violence had to be of previous chaste character in order for a rape charge to be sustained; and a survivor of sexual violence had to present testimony that could be corroborated by other independent evidence. The shroud of sexual mystique that is expressed within a systemic discriminatory context leads to social, moral, and legal notions that women secretly like to be raped and that they often provoke the act, or that a woman was indirectly "asking for it" by her choice of attire or location, or that "no really means yes." These values and beliefs were present in the Canadian and American criminal justice system in the past, and many of these same ideologies continue to be expressed today within some elements of the legal apparatus. These systemic discriminatory expressions can be exposed by the assessment of the types of responses a survivor of sexual violence receives from the legal apparatus, the priority given to crimes of sexual violence, and the allocation of human and technical resources assigned to respond to sexual violence.

The many reforms of sexual violence legislation in Canada and America have indeed developed some significant changes to legislative and legal policies and practices. Numerous commissions and task forces have been specifically charged with investigating the state of violence against women, quite often making the same recommendations as those produced by earlier groups. National-level attention to violence against women has most definitely increased in profile. Initiatives such as that by the National Academy of Sciences panel on the development of a research agenda on violence against women have occurred because of congressionally mandated studies arising from the Violence Against Women Act (VAWA) of 1994. Initially as part of the 1994 Crime Bill and then through its reauthorization in 2000, the VAWA has increased available funding for states to provide victim services and other initiatives aimed at the prevention, intervention, and eradication of violence against women. The level of funding available for research, programs, services, and evaluation represents a significant step forward as does the cooperative relationships between academics and practitioners. Violence against women in all its myriad forms is no longer invisible and of secondary concern to researchers across various disciplines working within the academy or to those practitioners and professionals in diverse fields.

The theme of this book is to provide an opportunity to critically assess and evaluate current criminal justice responses, policies, practices, and challenges as they relate to sexual violence. There have been significant reformations to the criminal justice apparatus response to sexual violence over the last twenty years. This book evaluates and assesses these changes in the criminal justice response to survivors of sexual violence, in order to provide an assessment of these reforms. Specifically, this book provides an inventory of changes in criminal justice practice and policy, current systemic criminal justice responses to sexual violence, specialized programs and agencies that address the needs of survivors of sexual violence, and arguments for enhanced developments and reformations of the criminal justice system in Canada and the United States. The subject areas that are explored in this effort are placed into the following categories: past practices and policies of the criminal justice response to sexual violence; current criminal justice responses to sexual violence; assessment and analysis of the criminal justice response to the sexual violence reform agenda; evaluation and analysis of victim advocacy programs and initiatives; and future reformations and developments of the criminal justice system to adequately respond to the crime of sexual violence in our communities. This reader includes original contributions from authors that address particular issues of relevance to the study of sexual violence in the United States and Canada. These fourteen chapters are original writings that address current and contemporary themes and issues of relevance to sexual violence, policies, practices, and challenges.

Following this introductory chapter, which has described the social, legal, and political context of sexual violence, the contributions to this volume are offered in the forthcoming thirteen chapters. Chapters 2 through 5 offer an examination of several issues within the context of recent theoretical and methodological debates. In chapter 2, "The Measurement of Rape," Debra S. Kelley details the evolution of efforts by survey researchers to better measure and assess the prevalence and incidence of rape. By focusing on the recent National Violence Against Women Survey and the more well-established National Crime Victimization Survey, Kelley explains the procedures used to measure rape and the rationales behind the decisions of researchers who use survey research to provide prevalence and incidence estimates of rape in the general population. An understanding of the methods behind rape measurements is crucial if a reasonable discourse is going to continue among academics, practitioners, and the general public concerning the extent of rape in society.

Similarly to the debates over the extent of rape in our society, debates have surrounded theoretical attempts to explain the causal factors that contribute to rape at the individual and societal level. One theoretical perspective on rape that has been the subject of much controversy is the evolutionary perspective on rape. In chapter 3, "Biology, Sex, and the Debate Over 'Chemical Castration,'" Craig T. Palmer, Randy Thornhill, and David N. DiBari begin by describing how many of the current arguments used in the debate over the value of castration in the treatment and punishment of sex offenders are based on the assertion that such a procedure will not be effective because (1) it is a biological procedure, and sex offenses are caused by *nonbiological* social, cultural, and psychological factors, and (2) it reduces sexual motivation, and sex offenses are not sexually motivated. This chapter demonstrates that both of these arguments are based on unsupported assertions and fundamental misunderstandings. This chapter asserts that both of these arguments should be expunged from the debate over antiandrogens in order that the debate be decided on more legitimate legal, ethical, and empirical issues.

The next two chapters explore areas that have either been ignored or under-developed. In chapter 4, "A Critical Critique of the Cultures of Control: A Case Study of Cyber Rape," Livy A. Visano examines the Internet as a site for new forms of rape. As the Internet becomes more and more at the center of our so-cial, cultural, and work lives, its influence on promoting violence against women must be examined. The aim of this chapter is to explore the relation-ships between law and cyber rape within wider cultural contexts of coercion. This chapter examines forms of "virtual" violence against women as a social harm that impacts on the identities and everyday life experiences of all women. Moreover, it is argued that any discussion of the regulation of rape pornography on the Internet must be contextualized within relations of domination that have been developed and fine-tuned by legal, economic forces and cultural forces. A case study of "cyber rape" demonstrates how the commonsense, naturalized, or taken-for-granted nature of misogyny is ultimately related to the contradictions in liberal democratic thought and invites Internet consumers to be aware of the online constructions of gendered identities. Specifically, this chapter highlights the limitations of law in dealing with the fundamental social problem of vio-lence against women.

In chapter 5, "Sexual Assault behind Bars: The Forgotten Victims," Charles Crawford asserts that incarcerated offenders in male correctional institutions constitute the "forgotten victims" of rape. Despite the documentation of rape within male prisons, our society continues to devalue the victimization of these individuals and to approach them as less than credible victims of rape.

Beginning with chapter 6, several chapters explore both the extent to which the legal landscape has changed in response to the demands of activists on the behalf of rape victims and the extent to which this change has produced perhaps only surface differences for victims. Chapter 6, "Rape Law Reform," by Fran-ces P. Bernat, analyzes rape reform laws from a historical and a contemporary perspective. This chapter includes an analysis of the common law, case and statutory law development on rape and sexual assault, changes in evidentiary standards and rape shield statutes, and other legal changes pertaining to rape and sexual assault laws (e.g., victim rights and their impact on rape cases). This chapter also discusses the latest U.S. Supreme Court ruling that curtails the rights of rape victims to seek federal redress under the federal Violence Against Women Act.

Continuing this line of inquiry, Margaret Denike in chapter 7, "Myths of Woman and the Rights of Man: The Politics of Credibility in Canadian Rape Law," presents the history of legal reform in Canada. Examining Canadian criminal sexual assault proceedings, this chapter traces the inscription of such ambivalence in and through the development of criminal jurisprudence and legislative reforms to sexual assault law. The dance of the legislature and the courts, which relies heavily on a sexual politics of truth, has performatively constituted and institutionalized the highly peculiar constructions of the "victims" and "pretenders" to this violation. The *de facto* assumptions about women's lack of credibility and insatiable sexuality are pervasive enough to entail that criminal proceedings for rape have historically and consistently displaced the threat that sexual violence poses to its victims and have attended primarily to the threat that presumed deceivers pose to the rights of the accused. The saga of sexual assault and its reforms tells of a struggle between the courts and the legislature to reconcile myths of woman with the rights of man.

Chapter 8, "Psychological Evidence in Sexual Assault Court Cases: The Use of Expert Testimony and Third-Party Records by Trial Court Judges," as offered by Giannetta Del Bove and Lana Stermac, asserts that the recent use of both expert testimony evidence and complainant's personal records in sexual assault trials has increased. The chapter argues that this practice must be examined in terms of recent Canadian rape shield reforms, and pervasive cultural myths regarding women and rape that have affected the judiciary's treatment of sexual assault complainants. Despite recognition in the literature that psychological evidence can have both positive and negative consequences for victims and the outcomes of a sexual assault trial, there is no research on the actual practice and effects of introducing this type of information. This chapter explores what kind of psychological information is being introduced in trials, why it is deemed relevant, and how judges are using the evidence. Fourteen Ontario Provincial Court cases heard during the period June 1997 to December 1999 are examined in this chapter. Judges' decisions are analyzed using the qualitative research paradigm of Glaser and Strauss's (1967) "constant comparison method." This chapter highlights that four major themes emerge from the data—specifically, ease of access to complainants' personal records, frequency of use in criminal trials, the use of expert testimony to discredit victims, and recognition of the evidentiary and equality rights of complainants. The results, within this chapter, are discussed within a social justice and feminist perspective, with a particular emphasis on issues of role socialization.

Chapter 9, "Reconceptualizing Sexual Assault from an Intractable Social Problem to a Manageable Process of Social Change," by K. Edward Renner, argues that over the past three decades there has been a gradual evolution in how adult sexual assault and child sexual abuse have been defined by the law, and how they are seen professionally and by the general public. As a result of these changes in awareness there is now a growing consensus that male sexual violence is a social problem of considerable magnitude. Despite this awareness, Renner argues, effective reform and social change have been hard to accomplish. Renner asserts that under the impact of the new legislation, more women started to report sexual assaults, but the response of the criminal justice system

remained virtually unchanged: a large proportion of the cases were still classified as unfounded by the police, were not charged by the prosecution, and were
not convicted by the courts. Clearly, the old problems remained despite the new
legislation. Over the intervening years several "rape shield" laws were passed
making it more difficult for the defense to raise questions about a victim's past
sexual history or gain access to her counseling records. These reforms were all
challenged and their applications limited by the Supreme Court.

In addition to changes in the legislative response to the crime of rape and the
plight of rape victims, agents of the criminal justice system have instituted policies and practices that have changed the response. In chapter 10, "Law Enforcement's Response to Sexual Assault: A Comparative Study of Nine Counties in
North Carolina," Vivian B. Lord and Gary Rassel note that after the major reforms of sexual assault laws between 1960 and 1975, a number of studies examined the changes in sexual assault reports to the police and the prosecution of
these cases; however, little research has studied changes in law enforcement investigative procedures of sexual assault cases. This chapter examines the process used in the investigation of sexual assault cases by police and sheriff
departments in nine counties of North Carolina. The procedures of these departments were compared with a set of practices identified as effective in earlier
assessments. These practices, or reforms, include specialized sexual assault investigative units, in-house victim/witness advocates, acceptance of anonymous
reports from victims who did not wish to prosecute, written procedures, multiple interviews, confidentiality of the victim from the media, specialized training for investigators as well as patrol officers, and specific criteria for the
selection of investigators. The law enforcement departments examined in this
chapter vary in their implementation of the reforms advocated in other assessments. This chapter finds that the relationships between specific characteristics
of the departments and the community and the variation in implementation
were not significant; however, the departments' association with the rape crisis
centers in their communities was significantly related to the existence of written procedures, a specialized unit, and the use of blind reports. This chapter
concludes that police sexual assault investigations to some degree continued to
focus on the issue of consent and the victims' behavior, but there did appear to
be an increase in officers' sensitivity to victims' needs.

In chapter 11, "Policing Sexual Violence: A Case Study of *Jane Doe v. the
Metropolitan Toronto Police*," James F. Hodgson offers a case study approach
of police response to rape in Canada by focusing on a case in which a survivor
of sexual violence successfully sued the Metropolitan Toronto Police in the
civil courts on the grounds that the police agency engaged in systemic discriminatory policies and practices when investigating sexual violence. This chapter
provides for an opportunity to assess systemic discriminatory process and practice as they are operationalized within the framework of police response to sex-

ual violence. Hodgson argues that the values and beliefs of the sexual mystique that historically have been fostered within the Canadian and American legal systems are the same ideologies that continue to be expressed today within some elements of the legal apparatus. Although much of the Canadian and American sexual violence legislation has undergone significant reform, many of the norms, values, and beliefs of the sexual mystique continue to be practiced and expressed in the application of the new legislation. The criminal justice apparatus is riddled with the pretense of assessing the believability of survivors of sexual violence. Again the traditional perspective as articulated by the criminal justice systemic response is that the victim cannot be trusted to tell the truth. A case study approach is utilized within this chapter to demonstrate practical applications of police sexual violence investigative strategies in which a systemic discriminatory response is most evident.

Chapter 12, "Assessing the Role of Sexual Assault Programs in Communities," by Elizabethann O'Sullivan, argues that sexual assault programs do more than counsel victims of rape. They document sexual violence in their community, keep it on the public agenda, and work toward lasting social change. Focusing exclusively on a program's client services may give an inaccurate picture of its effectiveness. More than one agency may provide crisis counseling, victim advocacy, in-service training, or community education; furthermore, many victims never report an assault or contact a rape crisis center. Drawing on a study of sixteen North Carolina sexual assault programs, this chapter presents a strategy to establish a program's role in its community. It details how a program can use information on its (1) definitions of sexual assault, (2) client mix (client demographics and type of incident), (3) interagency relations, and (4) community education to monitor, improve, and evaluate its impact on its community. The same information can be gathered from other community agencies to identify gaps and overlaps in community services.

The final two chapters address the implications of sex offender legislation. Chapter 13, "Megan's Law in California: The CD-ROM and the Changing Nature of Crime Control," by Suzette Cote examines the implementation of Megan's Law in California. Similar to other sex offender legislation introduced at both the state and federal level in the 1990s, Megan's Law focused attention on not what offenders had done but what they might do in the future based on past patterns of behavior. Consequently, this focus represented a shift in criminal justice policy, and Cote uses the specific site of Megan's Law to examine the nature of this philosophical and pragmatic shift within the criminal justice system. Through an examination of the implementation of Megan's Law in California, Cote pursues two goals: (1) a description of the general shift in crime control policies from open to hidden forms of social control; (2) a discussion of California's Megan's Law, specifically the history of sex offender registration and notification in California and the development, nature, and use of the

CD-ROM and 900 line as tools for dissemination. Essentially, California's law provides an effective example of an important legislative transformation toward the increased use of technology within and by members of communities in the effort to combat increased levels of risk among dangerous offenders.

In chapter 14, "Revisiting Megan's Law and Sex Offender Registration: Prevention or Problem," Robert E. Freeman-Longo argues that both convicted sex offenders and innocent citizens have experienced serious and negative consequences resulting from the implementation of the Jacob Wetterling Crimes Against Children and Sexually Violent Offender Registration Act, passed in 1994, which included national sex offender registration laws, and Megan's Law, passed in 1996, requiring public notification of sex offender release. This chapter revisits predictions made by the author in 1996 regarding these laws and the negative impact documented since their implementation.

Across the articles in this text, the goal is to generate a responsible discourse on sexual violence in our communities that will benefit the student, the practitioner, the academic, and the victim. The authors for this text are drawn from the disciplines of sociology, psychology, the law, activism, biology, anthropology, and what else here. In addition to the diversity of the authors' perspectives, the various areas and topics covered in this text reflect the editors' concern with examining the systemic responses of the criminal justice system to the pervasive issue of sexual violence in Canadian and American society.

REFERENCES

Bonta, James, and R. Karl Hanson. 1994. *Gauging the Risk for Violence: Measurement, Impact, and Strategies for Change*, available at *http://www.sgc.gc.ca/epub/corr/e199409/e199409.htm*.

Bureau of Justice Statistics. 2000. *Criminal Victimization, 1999*. Washington, DC: U.S. Department of Justice, Bureau of Justice Statistics.

Fagan, Jeffrey. 1997. "Continuity and Change in American Crime: Lessons from Three Decades," *The Challenge of Crime in a Free Society: Looking Back, Looking Forward*. Symposium on the 30th Anniversary of the President's Commission on Law Enforcement and Administration of Justice. June 19–21, 1997, Washington, DC. Washington, DC: U.S. Department of Justice, Office of Justice Programs.

Federal Bureau of Investigation. 2000. *Crime in the United States, 1999*. Washington, DC: U.S. Government Printing Office.

Johnson, Holly. 1996. *Dangerous Domains: Violence against Women in Canada*. Toronto: Nelson Canada.

Kilpatrick, Dean G., and B.E. Saunders. 1997. *Prevalence and Consequences of Child Victimization*. Washington, DC: National Institute of Justice, U.S. Department of Justice.

Kilpatrick, Dean G., C. Edmunds, and A. Seymour. 1992. *Rape in America: A Report to the Nation*. Arlington, VA: National Center for Victims of Crime;

Charleston, SC: Medical University of South Carolina, Crime Victims Research and Treatment Center.

Office of Justice Programs. 1998. *Women in Criminal Justice: A Twenty Year Update.* Washington, DC: Office of Justice Programs, U.S. Department of Justice.

Tjaden, Patricia, and Nancy Thoennes. 1998. *Prevalence, Incidence, and Consequences of Violence against Women: Findings from the National Violence against Women Survey.* Washington, DC: National Institute of Justice and U.S. Department of Health and Human Services, Centers for Disease Control and Prevention.

2

The Measurement of Rape

Debra S. Kelley

INTRODUCTION

In any given year, criminal victimization is a rare event. Based on victim reports for 1998, approximately 8.1 million violent crimes occurred or about thirty-seven violent victimizations per 1,000 persons age twelve or older. Rape victimizations of women have a lower incidence rate with not quite two attempted or completed rape incidents for every 1,000 persons age 12 or older reported, amounting to approximately 183,440 rape incidents (BJS 2000). Statements such as these and the statistics behind them have been controversial with much of the dissension centering on how the estimates are obtained. Though violence is a salient feature in the lives of women, this does not mean that all violence takes the form of rape or that violence is a simple phenomenon for researchers to capture. Research efforts focused on the extent of rape in our society are approached by a diverse group of researchers in terms of ideological commitment and uses for their research. In the final analysis, what constitutes a valid measure of rape will never satisfy all constituencies and will not be useful for all purposes. Understanding the methods behind the estimates is crucial because "the true prevalence of violence against women may be less important for policy and other decision makers than understanding the methodological differences that resulted in various estimates" (Crowell and Burgess 1996, 39).

This chapter details the survey procedures used to generate estimates of rape by comparing and contrasting the National Crime Victimization Survey (NCVS) and the National Violence Against Women Survey (NVAW). Variation in methodological features of the two surveys—including sampling procedures, survey context, respondent disclosure and recall, and measurement strategies—represent some of the key issues that have characterized the controversy over the methods used to generate incidence and prevalence statistics on rape. Recent research by Fisher and Cullen (2000) purposefully evaluating the accuracy of estimates using NVAW and NCVS strategies are discussed. Despite differences in research design between the surveys, they are both prime examples of how victimization surveys have become central to the estimation of rape.

THE CENTRALITY OF VICTIMIZATION SURVEYS

Research on victimization is best advanced if victimization surveys are placed in their proper context; what type of information on what groups is the method capable of obtaining? Victimization is an area that represents a complex array of concerns, and the necessary information to address these are not solely provided by victimization surveys; some are best addressed by official crime data, and others best addressed by data on clinical populations. Beginning in the 1970s, criminal justice researchers began to increasingly rely on victims rather than criminal justice agents as a source of information on crime. Many crimes occur in a context that inhibit reporting to the police; crimes involving victims and offenders that are known to each other, crimes in which victims perceive criminal justice agencies to be unsympathetic; crimes in which victims feel that reporting would retraumatize them, crimes in which victims feel that nothing will be gained by reporting. The contextual experience of victims interacts here with the perception of what police reporting will mean.

The crime of rape is a prime example of how certain types of experiences may not be well represented within the scope of official statistics. Victimization surveys emerged to further societal understanding of crime by addressing many of the deficits in Uniform Crime Reports (UCR) data[1] and providing more detail on the specific contexts of criminal events. The power of victimization surveys as a preferred strategy for studying crime victims is evidenced by the institutionalization of the NCVS as a federally sanctioned source of crime data and increased number of researchers who use self-report techniques for surveying individuals for a broad range of purposes.

THE NATIONAL CRIME VICTIMIZATION SURVEY (NCVS)

As a survey of crime victims, the National Crime Victimization Survey (NCVS) is a national probability survey of households conducted by the Bureau of Justice Statistics (BJS). Annually, approximately 42,895 persons in 77,759 households are interviewed every six months over a three-year period (Rennison, 2000). The first and fifth interviews are conducted in-person, and the others are conducted over the telephone. The use of Computer Assisted Telephone Interviewing (CATI) is becoming more a part of the research design (Perkins et al. 1996). Based on 1999 data, the NCVS "response rate is 93% of eligible households and 89% of eligible individuals" (Rennison 2000, 14), a remarkably high response rate for national-level data and one that has been consistently achieved. The NVCS collects information on the personal violent crimes of robbery, rape, and assault, including sexual assault. The property crimes covered in the survey include burglary, larceny, and theft, including motor vehicle theft. Individuals in sample households are asked through a questionnaire to self-report their victimization experiences.

Collection of this data began in 1972 as a means to provide a data source on crime that could serve as an alternative to the Uniform Crime Reports (UCR). Beginning in 1979, the NCVS[2] went through a redesign effort with one of the goals being to develop better measures of rape. The redesigned questionnaire was phased into the NCVS sample in 1992, and data from 1992–93 was first released in 1995 (Bachman and Saltzman 1995). Data from the redesigned survey did in fact produce higher estimates of several crimes, including rape. The number of reported rapes increased by 250 percent, an increase that exceeded those found for other crimes and one substantial enough to shed serious doubt on the accuracy of victimization statistics prior to the redesign (Lynch 1996b).

The National Crime Victimization Survey was not developed or designed to primarily focus on one particular type of crime. Because it emerged as an alternative data source to official statistics, many of the design decisions that were made regarding the NCVS have been based on research conducted on various forms of crime, very little of which until recently was research including sexual assault. The NVAW, in contrast, was a special focus survey, designed in large part to focus on violence against women.

THE NATIONAL VIOLENCE AGAINST WOMEN SURVEY (NVAW)

The National Violence Against Women (NVAW) survey was a one-time telephone survey on personal safety with two national probability samples, one of 8,005 men and the other of 8,000 women, both English- and Spanish-speaking. Funded by grants from two federal agencies, the U.S. Department of Justice and the U.S. Department of Health and Human Services' National Center for Injury Prevention and Control (NCIPC), cross-sectional self-report data was collected between November 1995 and May 1996. The NVAW included information on the extent and nature of violence against women and the effect of such experiences on individuals' lives. Violence was assessed broadly by asking respondents to self-report experiences ranging from emotional abuse to rape. The context in which victimization took place was evaluated by gathering detailed information on factors such as the victim and offender relationship, injury involved, and the location of victimization.

All interviews were conducted using a computer-assisted telephone interviewing (CATI) system, and the survey response rate was 72 percent, "excellent for a telephone interview that averaged 25 minutes and dealt with subjects that were sensitive and potentially upsetting to the respondent" (Tjaden and Boyle 1998, 54). One of the main goals of the NVAW was "to provide reliable estimates of the prevalence and incidence of many forms of violence against women, including rape" (Tjaden and Boyle 1998, 3). According to estimates from the NVAW, 17.6 percent of women self-reported either a completed or attempted rape at some point during their lifetime. The prevalence rate for the past year was 0.3 percent for attempted and completed rapes combined, which translates to slightly over 300,000 rape victims and 876,064 rape incidents annually in the population (Tjaden and Thoennes 1998). The NCVS and NVAW produce different estimates of rape, with the NVAW producing higher estimates. The extent to which these estimates result from survey design procedures is addressed in the sections that follow.

SAMPLING PROCEDURE

The use of large probability samples in survey research allows the researcher to develop estimates of social phenomena that are generalizable to those not directly surveyed. Thus, prevalence and incidence measures that are produced from the results of survey research are more useful for policy development than those produced with smaller, nonprobability samples.

While the NCVS and the NVAW are both nationally based probability samples, they differ in the response rate, target population, sample size, and sampling frame. These features are interrelated; for example, the higher participation rate of the NCVS (96 percent) compared to the NVAW (72 percent) means that the former is better able to generalize findings based on the sample back to the population of interest, the target population. The target population for the NCVS is all persons age twelve and over, whereas the target population for the NVAW is persons age eighteen and over. Because victimization risk varies by age, the difference in target populations will affect survey estimates. Furthermore, in a comparison of the NCVS with another survey, Lynch (1996b) has contended that even though research using official statistics has supported that rape rates are lower for those over the age of eighteen, this difference may be due to variations in reporting by age. Thus, if actual victimization follows reporting patterns, it would be expected that the NVAW would produce lower rape estimates than the NCVS.

The NCVS and NVAW use different sampling frames, which refers to the manner in which members of the target population are first specified for sampling purposes. The NCVS uses census addresses as the sampling frame and the NVAW uses telephone numbers (Perkins et al. 1996; Tjaden and Boyle 1998). Such a difference has been interpreted by Lynch (1996b) as having the potential effect of increasing victimization reports in the NCVS design because of the ability to reach groups who are known to have higher victimization rates, those without telephones.

The NCVS has a much larger sample size than the NVAW. Sample size is extremely important in surveys that attempt to capture rare phenomena, such as being the victim of a crime. In any given year, there may not be enough cases of a rare event to allow for statistical analysis, and hence the sample size must be large enough to capture enough cases for these purposes. The NCVS reports 183,440 as the number of rape incidents for 1999 (BJS 2000a), but this is an estimate based on the sample data; an estimate is not the number of incidents available for analysis. Surveys such as the NVAW, which have a much smaller sample size than the NCVS, are not capable of generating enough cases to allow for detailed data analysis.[3]

Sample size is also important in terms of sampling error. In probability sampling, the size of the sample will have a significant effect on how much sampling error exists because samples of larger size will have smaller standard errors, a factor that will affect the accuracy of estimates generated from the sample data. Given the much larger sample size of the NCVS compared to the NVAW, the NCVS will have a lower standard error. Therefore, even though larger estimates of the annual prevalence of rape were generated from NVAW data, if the size of the standard errors are taken into account, it is quite likely that a ninety-five confidence interval based on NCVS and NVAW data would overlap to some degree. In other words, once sampling error is taken into account, the estimates based on NCVS data and NVAW may in fact be within the same range.

SURVEY CONTEXT

The context of a survey refers to the way in which the survey is introduced to respondents. Survey context is more than just a reflection of the question content on the survey, it sets the domain of the survey and answers an initial question that may be in the mind of many respondents: "What is this survey about?" Because it sets the stage for how the respondent will think about the information being solicited, the context of the survey may reduce the willingness of respondent participation, either because it sounds to be unrelated to their lives, of no interest to them personally, or for other reasons. The NCVS is introduced to survey respondents as a survey of crime victims, whereas the NVAW was a survey on personal safety.

NCVS has been routinely criticized as providing a context in which disclosure of sensitive material is problematic, especially pertaining to rape and domestic violence (see Koss 1992, 1996 and Russell and Bolen 2000 for criticisms). Several researchers closely affiliated with the NCVS design have echoed the sentiments expressed by Lynch (1996a, 129) in stating that the context of NCVS as a crime survey may inhibit reporting of "grey area events where the circumstances do not conform to our stereotypic notions of crime." Though introducing respondents to the survey as one interested in criminal victimization, the NCVS does not ask about such experience by using crime categories. "Questions in the NCVS are not crime specific; rather they are behavior-specific" (Bachman and Taylor 1994, 510). The specific effect that survey context has on reporting has not been empirically addressed, at least not directly (Lynch 1996a). Given the high participation rate of NCVS, it is reasonable to conclude that the context of the survey does not initially impede respondent participation. But does the content of the survey as it unfolds elicit the information it is designed to elicit?

DISCLOSURE

The social world does not exist in a manner that makes it easily quantifiable, just as research subjects do not exist as passive actors ready and willing to disclose all to the researcher. Part of what the researcher must encounter in developing measures is how to get the respondent to disclose the information. This is especially challenging in research on sensitive topics where there exists a host of reasons why individuals might not want to disclose experiences. In fact, when the NCVS was first developed, "it was deemed inappropriate for a government-sponsored survey to ask respondents directly about rape" (Perkins et al. 1996, 150). Turner (1981, 22) contends that had NCVS initially developed questions directly asking about rape, "an inquiry phrased in such indelicate terms would likely promote public charges of the unbridled insensitivity of government snoopers as well as congressional outrage." More recently, the NCVS acknowledges that "public attitudes toward victims have changed, permitting more direct questioning about sexual assaults" (Perkins et al. 1996, 3). Widespread consensus on the appropriateness of such questioning is crucial for a study with the broad scope of the NCVS. The NCVS must consider not only how respondents are going to respond to certain types of questioning but also how that could possibly impact on respondent disclosure throughout the rest of the survey including willingness to finish the survey.

The entire content of the NVAW reflected sensitive material that placed a heavy burden on respondent disclosure and could also potentially have yielded a much lower participation rate by this very fact. The possibility that the survey content could retraumatize victims was taken very seriously in the research design, and numerous protocols were instituted to minimize this possibility. For example, female interviewers conducted all interviews with female respondents, extensive pretests were conducted with residents of a battered women's shelter, and interviewers were provided with resource material to utilize in cases of respondent's disclosure of violence (Tjaden and Boyle 1998).

INTERVIEWER TRAINING

For both the NCVS and NVAW, interviewers were trained extensively and protocols are in place to allow respondents to interrupt the interview and finish it at a later time (Perkins et al. 1996; Tjaden and Boyle 1998). The training of interviewers strengthens respondent disclosure. Allowing respondents to break off an interview also increases respondent disclosure because the respondent can reschedule to finish the interview at a more convenient time rather than stopping the interview completely. In surveys involving sensitive material, the option of rescheduling interviews is crucial because given the fact that the many interpersonal crimes of violence involve victims and offenders with some familiarity, the offender could actually be living in the household with the victim. Koss (1992, 73) contends that the protocols used in NCVS "continue to be conducted under suboptimal levels of rapport and confidentiality." Survey methodology certainly is not characterized by the same opportunity to develop rapport between the researcher and the subject as other methods. Though criticisms of either survey in terms of deficits in interviewer training are unfounded based on the documentation of procedures used and upon consideration of survey methodology, the degree of privacy afforded respondents could be improved. In the future, the NCVS will utilize emerging technology allowing respondents to self-administer the questionnaire on a computer. Experimental use of computer based self-completion components in the British Crime Survey revealed that women reported a higher number of sexual assault–type incidents than was the case with the use of the conventional administration of the questionnaire (Percy and Mayhew 1997). Percy and Mayhew (147) contend that this discrepancy is best explained by the fact that "the computer provided an anonymous mode which encouraged more open answers." Such techniques are a promising avenue for the future administration of surveys on sensitive topics in which disclosure is problematic (Tourangeau and Smith 1996).

RESPONDENT RECALL

Self-report measures ask individuals to recall their past, and respondent recall is not automatically accurate or reliable. Lynch (1996b, 413) states that "common wisdom in retrospective surveys is that respondents fail to report some eligible events and that designs that result in more mentions of these events are better." In even the most basic question asked, a survey "respondent has to do four things: interpret the question, recall relevant information, decide on an answer, and report the answer to the interviewer" (Czaja and Blair 1996, 52). Operationalizing a concept such as rape also means giving attention to how to best elicit respondent recall that is accurate and detailed because "the mere fact that a respondent answers a question provides no assurance that the answer is accurate" (Tourangeau and Smith 1996, 277). Measures must take into account the need to get respondents to think back and clearly remember particular pieces of information and specific experiences that are no longer in their historical context.

Even though there is no measurement procedure with enough precision to elicit full disclosure and prefect recall, there are techniques that are better than others for this purpose. A standard survey technique is to place a temporal reference period on questions that ask respondents to recall information from their past. This technique was used in both the NCVS and the NVAW, except the reference period in the former was the previous six months and in the latter the previous twelve months.

In the NCVS, the respondent is asked if the particular victimization at hand occurred within the last six months. Initial decisions regarding the use of appropriate reference periods and other techniques to better enable respondent recall were based on studies that revealed that victims of crime had a difficult time clearly recalling experiences from their past. Two key issues here are "memory decay" and "forward telescoping" (Lynch 1996b; Biderman and Lynch 1991; Dodge 1985).

Memory decay refers to the tendency for specific information regarding the victimization to erode over time; this may even result in the incident itself being forgotten. Critics of the application of this to violence against women have contended that it is inappropriate to conclude that women would forget being the victim of rape. This criticism fails to consider two key points: Research findings of poor respondent recall were not primarily based on the experiences of sexual assault victims, and research investigations of respondent recall made clear that it was not simply a case of individuals forgetting that they had been victimized but a more complex issue. Citing findings from the pilot studies of the NCVS, Cantor and Lynch (2000, 102) state that research that revealed the poor recall of respondents regarding criminal events did not conclude "they were unimportant events for the victims."

Forward telescoping is when survey respondents report an incident to "have taken place more recently than they actually occurred" (DOJ 1989, 3). In order to address this, bounding is used for interviews. In cross-sectional data such as the NVAW, bounding is not an option because only one interview is conducted with each respondent.

BOUNDING INTERVIEWS AND SHORT CUES

The NCVS attempts to stimulate respondent recall by bounding interviews and by providing short cues in the screen questions. If an interview is bounded it means that information from the first interview is used to establish a base line that allows the interviewer to guide and check the accuracy of further recall by the respondent. Bounding techniques are used because research on a variety of crime victims supported that they increase the accuracy of respondent recall (Biderman and Lynch 1991). Because information self-reported in the first interview is used for bounding purposes only, if a person reports an experience of rape in the first NCVS interview, that information is not used in the calculation of rape estimates for that year.[4] Unbounded data such as that used in the NVAW will produce higher estimates when compared to a survey using bounded data.

Though certain researchers (Koss 1992) have interpreted bounding techniques as excluding relevant rape experiences and thereby underestimating the extent of rape, this is neither the intent nor the interpretation used by NCVS. Bounding is a data control issue; NCVS uses bounding techniques as a strategy to facilitate accuracy of respondent recall and hence the accuracy of data used to generate rape estimates, especially because the NCVS focuses on generating incidence rather than prevalence rates (Taylor 1989).

Short cues are a type of probe, used as part of screening questions and designed to stimulate recall and "to provide respondents sufficient time to recall victimization and help in structuring the recall task" (BJS 1994, 4). Cues in the NCVS are intended to "stimulate the respondent into thinking about concrete life situations rather than abstractly about 'crime' " (Biderman 1980, 30). Through question wording, respondents are cued to think of experiences in everyday locales such as "at work" and with others known to them as being within the context of the survey. Just as important as the content of the cues used is the density level of cues used. Just as abstract concepts are best measured by more than one question, the greater number of cues function to stimulate respondent recall in a way that a smaller number scattered throughout the survey will not do (Lynch 1996a; Fisher and Cullen 2000).

SCREENING QUESTIONS AND COUNTING RULES

Both the NCVS and NVAW use multiple items to get respondents to disclose and recall rape. The two surveys use different strategies for both measuring rape and counting rape victimizations. The NVAW obtained lifetime and annual prevalence measures, and the NCVS focuses on incidence measures.

PREVALENCE AND INCIDENCE FIGURES

What appears on the surface to be a simple task—how to count experiences of rape—is far from that. The counting of victims and experiences is not even

the same thing. Rape estimates are phrased in terms of prevalence and incidence figures. The prevalence of rape refers to the number of persons who have
experienced a rape in a specified time frame, such as the past year. Incidence
rates of rape refer to the number of rape incidents that occur in a specified period of time relative to some population base, such as all persons of a particular
age (Sparks 1980; Lynch 1996a). Specifically in the NCVS, the incidence rate
of rape is the "ratio of the number of rape events reported in the survey to the
number of persons interviewed" (Lynch 1996b, 411). Prevalence and incidence rates for the same time period will be the same if each individual who experiences a rape experiences only one rape. However, the number of incidents
will always be greater than the number of persons who have experienced these
incidents because some individuals will have been raped more than once. This
difference need not be tremendous as illustrated in data from the NCVS where
the ratio of victimizations to incidents is 1.03 for rape, meaning that for every
one incident there are 1.03 victimizations (Perkins et al. 1996).

Whereas the NCVS is a survey of crime victims and the NVAW is phrased as a
survey of personal safety, both attempt to measure rape by standards corresponding
to legal definition without using questions that are heavily laden with legal terminology. However, the NCVS takes a different strategy from the NVAW in this regard.

THE NATIONAL VIOLENCE AGAINST WOMEN SURVEY

The NVAW questionnaire had fifteen sections, one being a section to assess rape
victimization, which contains the rape screening questions, and another being a detailed rape report. Affirmative responses to the rape screening questions were the
primary basis for counting rape incidents; responses were "yes/no." By using a series of questions, the complexity of the concept being measured is better assessed
than through a single question. Responses to questions are then used to count the
number of persons who have experienced the phenomena of interest.

The questions used in the NVAW are presented in Table 2.1 (Tjaden and
Boyle 1998). The questions on forcible rape were taken from the National
Women's Survey (Tjaden and Boyle 1998; Kilpatrick et al. 1992). Questions used
in the NVAW are more explicit than those used in the NCVS and are designed to
"leave little doubt in the respondents' minds as to the type of information being
sought" (Tjaden and Boyle 1998, 3). If a respondent on the NVAW responded
"yes" to either of the questions focused on rape or attempted rape, detailed information was solicited on the specifics of the incident and the offender but this information is not used to classify the incident as a rape or other offense, it is the
screening question itself that functions in this manner. This strategy for eliciting reports "assumes that coherent sets of questions that cover a given domain of conduct
(e.g., rape) . . . worded in a behaviorally specific way will yield accurate responses"
(Fisher and Cullen 2000, 356). Unlike the procedures used in the NCVS, the
NVAW counts responses to screening questions as the basis for rape estimates.

Table 2.1 NVAW Questions Used in Measurement of Rape

F1) We are particularly interested in learning about violence women experience, either by strangers, friends, relatives, or even by husbands and partners. I'm going to ask you some questions about unwanted sexual experiences you may have had either as an adult or as a child. You may find the questions disturbing but it is important we ask them this way so that everyone is clear about what we mean. Remember the information you are providing is confidential.

Regardless of how long ago it happened has a man or boy ever made you have sex by using force or threatening to harm you or someone close to you? Just so there is no mistake, by sex we mean putting a penis in your vagina.

F2) Has anyone, male or female, ever made you have oral sex by using force or threat of harm? Just so there is no mistake, by oral sex we mean that a man or boy put his penis in your mouth or someone, male or female, penetrated your vagina or anus with their mouth or tongue.

F3) Has anyone ever made you have anal sex by using force or threat of harm? Just so there is no mistake, by anal sex we mean that a man or boy put his penis in your anus.

F4) Has anyone, male or female, ever put fingers or objects in your vagina or anus against your will by using force or threats?

F6) Has anyone, male or female, ever attempted to make you have vaginal, oral, or anal sex against your will, but intercourse or penetration did not occur?

Note: Question numbers reflect actual questionnaire numbers.
Source: Tjaden, 1996.

THE NATIONAL CRIME VICTIMIZATION SURVEY (NCVS)

The NCVS questionnaire consists of a screening questionnaire and an incident report that work together to measure criminal victimization. The NCVS counts incidents of rape based on responses to the incident report, a detailed examination of each crime incident mentioned by the respondent on the screening questionnaire. Similar to their use in other surveys, screening questions are used to identify eligible respondents, those who fit the specifics of the sample to be surveyed. Through screening questions, researchers are able to direct the attention and focus of the respondent to exactly what the researcher wants (Dodge 1985). In the NCVS, screening questions also function as empirical "gatekeepers to the respondent proceeding on to complete an incident report" (Fisher and Cullen 2000, 327). It is responses to screen questions that determine whether an incident report will be administered to the respondent. If a respondent gives an affirmative response to any screening question, an incident report is administered for every separate experience of a particular victimization.

Within the incident report, respondents are asked for specific information that allows NCVS to categorize the incident in the appropriate crime category such as completed rape or attempted rape. The respondent then does not have to consider the incident to be a rape in order for the NCVS to classify it as such. If in response to questions on the incident report, the respondent reports that she was raped, the NCVS interviewer asks "Do you mean forced or coerced sexual intercourse including attempts?" If the respondent appears unsure or asks for further clarification, the following definition of rape from the NCVS interviewer manual is read:

Rape is forced sexual intercourse and includes both psychological coercion as well as physical force. Forced sexual intercourse means vaginal, anal, or oral penetration by the offender(s). This category also includes incidents where the penetration is from a foreign object such as a bottle. (Bachman and Saltzman 1995, 6)

Four screen questions are used to focus or potentially cue the respondent to self-report a rape experience. The current NCVS screen questions are presented in Table 2.2. These screening questions were part of the redesign efforts to the survey. The earlier screen questions had been deservedly criticized for being too vague to actually function as a cue for respondents to disclose a rape victimization (BJS 1994). Current NCVS screen questions do not use the sexually explicit language that is contained with the NVAW questions. To the extent that the explicit nature of questions furthers disclosure and recall by the respondent, the higher estimates in the NVAW are partially explained by question content. A related issue concerns series victimizations.

Series Incidents

The NCVS and the NVAW handle the counting of what are often referred to as series victimizations in different ways. The NCVS as opposed to the NVAW provides a specific definition to series victimizations, and this definition is applied to all crimes with this characteristic. According to NCVS, a series victimization is one in which the respondent reports more than one rape victimization but cannot recall specific details on each event. Currently if the respondent can clearly recall specific details of up to six incidents, then each incident is counted separately. If the respondent is unable to recall clearly, then the series victimization label is applied and counted as one incident (Perkins et al. 1996). The NVAW counted each incident in a series separately in counts used to produce estimates of rape (Tjaden and Boyle 1998). This way of counting series victimizations will by definition produce larger estimates in the NVAW compared to the NCVS.

One of the rationales behind NCVS handling of series victimizations relies on the qualitatively different experience of chronic violence compared to discrete incidents of violence. Similarly to definitions of battering, Biderman (1980, 29) emphasizes that series victimizations are "more readily approached as a condition than as an incident" and better assessed in prevalence rather than

Table 2.2 NCVS Screen Questions for Personal Violent Crimes (1992 - Present)

40a) (Other than any incidents already mentioned). Since ___ ___, 19__, were you attacked or threatened OR did you have something stolen from you -

    a) At home including the porch or yard -
    b) At or near a friend's, relative's, or neighbor's home-
    c) At work or school -
    d) In places such as storage shed or laundry room, a shopping mall, restaurant, bank, or airport-
    e) While riding in any vehicle
    f) On the street or in a parking lot-
    g) At such places as a party, theater, gym, picnic area, bowling lanes, or while fishing or hunting
            OR
    h) Did anyone ATTEMPT to attack or ATTEMPT to steal anything belonging to you from any of these places?

41a) (Other than incidents already mentioned,) has anyone attacked or threatened you in any of these ways (Exclude telephone threats)

    a) With any weapons, for instance, a gun or knife
    b) With anything like a baseball bat, frying pan, scissors, or stick
    c) By something thrown, such as a rock or bottle
    d) Include any grabbing, punching, or choking
    e) Any rape, attempted rape or other type of sexual attack
    f) Any face to face threats
        OR
    g) Any attack or threat or use of force by anyone at all? Please mention it even if you are not certain it was a crime.

42a) People often don't think of incidents committed by someone they know. (Other than any incidents already mentioned,) did you have something stolen from you OR were you attacked or threatened by (Exclude telephone threats)

    a) Someone at work or school
    b) A neighbor or friend
    c) A relative or family member
    d) Any other person you've met or known?

43a) Incidents involving forced or unwanted sexual acts are often difficult to talk about. (Other than any incidents already mentioned,) have you been forced or coerced to engage in unwanted sexual activity by

    a) Someone you didn't know before
    b) A casual acquaintance
        OR
    c) Someone you know well?

Source: NCVS Screen Questionnaire available http://www.ojp.usdoj.gov/bjs/pub/pdf/ncvs1.pdf
Note: Question numbers used reflect numbers found in questionnaire.

incidence figures. Because the NCVS involves repeated interviews with the household over the time it is in the sample, this approach may present unique problems in terms of respondent disclosure for those who report series victimizations from intimate partners. Currently, the NCVS is considering the possibility of having households drop out of the sample after the initial report of domestic violence (BJS 2000b).

FISHER AND CULLEN'S RESEARCH ON COLLEGE WOMEN

Whether a series of behaviorally specific questions such as those used by the NVAW provide more accurate rape estimates than the screen-incident approach of the NCVS is an empirical question recently investigated by Fisher and Cullen (2000). Two key questions that Fisher and Cullen address are important here: (1) How does the use of behaviorally specific screen questions affect the experiences of rape screened into incident reports? (2) Are rape estimates obtained through the current NCVS screen questions comparable to those obtained using more explicit questions?

Fisher and Cullen constructed two surveys, both probability surveys of college women at two- and four-year institutions of higher education, to compare the approach of the NCVS and NVAW to rape measurement. The first survey, National College Women Sexual Victimization Survey (NCWSV), was introduced to respondents as an investigation of unwanted sexual victimization. Combining approaches from the NVAW and NCVS, Fisher and Cullen measured rape through a series of behaviorally specific questions that were used as screen questions to cue the respondent. Incident reports were used to ask a number of specific questions that were used to characterize the incident as either an attempted rape, completed rape, sexual coercion, or stalking experience.

Fisher and Cullen compared the extent to which responses on screen questions correspond to the more detailed information in the incident report. For example, if women responded "yes" to a screen question designed to cue disclosure of a rape experience, did this continue to be classified as a rape through the incident report?

The results of Fisher and Cullen's comparison supported the strength of the screen-incident combination as a technique. Among reports of rape based on responses to screen questions, the detail provided on the incident report yielded a final classification of rape for only 25 percent with 50 percent of incidents being designated as sexual victimization other than rape and the other 25 percent as lacking the necessary detail for specific classification. The victimization for rape based on only responses to screen questions was higher than the rate based on the use of the incident report for counting rapes. Furthermore, Fisher and Cullen's research design provided for rape experiences to be so identified on the incident report even if it was not screened in from a rape experience. Almost half of all victimizations finally classified as rape did in fact screen into the incident report on "non-rape screen questions" (Fisher and Cullen 2000, 368). These findings illustrate the centrality of the incident report in accurate classification of rape victimizations. Experiences screened into an incident report may prove to be on closer examination experiences that do not meet the legal definition of rape. Conversely, experiences screened into the incident report based on responses to "non-rape" questions may prove to constitute the legal definition of rape under the closer scrutiny of incident report questions. In both cases, the screen questions and the incident report are functioning in the manner intended by NCVS.

In order to directly address the adequacy of the current NCVS screen questions, Fisher and Cullen designed another probability survey of college women that closely replicated the basic NCVS design. Conducted in the same time period as the NCWSV, the National Violence Against College Women (NVACW) had the same sampling design, cover letter protocol, and reference period but used the NCVS screen questions. This second survey of college women was presented as a study "to examine the extent and nature of violence among college women" (Fisher and Cullen 2000, 371). The response rate was 91.6 percent. The estimates of rape were lower in the second survey than in the first survey; 2.03 per 1,000 persons compared to 19.34 per 1,000 persons, and hence the authors conclude that the more explicit wording of the questions elicited more reports from respondents.

Fisher and Cullen (2000, 377) conclude with the general observation that future research on rape should "not seek methodologies that produce higher or lower estimates of sexual victimizations but, rather, to develop measures that are the most accurate possible." The authors offer several avenues for the direction for future research, but only a few will be highlighted here. While acknowledging the strength of explicit questions for rape measurement, Fisher and Cullen state that the meaning that phrases such as "have sex" within questions needs to be explored both generally and in reference to particular sociodemographic groups. The use of incident reports in combination with sexually explicit screen questions has numerous benefits, but significant issues remain for future investigation. In this regard, Fisher and Cullen maintain that question sequencing, underexplored sources of measurement error, and flexibility in probing of respondents remain areas that are not yet adequately addressed in research. Another recommendation made by Fisher and Cullen and one that echoes that of the National Academy of Sciences panel Violence Against Women is the systematic gathering and use of "structured qualitative questions" within victimization surveys (2000, 381).

CONCLUSION

Survey design features including sampling procedures, survey context, techniques for disclosure and recall, and measurement strategies all influence estimates generated by the data. Understanding why certain design features may produce higher or lower estimates than other design features is necessary if we are to continue to move beyond the simplistic notion that a higher estimate is the best estimate. The methods used to produce particular findings must be understood and evaluated within the context of the method used rather than by less empirically based criteria. Furthermore, specifically regarding the NCVS, numerous commentaries on its design over the years have noted that the "full potential of the victimization survey method" will not be realized until NCVS moves more fully away from the need to "mimic" features of the UCR (Biderman 1980, 29; Biderman and Lynch 1991). The ability of the NCVS to more fully delineate the context of victimization by providing detail on more complex crime classifications such as stranger-to-stranger crime as opposed to the strict focus on crime category classifications such as robbery should be strengthened (Biderman and Lynch 1991; Lynch 1996a).

Both researchers interested in sexual violence and practitioners working in the field share an interest in developing better ways and means to evaluate the prevalence and incidence of violence toward women. Researchers and practitioners may differ in their uses for such knowledge, in their goals for gaining such estimates, and in the ideological perspective that informs their interest—differences that often build barriers rather than bridges to knowledge and action. Such differences are not the result of trivial concerns. Practitioners often fear that the policy uses of particular research studies will harm their organizations and the populations they serve. As research has moved to a more cooperative base between the academy and the field, this has changed. It was the very need for such collaboration that has now been institutionalized and forms the necessary ingredient in much of the federal grant money available under the Violence Against Women Act (Crowell and Burgess 1996).

The extensive attention to improvement of survey procedures that has characterized the NCVS from its inception will continue to characterize this survey's evolution. However, concerns of how the NCVS handles detection of crimes such as rape will continue to be weighed in the context of what are the best procedures within the scope of the NCVS as a survey of crime victims. Furthermore, the institutional position of the NCVS as a federally funded source of crime data has meant that as new classes of legislatively mandated victims emerge, the NCVS must incorporate their experiences into the survey design. Most recently, the NCVS must add questions on victims with disabilities because the Crime Victims With Disabilities Awareness Act so directs such consideration (BJS 2000b).

Though the extent to which revisions will continue to be made to measurement strategies relating to rape in the NCVS is unknown, Fisher and Cullen's (2000) research supports that the NCVS will continue to generate estimates lower than other surveys using more sexually explicit screening questions. The

NCVS may yet include more sexually explicit questions as part of the screening questions used, but as with all changes to the NCVS, they will be intensely debated and extensively field-tested prior to survey inclusion. Given the fact that the use of screen questions related to rape and containing the type of sexually explicit language as that found within the NVAW have never been field tested for NCVS use (personal communication, James Lynch, October 9, 2000), this change is not to be expected right away. In the meantime, the strategy offered by Russell and Bolen (2000) that the NCVS abandon measuring rape because it does such a bad job is ill advised. The sponsors of NCVS would never seriously consider the possibility of dropping rape from its coverage, and the symbolic message that would be sent by such action would hinder rather than advance our understanding of rape. Even though discrepancies may continue to exist between the levels of rape found within NCVS and surveys such as NVAW, the patterns of rape in terms of greater likelihood of known victims and offenders, for example, identified in the NCVS correspond to other research. The NCVS remains a useful source of data on rape, and further improvements to the overall survey design will continue to strengthen the usefulness of the data.

NOTES

The author wishes to thank Dr. Janet Lauritsen for her review of an earlier draft of this manuscript and Dr. James Lynch for valuable assistance regarding the National Crime Victimization Survey.

1. For a complete discussion of problems in the UCR, the reader is referred to Biderman and Lynch (1991).

2. Prior to the redesign, the BJS victimization survey was named the National Crime Survey (NCS).

3. The NVAW reports an annual prevalence rate of 0.3 percent and 2.9 incidents as the average number per victim. With a sample size of 8000, this means that there are only approximately 70 cases available for analysis.

4. Because of the rotating panel design of NCVS, some persons will move into the sample after the first interview. In these situations, unbounded data is used in estimate; Lynch (1996a) estimates that approximately 15 to 18 percent of data in any given year is unbounded.

REFERENCES

Bachman, Ronet, and Linda E. Saltzman. 1995. *Violence against Women: Estimates from the Redesigned Survey*. Washington, DC: U.S. Department of Justice, Bureau of Justice Statistics. (NCJ 154348).

Bachman, R., and B. Taylor. 1994. The measurement of family violence and rape by the redesigned National Crime Victimization Survey. *Justice Quarterly* 11(3):499–512.

Biderman, Albert D. 1980. Notes on Measurement by Crime Victimization Surveys. In *Indicators of Crime and Criminal Justice: Quantitative Studies*, pp. 29–32. Edited by Stephen E. Fienberg and Albert J. Reiss, Jr, Washington, DC: U.S. Government Printing Office.

Biderman, Albert D., and James P. Lynch, with James Peterson. 1991. *Understanding Crime Incidence Statistics: Why the UCR diverges from the NCS*. New York: Springer-Verlag.

Bureau of Justice Statistics. 2000a. *Criminal Victimization in the United States, 1998 Statistical Tables*. Washington, DC: U.S. Department of Justice, Office of Justice Programs. (NCJ 181585).

——— . 2000b. *National Crime Victimization Survey Description and Summary of Proposed Changes*. Available at *http://www.ojp.usdoj.gov/bjs/pub/ pdf/ncvsdspc.pdf*.

——— . 1994. *Technical Background on the Redesigned National Crime Victimization Survey*. Washington, DC: U.S. Department of Justice. (NCJ 151172).

Cantor, David, and James P. Lynch. 2000. Self-report surveys as measures of crime and criminal victimization. In *Criminal Justice 2000: Measurement and Analysis of Crime and Justice*, pp. 85–138. Washington, DC: U.S. Department of Justice, Office of Justice Programs.

Crowell, Nancy A., and Ann W. Burgess. 1996. *Understanding Violence against Women*. Washington, DC: National Academy Press.

Czaja, Ronald, and Johnny Blair. 1996. *Designing Surveys: A Guide to Decisions and Procedures*. Thousand Oaks, CA: Pine Forge Press.

Department of Justice, 1989. *Redesign of the National Crime Survey*. Washington, DC: U.S. Department of Justice, Bureau of Justice Statistics. (NCJ 111457).

Dodge, Richard W. 1985. *Response to Screening Questions in the National Crime Survey*. Washington, DC: U.S. Department of Justice, Bureau of Justice Statistics. (NCJ 97624).

Fisher, Bonnie S., and Francis T. Cullen. 2000. Measuring the Sexual Victimization of Women: Evolution, Current Controversies, and Future Research. In *Criminal Justice 2000: Measurement and Analysis of Crime and Justice*, pp. 317–390. Washington, DC: U.S. Department of Justice, Office of Justice Programs.

Kilpatrick, Dean G., C.N. Edmunds, and A.K. Seymour. 1992. *Rape in America: A Report to the Nation*. Arlington, VA: National Victim Center.

Koss, Mary P. 1992. The Underdetection of Rape: Methodological Choices Influence Incidence Estimates. *Journal of Social Issues* 48(1):61–75.

——— . 1996. The Measurement of Rape Victimization in Crime Surveys. *Criminal Justice and Behavior* 23:55–69.

Lynch, James P. 1996a Understanding Differences in the Estimates of Rape from Self-Report Surveys. In Rita J. Simmon, ed., *From Data to Public Policy: Affirmative Action, Sexual Harrassment, Domestic Violence, and Social Welfare*, pp. 121–41. New York: Women's Freedom Network and University Press of America, Inc.

——— . 1996b. Clarifying Divergent Estimates of Rape from Two National Surveys. *Public Opinion Quarterly* 60: 410–30.

Percy, Andrew, and Pat Mayhew. 1997. Estimating Sexual Victimization in a National Crime Survey: A New Approach. *Studies on Crime and Crime Prevention* 6(2):125–150.

Perkins, Craig A., Patsy A. Klaus, Lisa D. Bastian, and Robyn L. Cohen. 1996. *Criminal Victimization in the United States, 1993.* Washington, DC: U.S. Department of Justice, Bureau of Justice Statistics. (NCJ 151657).

Rennison, Callie Marie. 2000. *Criminal Victimization 1999: Changes 1998–99 with Trends 1993–99.* Washington, DC: U.S. Department of Justice, Bureau of Justice Statistics. (NCJ 182734).

Russell, Diana E.H., and Rebecca M. Bolen. 2000. *The Epidemic of Rape and Child Sexual Abuse in the United States.* Thousand Oaks, CA: Sage.

Sparks, Richard F. 1980. Criminal Opportunities and Crime Rates. In *Indicators of Crime and Criminal Justice: Quantitative Studies*, Stephen E. Fienberg and Albert J. Reiss, Jr., eds., Washington, DC: U.S. Government Printing Office.

Taylor, Bruce M. 1989. *New Directions for the National Crime Survey.* Washington, DC: U.S. Department of Justice, Bureau of Justice Statistics. (NCJ 115571).

Tjaden, Patricia. 1996. *Violence and Threats of Violence against Women in America: Female Questionnaire.* Denver: Center for Policy Research.

Tjaden, Patricia, and John M. Boyle. 1998, July. *National Violence against Women: Survey Methodology Report Draft.* Unpublished manuscript. Denver: Center for Policy Research.

Tjaden, Patricia, and Nancy Thoennes. 1998. *Prevalence, Incidence, and Consequences of Violence against Women: Findings From the National Violence against Women Survey.* Washington, DC: U.S. Department of Justice, National Institute of Justice and U.S. Department of Health and Human Services, Centers for Disease Control and Prevention.

Tourangeau, Roger, and Tom W. Smith. 1996. Asking Sensitive Questions: The Impact of Data Collection Mode, Question Format, and Question Context. *Public Opinion Quarterly* 60:275–304.

Turner, Anthony G. 1981. The San Jose recall study. In Robert G. Lehnen and Wesley G. Skogan, eds., *The National Crime Survey: Working Papers, Volume 1: Current and Historical Perspectives*, pp. 22–27. Washington, DC: U.S. Department of Justice, Bureau of Justice Statistics.

3

Biology, Sex, and the Debate over "Chemical Castration"

Craig T. Palmer, Randy Thornhill, and David N. DiBari

INTRODUCTION

This chapter is not an argument for the use of surgical castration or the use of anti-androgens (often inaccurately referred to as "chemical castration") in the treatment or punishment of sex offenders. This chapter is an argument about what should and should not be used as reasons for or against such methods. Specifically, many of the current arguments against the use of anti-androgens and other hormonal and drug treatments are based on the assertion that they will not be effective because (1) they are *biological* procedures, and sex offenses are caused by *nonbiological* social, cultural and psychological factors, and (2) they reduce *sexual* motivation, and sex offenses are not sexually motivated. Both of these arguments are based on unsupported assertions and fundamental misunderstandings. Hence, both of these arguments should be expunged from the debate to allow for it to be decided on more legitimate issues.

LEGITIMATE CONCERNS ABOUT THE USE OF HORMONAL TREATMENTS

The reason we are not arguing for the use of anti-androgens is that this question, currently being debated in numerous states (see Miller 1998), hinges on a number of issues that either cannot be settled currently given existing evidence or that belong to the realm of ethics instead of science and, as scientists, we have no special qualifications to recommend such ethical decisions. Among the empirical issues that are relevant to the use of such procedures are the following: What is the exact effect of them on sexual behavior? There is some limited evidence indicating a decrease in some forms of sexual behavior following the use of various drugs, but the exact effects on sexual behavior, aggression, and violence are not completely understood (Archer 1991, 1994; Bain 1987; Bradford and Bourget 1987; Dabbs et al. 1995; Kouri et al. 1995; Raboch et al. 1987; Spalding 1998; Windle and Windle 1995). The existing data also are inconclusive on recidivism rates for both sexual and nonsexual offenses (Bradford 1988; Meyer et al. 1992; Willie and Beier 1989), and there may be reason to expect that the effectiveness of anti-androgens might vary between different types of sexual offenders (Pfafflin 1992; Polaschek et al. 1997; Vanderzyl 1994). There also is incomplete knowledge on side effects, including health problems and the disruption of sociosexual relationships. More work also is needed to determine the ability to ensure that sex offenders actually take the drug, and to evaluate means of preventing offenders from taking androgens that offset the effects of the treatments. Bailey and Greenberg (1998) provide an important recent review of the empirical status of the relationship between castration (both surgical and chemical) and reduced sexual-offense recidivism, which concludes that although more research is called for, existing evidence supports a moderate to strong relationship.

In addition to certain remaining empirical questions there are ethical and legal questions. Is the use of anti-androgens unconstitutional, due to it being cruel and unusual punishment or for various other reasons (Baker 1984; Fromson 1994; Green 1986; Hicks 1993; Icenogle 1994; Peters 1993; Prentky 1997; Rebish 1997; Spalding 1998)? As a punishment, is it too severe or too lenient for different types of sexual offenses (Hansen and Lykke-Olesen 1997; Icenogle 1994; Spalding 1998)? Bailey and Greenberg (1998) give an excellent discussion of many ethical and legal considerations surrounding the use of castration, both surgical and chemical, that could be a useful springboard for additional moralistic and legal analyses of the validity of castration for punishment or treatment of sex offenders.

Although the legitimate issues just discussed are often mentioned in current debates, they are too often overshadowed by the assertion that hormonal treatments will not be effective because they are *biological* means of influencing *sexual* motivation, whereas sex offenses are asserted to be caused by *nonbiological* factors and *nonsexual* motivations. For example, the first objection to the use of hormonal treatments listed in the literature review by Willie and Beier (1989, 109) is the argument that "it is not the sex hormones which represent the decisive driving force [in sex offenses], but psychological factors." This view that the "psychological factors" are somehow distinct from both "biological" and "sexual" factors such as hormones reflects fundamental misunderstandings about human biology. This chapter is aimed at correcting these misapprehensions so that the issue can be solved on the basis of the legitimate issues.

THE ARGUMENT THAT SEX OFFENSES DO NOT HAVE BIOLOGICAL CAUSES

The assertion that hormonal treatments will be ineffective because they are *biological* procedures that are fundamentally different from "nonbiological" social, cultural, and/or psychological procedures is based on a very common misunderstanding of biology that leads to a false dichotomy between biological and nonbiological influences on human behavior. For example, Icenogle (1994, 279) addressed the question of "whether a state may elect to sentence convicted sexual offenders to the use of a *biological* treatment, as opposed to incarceration or non-biological psychotherapy" [emphasis added]. Such a dichotomy of treatments is based on the misconception that the term "biological" refers to genetically determined factors internal to an organism, as opposed to nonbiological "environmental" factors that are external to the organism. For example, Tsang (1995, 409) argued against the view that "it is biology that determines pedophilia, not the environment." This false dichotomy lead Tsang (1995, 397) to argue against "biodeterminist and reductionist views of human sexuality" on the grounds that "human beings are not automatons propelled solely by 'uncontrollable' biological 'drives,' but are a species with highly developed brains." If knowledge is to serve as the basis for decisions about the use of hormonal treatments, it is crucial to replace a conception of biology that excludes the human brain with a more accurate understanding of the meaning of biology.

CRITIQUE OF THE ARGUMENT THAT SEX OFFENSES DO NOT HAVE BIOLOGICAL CAUSES

Biology is simply the scientific study of living things. Hence, to state that something is biological is only to assert that it is an aspect of a living thing. All aspects of living things are the result of both genes and the environment, because genes alone are incapable of even creating cells, much less organisms or the behavior of those organisms. This means that everything that is biological is the result of an interaction between genes *and* the environment, and that nothing biological is purely genetic or purely environmental. Hence, the common equation of biological with genetic, and the corresponding contrasting of biological with environmental, is totally at odds with current biological knowledge. Despite the truth of the assertion that biological (living) things are always the result of an interaction between genes and environmental factors, many social scientists continue to ignore the implications of this fact for explanations of human behavior (for further discussion, see Thornhill and Palmer 2000).

The first step in making explanations of human behavior congruent with current biological knowledge is to realize that the environment means everything external to the genes and that there is a vast number and range of things in the environment that are essential for the development of an organism. These include not only the multitude of things external to the individual (e.g., oxygen, water, nutrients, and so on), of which members of the same species (the social environment) are only a small (but often crucial) part but also the environment within the developing individual (e.g., other cells, tissues, organs, hormones, physiological systems, and so on).

The next step is the realization that the gene-environment functional co-relationship of interactions is too intimate to separate into genes and environment (social or otherwise). Hence, although it is possible to determine whether the *differences between individuals* are heritable, that is, to a significant degree due to *differences* in genes, the interactions between genes and environment during the development of any given organism are so intimately intertwined that it is not only meaningless to suggest that any trait of an individual, including an individual's brain, is environmentally or genetically "determined," it is not even valid to talk about a trait as being "primarily" genetic or environmental. Indeed, the modern biological view of ontogeny (an individual's developmental experiences) holds that the environmental and the genetic causes during development of any given organism are equally important and totally inseparable. Hence, neither environmental determinism (meaning only or primarily that the environment causes a certain behavior) nor genetic determinism (meaning only or primarily that genes cause a given behavior) are parts of modern biology. It is, however, quite scientifically valid to claim that any trait of an organism, regardless of the role played by specific environmental factors (including factors in the social environment), is biologically determined (see Daly and Wilson 1983).

Although the arguments used against hormonal treatments reveal how social science theory often views arbitrary learning as a complete, or an essentially complete, explanation of sexual offenses, the preceding discussion illustrates that learning is actually only a small, proximate part of the explanation at best, a part that cannot be isolated from genes, hormones, brain structures, and numerous other environmental factors that contribute to the human behavioral phenotype. Both the behavior referred to as "learned" and the behavior referred to as "innate" are equally the product of gene/environment interactions. In order to develop within an individual, both require certain genes interacting with countless things in the environment. In terms of causation, both are 100 percent environmental and 100 percent genetic. They are distinguished only by whether or not one specific identified aspect in the environment is part of the aspects of the environment that are necessary for the behavior to occur. The environmental factors necessary for "innate" behavior do not include a specific identified environmental factor in order for the behavior to occur, whereas a "learned" behavior does require an interaction with a specific identified environmental factor in order to occur (Alcock 1997; Symons 1979).

Once the meaning of biology is grasped, the absurdity of the argument that hormonal treatments should not be used because they would influence only the biological aspects of human behavior becomes obvious. Sexual offenses, like every other behavior of living organisms, are biological. Hence, by definition, any attempt to change this behavior will involve influencing human biology. Changes in the social environment (e.g., psychotherapy, education courses, imprisonment, counseling, public humiliation), changes in the levels of circulating hormones (e.g., chemical castration), or changes in the genetic makeup of an individual are all biological means of influencing behavior, and equally so.

THE ARGUMENT THAT SEX OFFENSES ARE NOT SEXUALLY MOTIVATED

Even more common than the argument that hormonal interventions will be ineffective because they are biological is the argument that they will be ineffective because they influence sexual motivations whereas sexual offenses are not sexually motivated. The assertion that sexual offenders, especially rapists, are not sexually motivated started in the late 1960s and early 1970s and became widely disseminated in Susan Brownmiller's book *Against Our Will* in 1975. It then became a "central theme" (Thornhill and Thornhill 1983, 163) in nearly every work written on sexual assault so quickly that by 1980 Warner (1980, 94) concluded that "it is now generally accepted by criminologists, psychologists, and other professionals working with rapists and rape victims that rape is not primarily a sexual crime, it is a crime of violence" (see Palmer 1988 for references). Although several evolutionists systematically exposed the flaws in the specific arguments used to support the "not sex" explanation (Ellis 1989; Hagen 1979; Palmer 1988; Symons 1979; Thornhill and Thornhill 1983), they were largely ignored or met with accusations that the authors were condoning rape (e.g., Fausto-Sterling 1985). Hence, in 1990 Felson and Krohn (1990, 222) were still able to observe that despite the lack of supporting evidence, "Since the mid-1970s, the motivation for rape has usually been explained in terms of hostility and power rather than sex."

An unbroken repetition of the "not sex" position, and the portrayal of this position as a defining part of the "feminist" theory of rape and other sexual offenses, has continued throughout the 1990s in the popular press (see Murphey 1992), academic textbooks (e.g., Davidson and Neale 1996; Parillo et al. 1985; Robertson 1981) and research articles (e.g., Blatt 1992; Brownmiller and Mehrhof 1992; Buchwald et al. 1993; Davies 1997; Donat and D'Emillio 1992;

Drake 1990; Fonow et al. 1992; Herman 1990; Jones 1990; Miccio 1994; Parrot 1991; Polaschek et al. 1997; Sanday 1990; Scott 1993; Stock 1991; Syzmanski et al. 1993; Ward 1995). As a result of this repetition, the claim that rapists are not sexually motivated has became an unquestioned premise in much of the literature on sexual offenses: "Feminist *assumptions*, for example, generally deemphasize the potential contribution that biologically driven sexual motives may play in the commitment of sexual assault" (White and Farmer 1992, 47; emphasis added). The strength and pervasiveness of these *assumptions* is indicated by Sorenson and White's (1992, 3–4) statement "We cannot overestimate the influence of feminist theorists such as Brownmiller upon the thinking of current researchers. Many investigators, while not necessarily testing the assumption in their studies, *presume* that rape is a manifestation of male dominance over and control of women" [emphasis added]. (See Thornhill and Palmer 2000, for a full review of the history and influence of the "not sex" view of rape.)

It is also important to note that even the "radical feminists" (e.g., Dworkin 1989, 1990; MacKinnon 1983, 1987, 1989, 1990, 1993) who assert "rape is sex" are not arguing that sex offenders are using violence and power to obtain the distinct goal of the biological sensation known as sexual stimulation. As Bell (1991, 88) pointed out, when these radical feminists assert that rape is sexual they mean that "It is *social* sex, not biological sex that rape is about" [emphasis in original]. This is because these authors assert that since sex has no inherent biological reality, it can be socially constructed in an infinite number of ways. In patriarchal cultures, according to radical feminists such as MacKinnon (1989, 113), "sexuality . . . is a form of power" and "violence is sex" (MacKinnon 1989, 134; see also Dworkin 1989, 165; MacKinnon 1987, 6; A Southern Women's Writing Collective, 1990, 143). Hence, far from opposing the view that violence and power are the goals of rapists, these authors are actually arguing that power and violence are not only the goals of males engaged in sexual offenses, they are also the goals of males engaged in all forms of sex. Instead of really arguing that Brownmiller was wrong about rape when she claimed that it wasn't sexually motivated, the position of these radical feminists "in effect extends Brownmiller's definition of rape to the sex act itself" (Podhoretz 1991, 31). Hence, the radical feminists share the fundamental assumption that the motivations of sex offenders are a desire for violence and power that, according to their social constructionist theory, just happen to be the same thing as sex. Hence, Paglia's (1994, 41) assertion that for most feminists "the rape discourse derailed itself early on by its nonsensical formulation. 'Rape is a crime of violence but not of sex,' a mantra that blanketed the American media . . . ," applies even to the radical feminists (see Thornhill and Palmer 2000, for additional discussion).

Given the pervasiveness of the view that sexual offenders are not sexually motivated, it is not surprising as noted by Hicks (1993, 647) that "many experts say that castration will not work because rape is not a crime about sex, but rather a crime about power and violence." For example, Estrich (1987, 82) argued against the use of chemical castration because the position that "convicted rapists should have a choice between castration and imprisonment, [is] a choice which makes sense only if their crime . . . is understood as a problem . . . of . . . sexual desire." Goldfarb also quoted Groth as stating that offering rapists the option of chemical castration "reflects the misconception that most sex offenders are raping out of some type of sexual desire" (quoted in Goldfarb 1984, 4). Similarly, Vachss (1994, 112) argued against the use of castration as a form of treatment by stating that such a "remedy" ignores reality. Sexual violence is not sex gone too far; it is violence with sex as its instrument. Tsang (1995, 400) also pointed out that "[s]uch drug therapy for rape cases . . . goes against the feminist view of rape as a crime involving violence and domination of women, and assumes rape to be primarily a sexual act. . . . Feminists would argue that reducing the 'libido' would do nothing to reduce the threat of violence." Spalding (1998, 132–33) even asserted that "because [rapists] are motivated not by sexual drive, but by intense feelings of hatred and hostility, the procedure [of chemical castration] may cause an increase in the occurrences of this type of sexual battery."

CRITIQUE OF THE ARGUMENT THAT SEX OFFENSES ARE NOT SEXUALLY MOTIVATED

The problem with the "not sex" explanation of sexual offenses is that there is little, if any, empirical support for the claim that sexual offenders are not sexually motivated (see Palmer 1988; Felson and Krohn 1990) and a vast amount of evidence concerning the crucial role of sexual arousal in sex offender behavior (see Lalumiére and Quinsey 1994). Indeed, the arguments used to support the claim that sexual offenses such as rape are not sexually motivated are riddled with logical flaws and unsupported assertions, and numerous researchers have demonstrated that these arguments can be accepted only if one accepts a definition of "sexual" that is vastly different from how the word is literally used and suspends logic when evaluating the arguments (Ellis 1989; Felson and Krohn 1990; Hagen 1979; Palmer 1988; Symons 1979; Thornhill and Thornhill 1983) (see Thornhill and Palmer 2000, for a full discussion).

An example of an argument based on a very atypical definition of the word "sexual" is offered by Shields and Shields (1983, 122):

When they say sex or sexual, these social scientists and feminists [who argue that sex offenses are not sexually motivated] mean the *motivation*, moods, or drives associated with honest courtship and pair bonding. In such situations, males report feelings of ten-

derness, affection, joy and so on. . . . It is this sort of pleasurable motivation that the
socioculturists (and feminists) denote as sexuality. [emphasis in original]

The problem with this argument is that there is considerable evidence that
this definition of "sex" is much narrower than what the word "sex" typically refers to. First, as offered by Hagen (1979, 158–59):

it is abundantly self evident . . . that a large percentage of males have no difficulty in di-
vorcing sex from love. Whistles and wolf-calls, attendance at burlesque shows, patron-
izing of callgirls and prostitutes—all of these are probably manifestations of a sexual
urge totally or largely bereft of romantic feelings.

More fundamentally, the word "sexual" (but not necessarily "tenderness,"
"affection," or "joy") is used routinely by both men and women to refer to the
motivation of nonhuman animals involved in reproductive acts.

An example of an argument that requires the suspension of skeptical thought
is the statement that sexual offenses are not sexually motivated because "most
rapists have stable sexual partners" (Sanford and Fetter 1979, 8). This widely
mentioned argument hinges on the assumption that a male's sexual desire is exhausted by a single "outlet." In addition to being contrary to our knowledge of
the evolution of human sexuality, this assumption is obviously inconsistent
with the observation as noted by Symons (1979, 280) that "most patrons of
prostitutes, adult bookstores, and adult movie theatres are married men, but this
is not considered evidence for lack of sexual motivation." Another example is
the widely quoted argument (see Palmer 1988 for citations) that rapists are not
sexually motivated because young children and elderly women are sometimes
raped. Those making this argument conveniently ignore the close correlation
between the age distribution of rape victims (but not the victims of other violent
crimes) and the ages of peak female sexual attractiveness (see Thornhill and
Palmer 2000 for critiques of other arguments).

Despite such flawed arguments, many social scientists maintain the view
that the occurrence of rape and other sexual offenses cannot be accounted for by
the hypothesis that sexual stimulation is the goal of offenders. That is, sexual
desire is claimed to be neither a sufficient nor even a necessary motivation for
the sexual offense to occur. Instead, these social scientists cling to the view that
the occurrence of sexual offenses such as rape can be explained only by the hypothesis that sex is just a means used to attain the goals of power, control, domination, and/or violence. Hence, according to this social science theory of sexual
offenses, a nonsexual motivation (such as a desire for power, control, domination, and/or violence) is necessary for a rape to occur, and such nonsexual motivation also is a sufficient motivation for a rape to occur. Contrary to this view,
though any number of motivations may be involved in a given sexual offense,
evidence indicates that sexual desire is sometimes a sufficient motivation to

produce the sexual offense and that sexual desire is always a necessary motivation for a sexual offense to occur (Palmer 1988, 1989). Although this necessary role of sexual arousal in sex offenses does not guarantee that any specific drug treatments will be effective in preventing offenses due to the complexity of the chemical factors influencing sexual behavior, there is no justification for the assumption that castration procedures will be ineffective simply because they influence the sexual drive of offenders.

Several reasons have been proposed to account for why such an unsupported position as the "not sex" aspect of the social science explanation of rape could have achieved, and maintained, such popularity. Perhaps it is just the illogic of the naturalistic fallacy leading to the assumption that if sexual offenses are motivated by something as natural as sexual desire they must be good, or at least excusable. This is suggested by Symons (1979), who proposes that the "not sex" argument is the result of the view that sex is good and therefore cannot be involved in something bad like rape. Another possibility, suggested by Thornhill and Thornhill (1983), is that viewing rape as distinct from sex is the result of the importance of female choice throughout much of our evolutionary history. If female sexual arousal has been designed to occur when females find a male who has the qualities and behavior of a high-quality mate, rape is unlikely to be sexually arousing to females. Thus, for females, the experience is very different from sexual acts with a desired mate.

The main reason, however, for the denial of sexual motivation on behalf of sexual offenders, especially rapists, almost certainly stems from greater concern with political ideology than accurate knowledge. That is, debates over the question of what is the motivation of rapists have been evaluated not on logic and evidence, but on how the different positions might influence people to behave. For example, Muehlenhard et al. (1996, 130) states, "The question of how to conceptualize rape has important legal, scientific, clinical, and interpersonal implications. It has sometimes been assumed that conceptualizing rape as sex has solely negative implications for women, whereas conceptualizing rape as violence has solely positive implications." Given this association, many feminist theorists "argued for *utility* of conceptualizing rape as violence" (Muehlenhard et al. 1996, 123; emphasis added). This focus on the ability of explanations to influence behavior, instead of the congruence of explanations with evidence, is illustrated by Blackman's (1985, 1118) criticism of the attempts by evolutionists to put forth an objective scientific explanation of rape, not for a failure to account for the data but for "de-politicizing" the word rape: "To use the word rape in a de-politicized context functions to undermine ten years of feminist consciousness-raising." Whether or not "consciousness raising" is undermined, viewing rape as sexually, instead of politically, motivated does undermine what has been an effective argument for ending the patriarchal domination of American society.

Who could oppose ending the male political domination of women if it is the cause of the horrible crime of rape? If the causes of rape are to be found not in the political structure of American society but in the evolved mechanisms of the human sexual psyche, other reasons must be given for ending patriarchy. The tragedy is that such other reasons, in our opinions, abound, and clinging to unsubstantiated and illogical explanations of the causes of rape only hinders attempts to prevent rape. Indeed, successfully reducing the occurrence of rape may require the de-politicization of rape from the "master symbol of women's oppression" (Schwendinger and Schwendinger 1985, 93) to a behavior that needs to be prevented through the identification of its causes. It is particularly crucial to do this in regard to the issue of sexual motivation because, as argued by Muehlenhard et al. (1996, 130), "the extent that men's sexual arousal to rape cues precipitates rape, assessment and treatment of such sexual arousal may help prevent rape." This is why Hartung (1992, 392) stated that "if those who think that rape is not a sexual act . . . were only a danger to themselves, we could let them play. But this is not the case, and rape is not a game."

CONCLUSION

The use of surgical castration and related procedures in the treatment/punishment of sex offenders is a very controversial issue, and deservedly so. At the moment there simply is not sufficient evidence for or against the effectiveness of these procedures. Further, their use raises legitimate ethical and legal concerns. On the other hand, the relative ineffectiveness of alternative methods of preventing sexual offenses clearly justifies further research to determine the possible uses of such methods (see also Bailey and Greenberg 1998).

Given the practical importance of the issue, we find it tragic that so much of the debate over this issue involves fundamental misunderstandings of the meaning of biology, and ideologically driven denials of the role of sexual motivation in the perpetration of sexual offenses. The extent of these two misguided positions is reflected in the statement by Thiessen and Young (1994, 63) who, after reviewing 1,610 recent studies on sexual coercion, concluded that "reference to biology is taboo, for to recognize its influence would . . . destroy the ideological fabric that cloaks the entire area of women's issues." We are attempting to change this situation, not because we oppose the ideological goals of feminism but because we share many of them, especially the goal of decreasing the frequency of sexual offenses. The tragedy of the current situations lies in the observation as offered by Wright (1994, 34) that "[h]istory has not been kind to ideologies that rested on patently false beliefs about human nature." In this case, history is likely to be unkind if we base the decision of whether or not to use certain methods of treatment on patently false beliefs about biology and the motivation of sex offenders.

NOTE

The authors would like to thank Martin Lalumiére and Vernon Quinsey for helpful comments on an earlier version of this chapter.

REFERENCES

Alcock, J. 1997. *Animal Behavior*, 6th edition. Sunderland, MA: Sinaur Associates.

Archer, J. 1991. The influence of testosterone on human aggression. *British Journal of Psychology* 82: 1–28.

————. 1994. Testosterone and aggression. In *The Psychobiology of Aggression* (pp. 3–25), edited by M. Hillbrand and N. Pallone. New York: The Haworth Press.

Bailey, M., and A.S. Greenberg. 1998. The science and ethics of castration: Lessons from the Morse case. *Northwestern University Law Review* 92: 1–21.

Bain, J. 1987. Hormones and sexual aggression in the male. *Integrated Psychiatry* 5: 82–93.

Baker, W.J. 1984. Castration of the male sex offender: A legally impermissible alternative. *Loyola Law Review* 30: 377–87.

Bell, V. 1991. Beyond the 'Thorny Question': Feminism, Foucault, and the desexualisation of rape. *International Journal of the Sociology of Law* 19: 83–100.

Blackman, J. 1985. The language of sexual violence: More than a matter of semantics. In *Violence against Women: A Critique of the Sociobiology of Rape* (pp. 115–28), edited by S.R. Sunday and E. Tobach. New York: Gordian Press.

Blatt, D. 1992. Recognizing rape as a method of torture. *Review of Law Social Change* 19(4): 821–65.

Bradford, J.M.W. 1988. Organic treatment for the male sexual offender. In *Human Sexual Aggression: Current Perspectives* (pp.193–202), edited by Robert A. Prentky and Vernon L. Quinsey. New York: The New York Academy of Sciences.

Bradford, J.M.W., and D. Bourget. 1987. Sexually aggressive men. *Psychiatric Journal of the University of Ottawa* 12(3): 169–75.

Brownmiller, S. 1975. *Against Our Will: Men, Women, and Rape*. New York: Bantam Books.

Brownmiller, S., and B. Mehrhof. 1992. A feminist response to rape as an adaptation. *Behavioral and Brain Sciences* 15: 381–82.

Buchwald, E., P.R. Fletcher, and M. Roth. 1993. Editor's Preface. In *Transforming a Rape Culture* (pp. 1–2). Edited by E. Buchwald, P.R. Fletcher, and M. Roth. Minneapolis, MN: Milkweed Editions.

Dabbs, J.M. Jr., T.S. Carr, R.L. Frady, and J.K. Riad. 1995. Testosterone, crime, and misbehavior among 692 male prison inmates. *Personality and Individual Differences* 18(5): 627–33.

Daly, M., and M. Wilson, 1983. *Sex, Evolution and Behavior*, 2nd edition. Belmont, CA: Wadsworth.

Davidson, G.C., and J.M. Neale. (1996). *Abnormal Psychology*. New York: John Wiley and Sons, Inc.

Davies, K.A. 1997. Voluntary exposure to pornography and men's attitudes toward feminism and rape. *The Journal of Sex Research* 34(2): 131–37.

Donat, P.L.N., and J. D'Emillio. 1992. A feminist redefinition of rape and sexual assault: Historical foundations and change. *Journal of Social Issues* 48(1): 9–22.

Drake, J.L. (1990). Sexual aggression: Achieving power through humiliation. In *Handbook of Sexual Assault: Issues, Theories, and Treatment of the Offender* (pp. 55–72), edited by W.L. Marshall, D.R. Laws, and H.E. Barbaree. New York: Plenum.

Dworkin, A. 1989. *Pornography: Men Possessing Women*. New York: E.P. Dutton.

———. 1990. Resistance. In *The Sexual Liberals and the Attack on Feminism* (pp. 136–39), edited by D. Leidholdt and J.G. Raymond. New York: Pergamon Press.

Ellis, L. 1989. *Theories of Rape: Inquiries into the Causes of Sexual Aggression*. New York: Hemisphere.

Estrich, S. 1987. *Real Rape*. Cambridge: Harvard University Press.

Fausto-Sterling, A. 1985. *Myths of Gender: Biological Theories about Women and Men*. New York: Basic Books.

Felson, R.D., and M. Krohn. 1990. Motives for rape. *Journal of Research in Crime and Delinquency* 27: 222–42.

Fonow, M.M., L. Richardson, and V.A. Wemmerus. 1992. Feminist rape education: Does it work? *Gender and Society* 6(1): 108–21.

Fromson, K.B. 1994. Beyond an eye for an eye: Castration as an alternative sentencing measure. *New York Law School Journal of Human Rights* 11: 311–21.

Goldfarb, C. 1984. Practice of using castration in sentence being questioned. *Criminal Justice Newsletter* 15 (February 15): 3–4.

Green, W. 1986. Depo-Provera, castration and the probation of rape offenders: Statutory and constitutional issues. *University of Dayton Law Review* 12: 1–10.

Hagen, R. 1979. *The Biosexual Factor*. New York: Doubleday.

Hansen, H., and L. Lykke-Olesen. 1997. Treatment of dangerous sexual offenders in Denmark. *The Journal of Forensic Psychiatry* 8(1): 195–99.

Hartung, J. 1992. Getting real about rape. *Behavioral and Brain Sciences* 15: 390–92.

Herman, J.L. 1990. Sex offenders: A feminist perspective. In *Handbook of Sexual Assault: Issues, Theories, and Treatment of the Offender* (pp. 117–93), edited by W.L. Marshall, D.R. Laws, and H.E. Barbaree. New York: Plenum.

Hicks, P. 1993. Comment, Castration of sexual offenders, legal and ethical issues. *Journal of Legal Medicine* 14: 641–51.

Icenogle, D.L. 1994. Sentencing male sex offenders to the use of biological treatments: A constitutional analysis. *The Journal of Legal Medicine* 15: 279–304.

Jones, A. 1990. Family matters. In *The Sexual Liberals and the Attack on Feminism* (pp. 61–66), edited by D. Leidholdt and J.G. Raymond. New York: Pergamon Press.

Kouri, E.M., S.E. Lukas, H.G. Pope, Jr., and P.S. Oliva. 1995. Increased aggressive responding in male volunteers following the administration of gradually increasing doses of testosterone cypionate. *Drug and Alcohol Dependence* 40: 73–79.

Lalumiére, M.L., and V.L. Quinsey. 1994. The discriminability of rapists from non-sex offenders using phallometric measures: A meta-analysis. *Criminal Justice and Behavior* 21(1): 150–175.

MacKinnon, C.A. 1983. Feminism, Marxism, method, and the state: Toward feminist jurisprudence. *Signs: Journal of Women in Culture and Society* 8(4): 635–58.

———. 1987. *Feminism Unmodified: Discourses on Life and Law*. Cambridge, MA: Harvard University Press.

———. 1989. *Toward a Feminist Theory of State*. Cambridge, MA: Harvard University Press.

———. 1990. Liberalism and the death of feminism. In *The Sexual Liberals and the Attack on Feminism* (pp. 3–13), edited by D. Leidholdt and J.G. Raymond. New York: Pergamon Press.

———. 1993. *Only Words*. Cambridge, MA: Harvard University Press.

Meyer, W.J. III, C. Cole, and E. Emory. 1992. Depo Provera treatment for sex offending behavior: An evaluation of outcome. *Bulletin of the American Academy of Psychiatry Law* 20(3): 249–59.

Miccio, K. 1994. Rape is a gender based crime. In *Crimes of Gender: Violence against Women* (pp. 80–84), edited by G.E. McCuen. Hudson, WI: Gary McCuen Publications, Inc.

Miller, B. 1998. A review of sex offender legislation. *Kansas Journal of Law and Public Policy* 7: 40–50.

Muehlenhard, C.L., S. Danoff-Burgg, and I.G. Powch. 1996. Is rape sex or violence? Conceptual issues and implications. In *Sex, Power, Conflict: Evolutionary and Feminist Perspectives* (pp. 119–37), edited by D.M. Buss and N.M. Malamuth. New York: Oxford University Press.

Murphey, D.D. 1992. Feminism and rape. *The Journal of Social, Political and Economic Studies* 17(1):13–27.

Paglia, C. 1994. *Vamps and Tramps*. New York: Random House.

Palmer, C.T. 1988. Twelve reasons why rape is not sexually motivated: A skeptical examination. *The Journal of Sex Research* 25(4): 512–30.

———. 1989. Is rape a cultural universal? A re-examination of the ethnographic evidence. *Ethnology* 28: 1–16.

Parillo, V.N., J. Stimson, and A. Stimson. 1985. *Contemporary Social Problems*. New York: John Wiley and Sons, Inc.

Parrot, A. 1991. Vital childhood lessons: The role of parenting in preventing sexual coercion. In *Sexual Coercion* (pp. 123–32), edited by E. Grauerholz and M.A. Koralewski. Lexington, MA: Lexington Books.

Peters, K.A. 1993. Chemical castration: An alternative to incarceration. *Duquesne Law Review* 31: 307–17.

Pfafflin, F. 1992. What is in a symptom? A conservative approach in the therapy of sex offenders. *Journal of Offender Rehabilitation* 18(3/4): 5–17.

Podhoretz, N. 1991. Rape in feminist eyes. *Commentary* 92(4):29–35.

Polasheck, D.L.L., T. Ward, and S.M. Hudson, 1997. Rape and rapists: Theory and treatment. *Clinical Psychology Review* 17(2): 117–44.

Prentky, R.A. 1997. Arousal reduction in sexual offenders: A review of antiandrogen interventions. *Sexual Abuse: A Journal of Research and Treatment* 9(4): 335–47.

Raboch, J., H. Cerna, and P. Zemek, 1987. Sexual aggressivity and androgens. *British Journal of Psychiatry* 151: 398–400.

Rebish, K.J. 1997. Nipping the problem in the bud: The constitutionality of California's castration law. *New York Law School Journal of Human Rights* 14: 507–17.

Robertson, I. 1981. *Sociology*. New York: Worth Publishers, Inc.

Sanday, P. 1990. *Fraternity Gang Rape*. New York: New York University Press.

Sanford, L T., and A. Fetter. 1979. *In Defense of Ourselves*. New York: Doubleday.

Schwendinger, J.R., and J. Schwendinger. 1985. Homoeconmicus as rapist. In *Violence against Women: A Critique of the Sociobiology of Rape* (pp. 85–114), edited by S.R. Sunday and E. Tobach. New York: Gordian Press.

Scott, E.K. 1993. How to stop rapists? A question of strategy in two rape crisis centers. *Social Problems* 40(3): 343–61.

Shields, W.M., and L.M. Shields. 1983. Forcible rape: An evolutionary perspective. *Ethology and Sociobiology* 4: 115–36.

Sorenson, S.B., and J.W. White. 1992. Adult sexual assault: Overview of research. *Journal of Social Issues* 48(1): 1–8.

A Southern Women's Writing Collective. 1990. Sex resistance in heterosexual arrangements. In *The Sexual Liberals and the Attack on Feminism* (pp. 140–47), edited by D. Leidholdt and J.G. Raymond. New York: Pergamon Press.

Spalding, L.H. 1998. Florida's 1997 chemical castration law: A return to the dark ages. *Florida State University Law Review* 25:1–11.

Stock, W. 1991. Feminist explanations: Male power, hostility and sexual coercion. In *Sexual Coercion* (pp. 61–74), edited by E. Grauerholz and M.A. Koralewski. Lexington, MA: Lexington Books.

Symons, D. 1979. *The Evolution of Human Sexuality*. New York: Oxford University Press.

Syzmanski, L.A., A.S. Devlin, J.C. Chrisler, and S.A. Vyse. 1993. Gender role and attitudes toward rape in male and female college students. *Sex Roles* 29 (1/2): 37–57.

Thiessen, D., and R.K. Young. 1994. Investigating sexual coercion. *Society* (March/April): 60–63.

Thornhill, R., and C.T. Palmer. 2000. *A Natural History of Rape: Biological Bases of Sexual Coercion*. Cambridge, MA: MIT Press.

Thornhill, R., and N.W. Thornhill. 1983. Human rape: An evolutionary analysis. *Ethology and Sociobiology* 4: 137–73.

Tsang, D. C. 1995. Policing 'perversions': Depo-Provera and John Money's new sexual order. In *Sex, Cells, and Same-Sex Desire: The Biology of Sexual Prefer-*

ence (pp. 397–426), edited by J.P. De Ceddo and D.A. Parker. New York: The Haworth Press, Inc.

Vachss, A. 1994. Treating sexual offenders: The point. In *Crimes of Gender: Violence against Women* (pp. 109–13), edited by G.E. McCuen. Hudson, WI: Gary McCuen Publications, Inc.

Vanderzyl, K.A. 1994. Castration as an alternative to incarceration: An impotent approach to the punishment of sex offenders. *Northern Illinois Law Review* 15: 107–17.

Ward, C.A. 1995. *Attitudes toward Rape: Feminist and Social Psychological Perspectives*. London: Sage Publications.

Warner, C.G. 1980. *Rape and Sexual Assault: Management and Intervention*. Germantown, MD: Aspen Publications.

White, J.W., and R. Farmer. 1992. Research methods: How they shape views of sexual violence. *Journal of Social Issues* 48(1): 45–59.

Willie, R., and K.M. Beier. 1989. Castration in Germany. *Annals of Sex Research* 2: 103–33.

Windle, R.C., and M. Windle. 1995. Longitudinal patterns of physical aggression: Associations with adult social, psychiatric, and personality functioning and testosterone levels. *Development and Psychopathology* 7: 563–85.

Wright, R. 1994. Feminists, meet Mr. Darwin. *The New Republic* (November 24): 34–46.

4

A Critical Critique of the Cultures of Control: A Case Study of Cyber Rape

Livy A. Visano

Rape is . . . nothing more or less than a conscious process of intimidation by which all men keep all women in a state of fear.

Susan Brownmiller (1975, 58)

INTRODUCTION: CULTURE, CAPITAL, AND COERCION

Violence against women is a form of social control. All aspects of male intimidation—physical, emotional and psychological—seek to maintain masculine privilege, that is male supremacy (Stanko 1985, 9; Beirne and Messerschmidt 1991, 52; Davies 1997). This power to victimize women is socially structured in ways that accommodate patriarchy and the advances of capitalism, which together ensure the continued vulnerability of women. Accordingly, it is essential to examine how social, economic, and political orders sustain a dominant culture of inequality between the sexes.

Rape, a male invention, is a sociopolitical consequence of inequality. The celebration of rape on the Internet is one of the most insidious instruments of violence against women. Cyber rape commoditizes women for the "entertainment" of men thereby promoting the hatred of women. Rape is an act of power or a "pseudosexual act" rather than an act of erotic or biological desire (Ellis 1989, 11). The aim of this chapter is to explore the relationships between law and cyber rape within wider cultural contexts of coercion. This chapter examines forms of "virtual" violence against women as a social harm that impacts on the authentic identities and everyday life experiences of all women. Moreover, it is argued that any discussion of the regulation of rape pornography on the Internet must be contextualized within relations of domination that have been developed and fine-tuned by legal, economic forces and cultural forces. Our case study of "cyber rape" demonstrates how the commonsense, naturalized or taken-for-granted nature of misogyny is ultimately related to the contradictions in liberal democratic thought and invites Internet consumers to be aware of the online constructions of gendered identities. Specifically, this study highlights the limitations of law in dealing with the fundamental social problem of violence against women.

It is, however, beyond the scope of this chapter to undertake a complete socio-history of rape, which enjoys a rich intellectual history. Likewise, this chapter does not engage in a debate regarding the relationship between exposure to sexually explicit materials and abuse, a topic that has also received considerable attention and about which the results of studies are inconclusive and inconsistent (Check 1984; Dworkin 1981; MacKinnon, C. 1984; MacKinnon, R. 1997a; Schwartz and DeKeseredy 1998; Scott and Cuvelier 1993).

INTERNET AS A MEDIATING CONTEXT

The Internet is a technological innovation that can be utilized as an informative, educational, and entertaining tool. At the beginning of the 1990s, the World Wide Web, with its communications paths, edges, and nodes, actually promised the possibility of alternative links and experiences, in opposition to the monopoly of the traditional media (Strehovec 1997). This information superhighway has ushered in new levels in communications and informational retrieval. This new information technology is rapidly and directly affecting the nature of economic, political, and social relations. From the technological advances that allow the immediate and global transfer of information and "money" to the more local ideas of how we see ourselves as connected individuals, the Internet is having a major social impact.

Briefly, the Internet is an international computer network that links more than tens of thousands of independently managed computer networks (Rimm 1995), local networks around the world, used by millions of people. This information highway provides access to an endless variety of topics with the simple "click" of a mouse. Cyberspace is a globally networked, computer-sustained, computer-accessed, and computer-generated, multidimensional, artificial, or "virtual" reality. In this reality, to which every computer is a window, seen or heard objects are neither physical nor, necessarily, representations of physical objects but are rather characters and action, made up of data of pure information. Web sites, documents on the Internet with information on particular topics, are found by using a specific address or by searching key words linked to other documents (Web sites) on the Internet. There are over 200 million world-wide users of the Internet (Simon 1998). No single person or organization controls or administers the Internet and its enormous amount of information transmitted over the system—it exists because individuals have chosen voluntarily to use common data transfer protocols to transmit information. Remote information retrieval, perhaps the most familiar means of Internet communication, allows users to search for and retrieve information located on remote computers (Simon 1998). There are three basic methods of locating and retrieving information. First, file transfer protocol (ftp) lists the names of computer files on remote computers and transfers those files to a local computer. Second, gopher guides a user's search through the available resources on a remote computer. And third, the World Wide Web's (WWW) increasingly dominant method utilizes a hypertext markup language (HTML) and programs that browse the Web displaying HTML documents containing text, images, sound, animation, and moving video. HTML documents often include links to other resources. Search engines seek out Web sites with certain related categories of information or key words.

From this overview, it is apparent that the Internet is a powerful medium of communication. Herein lies the problem. As Neil Postman writes, technology "creates a culture without a moral foundation, undermining certain mental processes and social relations that make human life worth living" (Postman 1992, xii). The Internet has become the largest pornography shop in the world with an incredibly large inventory of pornographic imagery. The current technology allows millions of personal computer users to utilize a home computer, color video monitor, and modem to download and display pornographic images. Pornography on the Internet is widely available in different formats. These range from pictures and short animated movies, to sound files and stories. Most of this kind of pornographic content is available through World Wide Web (WWW) pages; but sometimes they are also distributed through an older communication process, Usenet newsgroups. The Internet also makes it possible to discuss sex, see live sex acts, and arrange sexual activities from computer screens. There are also sex-related discussions on the Internet Relay Chat (IRC) channels where users in small groups or in private channels exchange messages and files. But as with the Web and the Usenet, only a small fraction of the IRC channels are dedicated to sex.

Most images are stored in common computer graphic formats, which can be easily opened and viewed on virtually any computer sold today. The two most popular formats for representing images on a computer are the Graphics Interchange Format (GIF) and Joint Photographic Experts Group (JPEG) formats, indicated by the .gif or .jpg file extensions.

According to Nielsen NetRatings, 17.5 million surfers visited porn sites from their homes in January 2000—a 40 percent increase compared with four months earlier. The top E-Porn site—PornCity.net—boasted more visitors in January than ESPN.com, CDNOW, or barnesandnoble.com. (Koerner 2000, 36). By both online and offline standards, E-porn is also a massive money-maker (Rimm 1995). There are now at least 40,000 sex-oriented sites on the Web, and probably thousands more (Koerner 2000, 36). Computer transmission of obscene material, including text, chat, bulletin boards, and newsgroups exist in cyberspace in an ever-expansive spatial and inclusive temporal terrain that extends beyond all national borders. In the early to mid-1990s, up to 80 percent of all Internet traffic was adult related, and service providers were quick to discover profit opportunities (Koerner 2000, 36).

IDENTIFYING THE PROBLEM: A CASE STUDY OF CYBER RAPE

This study is part of a larger ongoing longitudinal project investigating the impact of law on the culture of cyber pornography. Over a six-month period, a sample was collected primarily by a simple "snowball" technique of "net surfing," which generated leads to more developed Web sites. Searches were conducted by going directly to various engines (Google, Excite, Yahoo!), which provided various cyber cultural articulations of rape. A content analysis of rape photos and stories was conducted, using a flexible "theoretical sampling" scheme that was well-suited and convenient. This study examined the treatment of female characters in cyber rape, analyzing 12,452 freely available sites and vignettes from forty different porn providers. Stories accompanying images were assessed in order to evaluate violent depictions. Images were all coded and categorized. By simply spelling out the word "rape" and clicking on to a Web site, thousands of sites were easily accessed. "Chat rooms" (areas in which Internet users converse with each other on rape subjects) and commercial Bulletin Board Systems (BBS) requiring membership by fee or e-mail address were excluded.

Note the following representative entries of a random sample search yielded simply by typing the word "rape" on the Google search engine, which resulted 32,300 for xxx Rape in a search that took 0.05 second.

Sex Stories free stories of xxx, incest, rape . . . porn stories are of incest, rape, sex, xxx, and Sex. Click here to . . . www.baldbastards.com/stories/daddy.html,

cheerleader free xxx free xxx rape totally free explicit juicy free xxx cutoffs I knew I was very free xxx . . . free-xxx.sextazied.com/

private xxx pics xxx pics sample free rape xxx . . . xxx-pics.sexycocktail.com/

free teen xxx password xxx passwords free rape. . . . xxx-password.sexmegalopolis.com/

gang rape pictures xxx rape stories free only rape.bikiniparadise.net/

forcible rape videos xxx free online rape videos. . . . rape-video.q-e.net/

the rape zone xxx anime teen rape raped sexual assault rape.sexcounsellor.com/

sexx.free.xxx-thumbs.com! Adult Rape Rape . . .

sexx.free.xxx-thumbs.com/free/rape-video-girl/index34.html

forced rape xxx free xxx free pictures of nude lolitas xxx-free.celebritygrils.com/-

www.redlighthost.com/xxx/alexxx/rape.html RedLlightHost - Adult Web Hosting -

xxx-rape.strongcash.com/

xxx comic teen rape . . . www.xxx-files.com/homeav17.htm

free xxx vivo Video movies xxx vivo vivo filles video, black,

"RAPE.HTM">video adult free sample avi a href="SAMPLE.HTM>"xxx . . . gang
rape www.babydoll.com.au/anal05.html

hardcore rape xxx hardcore rape video free hardcore . . . explicit juicy hardcore rape .
hardcore-rape.5zeros.com/

Make Her Squeal!

Welcome On Rape Street!

Zoon 1K+ S The Hottest Free Rape Site on the Web - Site Link

Rake 15 T Rape

Jackal 17 T Rape

===TEEN RAPE===BRUTAL Inhuman Torture & RAPE Fantasy! Extreme Graphic

*** 10000+ PICS OF FETISH, VIOLENT RAPE FANTASY, TORTURE, SLAVES
FROM PRIVATE COLLECTORS.

RAPED AND ABUSED - 40+ FREE PICS RAPE, ABUSE & TORTURE, FAN-
TASIES.

ASIAN, WESTERN & OLDIES SLAVES. FREE PICS (AVS)

Rape Fantasy . . . Abduction Fantasy

In general, findings reveal that all images had sexually violent or dehuman-
izing/degrading themes. The most common thread was nonconsensual
sex-rape, forced physical and mental submission of women. Interestingly, in
the large number of sites sampled, there were no rapes of men. All rape depictions had explicit acts of domination or violent exploitation—women were tortured, gagged, tied, or restrained by other men. Gang rapes constitute a third of
the depictions. Graphic images of rape scenes are frequently accompanied by
equally dehumanizing scripts, titles, headings (captions) such as references to
"whore," "bitch," "skank," or "slut" who needs to be punished. These forms of
degradation are depicted as objects for sexual pleasure. Rape eroticizes power,
as argued by Smart (1989, 117). In our analysis of rape pornography, all males
are depicted as angrily posturing over females, while females are portrayed in a
series of contradictory emotions ranging from pain to pleasure and always in
the foreground. All images concentrate on the objectification of the woman's
body and the phallic subjectivity of men. Specific findings highlight a variety

of messages that further perpetuate inequalities and promote a host of stereotypes.

Social Inequalities

Racism. The results indicate that black women experienced more violence
from both white and black men than was the case for white women. The use of
black women followed by Asian (Japanese especially) reinforces racist stereotypes. Racial and ethnic bigotry accompany acts of physical aggression. The
concept of beauty is based on white values. For example, black women are
made to look white or alternatively serve as a contrast "white purity" of white
women. Note the following racist captions expressed in both rape-specific and
general pornographic depictions:

"give a horny gook some paint and this is what he comes up with" (6/20/00)

vintage spook (6/20/00)

"gooks in bondage . . . dumb c—" (6/19/00)

the ugliest niggah i have ever seen . . . george foster not (11/1/00)

a teen gook in this hardcore series (11/1/00)

if god wanted gooks to have blonde hair you would be able to grow rice in switzerland
(10/31/00)

a beautiful dink with little yellow tits . . . ahhh, to be back in nam again . . . donlinger and
i would f— and kill, f— and kill, f— and kill, f— and kill . . . man, it was pure magic
(10/30/00)

pix of an amateur slut . . . she looks a lot like a nurse i used to plow back in nam . . . she
dumped me when i showed her my necklace made out of the ears of freshly killed gook

Ableism. "it's way too late for this dumb fat c— to lose weight . . . i suggest suicide . . .
death to the obese and people with cerebral palsy" (6/19/00)

Heterosexism. There were dozens of depictions suggesting that lesbians should be
raped by men.

"it's ok to kill transvestites . . . god told me so" (6/20/00)

Ageism. Older white women, in fact, experienced more violence than younger white
and black women. Depictions valorize youth, especially white teenage girls. Note the
following:

"someone remind me to date rape this sweet teen in pink" (4/5/00)

"pix of an old hag named barbara" (6/20/00)

Classism. Approximately 5 percent of images depicted poorer women as "trailer
trash" deserving of brutal violence.

Objectification

The data indicate that in all depictions of rape, gender-specific violence reinscribes male domination. Three interrelated subthemes emerge: framing the body, denying the body, and women as no "body." In rape depictions men compel women to adopt a docile role, thereby forcing women to comply to the disciplinary cadence of male obsession with women's bodies. Within these depictions, women's body parts are amplified, dissected, and reconstructed in images that satisfy male power. Men in turn are judged whether they project an appearance of power and authority. This power can by physical, as communicated through muscles and broad shoulders in a "tough" leather jacket, and macho blue jeans.

Objectification is used to dehumanize women as pleasure objects thereby facilitating rape. Accordingly, as sexual objects, things, or commodities, images suggest to consumers that women do not suffer pain or humiliation. Moreover, as objects of male gratification they are reduced to body parts, penetrated by objects or animals. The identities (male and female) are separated from physical bodies. The conferring of inferiorized identities on women as "filthy" and "stupid" serves to justify sexual submission, tied up, cut up, mutilated, bruised, or any physical injury.

The facial expressions and body language of women in all rape scenes suggest that male power assaults the body and mind (physical, emotional, psychological). This monopoly over violence and its concomitant fear ensure that the body of a woman is owned exclusively by men who do as they please—invade, colonize, and exploit passive victims. The image depicted is both ahistorical and essentialized. That is, the woman's body is never authentic, but rather it is solely a site of coercive compliance. On the other hand, the facial expressions and the body language of men communicate a rule of force. Herein, the woman's body is male property. According to this imagery, in the rape scene the male is claiming sole ownership of property rights.

Phallocentric discourses dominate in a manner that celebrate the violent performances. The phallocentric gestures are weapons used not only to penetrate the female body but also to manipulate the conscious and unconscious desires of women. Note the following:

stupid bitches getting blasted (11/1/00)

as you know i'm not a violent man . . . but something about this allison bitch just makes me want to poke her in the eyes and kick her in the c— (10/31/00)

note to self: stalk this bitch . . . (10/30/00)

i'd sure like to suck the nipples on this trashy teen, after i kick her in the . . . of course. (10/29/00)

The promotion of rape myths is rampant. In images and texts, women are also depicted as enjoying the domination and find it sexually exciting. Images portray victims as smiling during different stages of the rape act. The body language and images of women subsequent to the brutal torture suggest consent, appreciation, and desire. In 50 percent of images, female victims are often depicted as expressing pleasure during and after being raped, suggesting that women enjoy such treatment. According to these insidious images, women enjoy sexual degradation, injury, and torture acts. In summary, these findings corroborate MacKinnon's thesis that "pornography codes how to look at women, so you know what you can do with one when you see one" (MacKinnon 1985, 19). That is, pornography structures the manner in which women are perceived. The data indicate the following about the user/consumer.

Cowardice, Convenience, and Commerce

The Internet pornographers provide consumers with the anonymity they cannot receive from any other medium. This guarantee of anonymity adds to a sense of license. Consumers can choose screen names that disguise their identities. This privacy easily avoids the potential embarrassment of walking into an "adult" store to acquire pornography. Also, consumers can easily conceal their stored images from family members, friends, and associates. Sites are free and easily accessible requiring only limited knowledge of the Internet. These low barriers to entry and the ability to download conveniently provide relatively unlimited consumption to anyone of any age. Internet pornographers market their product in increasingly sophisticated ways by offering a large sample of free images. As noted earlier, the commerce in cyber porn is a billion-dollar industry that promotes consumption. Once the free images are exhausted, providers encourage users to subscribe and pay monthly fees of $30 for the privilege of viewing even "higher quality" X-rated material. Commercial pornographers also typically charge $2.95 to $5.95 (credit card) for one time viewing of sites. Because the use of credit cards compromises anonymity, the industry could be expected to develop e-money as the alternative.

Rape depictions are more than just cross-cultural appropriations disguised as pornographic pleasures. The range of discourses used to construct rape consists of ideological practices that typically articulate a narrative of danger, doubt, and dependency. The text of rape, as a localized script of violence, is written within a larger narrative on misogyny.

THE LIMITS OF LAW: BEYOND THE LIBERAL BANTER

The regulation of cyber rape has ushered in an intense debate on equality and individual rights. On the one hand, the supreme laws of the United States and Canada, their respective constitutions, relentlessly dwell on the inviolability of individual rights, freedom from government interference (Visano 1998). On the other hand, there is a proliferation of legal discourse on equality (the distribution of opportunities), collective rights, and human rights, especially women's rights. The "freedoms versus equality" debates, however, continue to avoid how law is inimical to social justice and how this exaggerated dichotomy of freedom and equality exacerbates attempts to regulate cyber rape.

Legal protections of equality and freedom are of dubious value when unaccompanied by meaningful initiatives or programs. Instead, the law as enshrined in the lofty, nostalgic, and tantalizing moral preambles of the Canadian and American Constitutions tends to resort to attractive legal palliatives and convenient mythologies. What is concealed in the public pronouncements of law and revealed in actual practice of law is the celebration of "possessive individualism," a myopic legal emphasis that historically anchors the culture of capitalism and currently drives the engine of neoliberalism.

The main concern of both Canadian and American jurisprudence in relation to Internet content is child pornography, rather than other forms of pornographic content. In the United States, the regulation of cyberporn has raised many First Amendment questions as the federal and state governments attempt to criminalize, let alone outlaw cyber rape. According to the First Amendment to the Bill of Rights, Congress shall make no law respecting an establishment of religion, or prohibiting the free exercise thereof, or abridging the freedom of speech, or of the press; or the right of the people peaceably to assemble, and to petition the government for a redress of grievances. The First Amendment has been interpreted by the Supreme Court to mean that the federal and state governments should not pass laws that interfere with speech unless it is necessary to protect some perceived public interest. Simply, this legal logic maintains that the censorship of cyber rape is a violation of constitutionally protected "speech" rights. Speech in the context of an adult Web site includes text, images, sound and video files, and other visual and aural forms of communication. "Public interest" means whatever the Court says it means. Much of the current legal definition of obscenity is found in the 1973 case of *Miller v. California* (413 U.S. 15, 1973). Under the so-called "Miller Test," a jury from the jurisdiction where an obscenity charge is brought will decide whether the content in question is obscene by asking whether:

1. The average person, applying contemporary community standards, would find that the work, taken as a whole, appeals to the prurient interests.
2. The work depicts or describes, in a patently offensive way, sexual conduct specifically defined by the applicable state (or federal) law, and
3. The work taken as a whole, lacks serious, artistic, political or scientific value (Report of the Attorney General's Commission on Pornography 1986).

Such a test gives a jury a large role in a case in determining "contemporary community standards." Pornographic material, therefore, can be prohibited if it meets the legal definition of obscenity.

In addition, the U.S. Congress passed the Communications Decency Act of 1996 (CDA). The CDA, as codified in Title V of the Telecommunications Act of 1996, prevents minors from sexually explicit material over the Internet—a goal furthered by the use of criminal sanctions (Simon 1998). In particular the CDA specified that it covered content available via an "interactive computer service." This obviously included materials available on the Internet. In the United States, speech that is not considered "obscene" but is indecent enjoys First Amendment protection, though it can still be regulated where there is a sufficient governmental interest. The fact that the CDA was intended to prohibit "indecent speech" would have had an unprecedented effect on the Internet (Akdeniz 1997).

Thus, immediately after former President Clinton signed the Communications Decency Act into law on February 8, 1996, the American Civil Liberties Union (ACLU) and other civil liberties groups filed a lawsuit against United States Attorney General Janet Reno and the United States Justice Department challenging the CDA as an unconstitutional restraint on free speech on the Internet. The final appeal in the ACLU case resulted in a historic ruling on June 26, 1997, in which by a seven to two vote, the online censorship provisions of the CDA were struck down. The U.S. Supreme Court unanimously ruled that the Communications Decency Act violated the First Amendment. In *Reno v. ACLU*, the U.S. Supreme Court granted the highest level of First Amendment protection to the Internet. The Communications Decency Act of 1996 was found to be unconstitutional due to its statutory ambiguity or vagueness and the chilling effect that government intrusions would have on Internet communications. Despite the Supreme Court's ruling, governments are anxiously crafting censorship laws such as the "Internet Freedom and Family Empowerment Act," the "Protection of Children from Computer Pornography Act," "The Internet School Filtering Act," The "Safe Schools Internet Act," "Child Online Protection Act," "Family-Friendly Internet Access Act of 1997," "Internet Freedom and Child Protection Act of 1997," etc. Many state censorship laws are unconstitutional because they violate the Constitution's Commerce Clause because they criminalize online conversations that occur entirely outside the state's borders and burden interstate commerce.

In Canada, the privacy rights guaranteed under section 8 of the Canadian Charter of Rights and Freedoms are weighed against Her Majesty's interest in collecting electronic evidence in order to facilitate criminal proceedings against an individual who is accused of using email to gain possession of child pornography. As written, section 163 of the Criminal Code defines obscenity as "the undue exploitation of sex" or of sex in combination with crime, horror, cruelty, or violence. This definition is very vague; it remains difficult to determine what "undue" means. Jurisprudence maintains that material must meet the community standards test. On February 27, 1992, in a nine to zero landmark decision in *R. v. Butler*, the Supreme Court upheld the obscenity provision of the Code as constitutional, but it sent the case of a Winnipeg vendor of explicit videotapes, convicted of eight counts of violating Canada's obscenity laws, back for retrial because of new judicial guidelines for assessing obscenity. The Butler case represents a major shift in emphasis in the nation's obscenity laws and adopts many arguments made by the intervenor, Women's Legal Education and Action Fund. In the judgment, Mr. Justice Sopinka, who gave lead opinion that was endorsed by other justices of the Court, spelled out what undue exploitation means. For Sopinka, if true equality between male and female persons is to be achieved, we cannot ignore the threat to equality resulting from exposure to audiences of certain types of violent and degrading materials (Johnson 1995). Materials portraying women as a class as objects for sexual exploitation and abuse have a negative impact on the individual's sense of self-worth and acceptance. The Court defined "undue exploitation" as explicit sex coupled with violence will "almost always" constitute undue exploitation of sex, and explicit sex that is "degrading or dehumanizing" will be undue exploitation if it creates a substantial risk of harm, especially to women. Harm is defined as materials leading to attitudinal changes that may predispose a person to act in an antisocial manner. Degrading or dehumanizing means processes of subordination, servile submission, or humiliation. Canada's obscenity laws are aimed at preventing harm to women and children rather than maintaining conventional standards of sexual propriety.

Interestingly, in the 1992 *Butler* ruling, the Supreme Court of Canada unanimously adopted an equality approach to interpreting the dangers of pornography. Unlike the U.S. Constitution, which does not enjoy an Equal Rights Amendment, the Canadian Charter specifically guarantees sex equality. In *Her Majesty R. v. Butler*, Canada's Supreme Court ruled that society's interest in sex equality outweighs the pornographer's speech rights. The court held that the obscenity law was unconstitutional if used to restrict materials on a moral basis, but constitutional if used to promote sex equality. In reaching the *Butler* decision, the Supreme Court acknowledged that it was violating freedom of speech, but it deemed the possible harm that pornography could inflict on women to be of greater legal significance. Through its decision in the *Butler vs. Her Majesty* case, the Supreme Court of Canada adopted Catherine MacKinnon's definition of obscenity nearly word for word into Canadian law. The Canadian Supreme Court endorsed MacKinnon's view that some sexually explicit material that is "violent and degrading" harms women. MacKinnon, a prominent legal scholar in the United States, was a cofounder of the Women's Legal Action Fund, the Canadian group whose brief shaped the new definition. Her influence was clear in the court's definition of "degrading" materials as those that place women (and sometimes men) in positions of subordination, servile submission, or humiliation (Johnson 1995). MacKinnon proposed a strategy for circumventing constitutional guarantees. She suggested that because pornography subordinates women to men, it is a form of discrimination on the basis of sex. By arguing that censorship is a legitimate tool for attaining civil rights, she has struggled for decades to limit the protection of the First Amendment; MacKinnon's arguments were committed to using censorship as a means of attaining equality. Again for MacKinnon (1993), pornography as hate speech should be restricted. The rights of women to equality should limit constitutional protections to free speech. The law of equality and the law of freedom of speech are on a collision course in this country" (MacKinnon 1993).

This 1992 court decision—which was vigorously championed by most feminists in Canada and the United States—allows Canadian customs to seize what it judges to be pornography at the border as the material is being imported. In reaching the *Butler* decision, the Supreme Court acknowledged that it was violating freedom of speech, but it deemed the possible harm that pornography could inflict on women to be of greater legal significance. In June 1993, the House of Commons passed one of the toughest child pornography laws in the Western world, making it a crime punishable by up to ten years in prison to possess (including computer images), produce, sell, or import child pornography. In Canada, pornography is only illegal if it is criminally "obscene," a term so obscure that, in practice, very little material falls within its definition. In 1993, the Supreme Court of Canada held that criminal obscenity is something that an ordinary adult would consider intolerable not just in his or her own house, but in any house. This is now referred to as the "community standards test." The Supreme Court of Canada faced the difficult task of sorting out Canada's troubled law on the possession of child pornography. But, the government of British Columbia appealed a ruling by a provincial court regarding Canada's controversial child-pornography law that was declared unconstitutional by the British Columbia Court of Appeal in 1999 on the basis that laws against possession of child porn violated the right to freedom of expression. The law has been criticized as being too broad and too constraining on personal freedom of expression.

On January 26, 2001, the Supreme Court of Canada upheld a law criminalizing the possession of child pornography—but it carved out narrow exceptions to protect private works of the imagination or photographic depictions of oneself (Makin 2001). According to the Supreme Court of Canada, "It is a fine line that separates a state attempt to control the private possession of self-created expressive materials from a state attempt to control thought and opinion" (Makin 2001, A1). The judgment reinstated two child pornography possession charges against a sixty-seven-year-old Vancouver man—John

Robin Sharpe—that had been dismissed in 1999. Sharpe challenged the constitutionality of the law, arguing that banning simple possession of child pornography violates the Charter of Rights. The Canadian Civil Liberties Association noted that the court failed to clarify whether someone who views child porn on the Internet without downloading or printing it is guilty of possession (ibid). All nine Supreme Court judges agreed that outlawing the possession of child pornography is a "reasonable limit" on freedom of expression. This means that the Charter of Rights can never be used again to justify the possession of child pornography. The Charter of Rights does not condone, excuse, or allow any activity that feeds on the sexual exploitation of children.

From this legal overview, it is obvious that there is no settled definition of pornography where cultural, moral, and legal variations make it difficult to define "pornographic content" in a way acceptable to all. What is considered simply sexually explicit but not obscene in one country may well be obscene in many other countries. There appears to be no single solution to the regulation of illegal and harmful content on the Internet because, for example, the exact definition of offences such as pornography varies from one country to another and also what is considered harmful will depend upon cultural differences.

The Internet is a complex, anarchic, and multinational environment where old concepts of regulation, reliant as they are upon tangibility in time and space, may not be easily applicable or enforceable (Akdeniz 1997). The regulation of cyberspace has been ineffective for reasons also relating to technological difficulties. Computer-generated criminal behavior is hard to trace and track down because of the Internet's wide scope (Lamb 1998). The Internet is a new technological advancement, and its very lack of frontiers makes law enforcement extremely difficult. No one institution owns and controls the Internet. Messages are passed from one computer system to another in milliseconds and the network resembles a web of computers and telephone lines. Therefore, one of the problems regarding regulation is legal jurisdiction. For example, the following questions warrant inquiry. How are sources (point-of-origin) and destination (point-of-access) of offensive practices monitored? In the absence of legitimate international law and policing, how do differential legal and cultural standards of different countries vitiate effective enforcement? The infringement of human rights goes beyond local North American concerns. How do American and Canadian police forces secure the cooperation of foreign investigators? These and other dilemmas created by the nonphysical, nongeographical reality of cyberspace exacerbate a community standard approach. Local or national attempts to regulate content on cybernet contradict current initiatives facilitating the electronic mobility of capital, goods and services, and labor. Even after child pornographic GIFs or JPEGs (image files) are located and seized, they may be unreadable. Due to increasing availability of sophisticated encryption technology, all computer files, including GIFs, can be "scrambled" so thoroughly that they are virtually impossible for law enforcers to unscramble without sophisticated decoders.

Clearly, the concept justice has become confined narrowly within a juridic framework of ambiguous rules. Law is constructed in reference to well-established, albeit poorly understood, impressions that are grounded in mythologies of equality and sibling freedom. Legal protections and initiatives are of dubious value when unaccompanied by meaningful programs that embrace universal entitlements. Kristol (1999), Lacombe (1994), and Easton (1994), therefore, question the ability of law to intervene in the pornographic social construction of sexualized gender relations. The domain of legal authority has failed to modify community values, moral practices, and norms of interpersonal conduct (Tatalovich and Daynes 1988).

Laws have not been effective in regulating the pornography industry. Quite the contrary, Internet pornography has enjoyed unparalleled growth. It is not possible to access the Internet without the services of an Internet Service Provider (ISP), and thus the role of ISPs in content regulation of the Internet is crucial. The preferred option for governments in relation to the regulation of ISPs is one of self-regulation rather than control by legislation (Akdeniz 1997). ISPs have been encouraged to produce codes of practice to control access to illegal and unsuitable material. To allay criticisms, this industry has been active in promoting self-policing through a series of voluntary steps (Gruenwald 1998). The Internet providers argue that there is no way that they can control the information that crosses their networks. They hope that they will eventually be considered common carriers, as the telephone companies are, and therefore not be liable for what transpires over their networks. Examples of software released in recent years to limit Internet access to children include: Cyber Patrol; CYBERsitter; The Internet Filter; Net Nanny; Parental Guidance; SurfWatch; Netscape Proxy Server; and WebTrack. CYBERsitter programs limiting access to these sites. Take for example, http://www.free-voyeurism.com/, which on October 28, 2000, noted

You are responsible for what your child is exposed to on the Internet. There is an abundance of great tools available to help you regulate what your child has access to on the net. We strongly encourage you to explore these options. Links to the top resources have been supplied below:

SurfWatch

NetNanny

Cyber Patrol

Cyber Sentinel

CyberSitter

Internet Filter Suite

This charade, disguised as industry self-regulation, demonstrates the continued shift in control from government to self-serving private interests that have kept pace with rapid changes in technology (Samoriski, Huffman, and Trauth 1997).

CRITICAL CULTURAL THEORY: A QUESTION OF VALUES

Law as a normative guide provides society with diverse proscriptions of propriety. More importantly, law also articulates the dominant culture. Although presented publicly as objective, neutral, and independent, law is not a "disembodied spectacle" (O'Neill 1985), divorced from its larger social anchors—culture, history, and economics. As Habermas (1974) indicated, the meanings and symbols of the dominant ideology prevent critical thinking by penetrating social processes, language, and individual consciousness. Consequently, recourse to law is rarely the most effective way to deal with social problems. To fully appreciate the conditions and consequences of cyber rape, it is necessary to understand how this phenomenon is contextualized culturally, mediated politically, and legitimated legally. An understanding of the way in which women are culturally perceived is crucial to an understanding of the whole problem of rape pornography, a subject that has been woefully ignored by law. As Johnson (1995) argues in reference to pornography generally:

I suggest that agents of the state responsible for judicial practice fail to comprehend the complexity of pornography. Owing to this failure, the law tends to persist in legitimizing, and thereby normalizing, what I refer to as currently unequal socio-subjectivity and practices. Thus porn law has reproduced rather than changed gender power relations. (p. 7)

Lastly, this chapter suggests that the processes and structures of cyber rape are indistinguishable from generic forms of gender representation. Critical cultural approaches provide an alternative framework in appreciating the form and content of pornography as a major component of American popular culture (Schlosser 1997). Cyber rape should be analyzed in light of larger patterns of political, economic, and social inequalities along gender, race, class, and sexual orientation lines thereby challenging many of the hegemonic narratives of inequality that operate in modern culture.

Within North American popular culture, gender relations are based on various forms of domination (Baxandall 1995). The traffic and consumption of cyber rape are constitutive and reflective of both patriarchy and capitalism, which in turn succeed in producing their own fictive justifications replete with language, attitudes, and ideas that define away the essence of a woman's body. Cyber rape is a representation of patriarchal symbols and practices that indicate the particular social location of women. Simply, cyber rape is a male invention, designed to dehumanize women and to reduce the female to an object of sexual access. Consumed as cultural controls, the woman's pain is the man's pleasure. The staple of cyber rape is brutality—the woman's tortured mind (will) and body (breasts and genitals) are sites of domination. These images and stereotypes are ingrained in a popular culture that promotes illusions of phallic masculinity. If women are presented purely in terms of their genitals, how can they be seen as fully human and men's equals (Willis 1997; MacKinnon 1993)? A critical cultural perspective overcomes the limitations of the subject-object, consumer-product dichotomies by encouraging an awareness of the links between popular pleasures and collective political struggles (Walters 1999). Central to this theorizing is the delineation of modern consumption and the nature of female embodiment in Western culture (Falk 1994). As feminists note, explicit sexual imagery can offer more positive opportunity than harm for women (Valverde 1991) such as female sexual freedom and pleasure pitted against victimization, danger, and repression.

To appreciate the violence against women, one should look at the political and economic systems that keep women powerless. Instead of fighting pornography alone, Pally (1985) encourages women to fight for equal and comparable pay, for a feminist presence in politics, sex education, nontraditional jobs, abortion, self-defense classes, better birth control dissemination, and for much more. The Internet, like any other institution of society, reflects the values of the larger society (Stewart 1977) with such concepts of capital, circulation, and "rational" exploitation of markets gaining considerable currency. The main catharsis driving the pornography industry is profit: consumption as governed by the laws of supply and demand. Schlosser (1997) states that the American sex industry offers a textbook example of how a free market system can efficiently harness production to meet consumer demand. Pornography satisfies the requirements of capitalism with its emphasis on rationality, market forces, anonymity, profit, and a quasi-industrial instruction in efficient production.

Although the United States has some of the toughest restrictions on pornography, tougher than any other Western industrialized nation, it is nonetheless the world's largest producer of pornography (Schlosser 1997). Pornography has been part of North American society for many decades and will continue unabatedly until there is no demand. In other words, economic profit is derived from male sexual power. According to Keith Condon, vice president of Atlas Multimedia, whose holdings include LivePorn.com, "a large, mainstream E-commerce company needs to go out of its way to create demand, [to] explain why it is important. . . . We don't. We work on filling demand that's already there" (Koerner 2000, 36). Overall, Web surfers spent $970 million on access to adult-content sites in 1998, according to the research firm Datamonitor, and that figure could rise to more than $3 billion by 2003. A Forrester Research report estimates that cyberporn sales accounted for 8 percent of last year's $18 billion E-commerce pie. That's about the same as the amount spent online for books ($1.3 billion in 1999) and more than plane tickets (less than $800 million). With low advertising and labor costs, adult sites typically enjoy profit margins of 30 percent or more. Online brokerages, among the few Internet ventures to rival adult sites in popularity, are far less lucrative. The 1998 profit margin for Ameritrade, for example, was just 0.2 percent. America Online, which tirelessly promotes itself as family friendly, owes a great deal to sex; its early survival depended on E-porn and spicy chat, the latter of which brought in an estimated $7 million per month at one point (Koerner 2000, 36).

Instead of wondering how to control the Internet, it may be appropriate to examine what Baudrillard calls a seduction, "a locus of that which eludes you, and whereby you elude yourself and your own truth" (Baudrillard 1988, 66). Specifically, it is imperative that as researchers we challenge the pervasive pathology of fragmentation and its attendant theory of possessive individualism, the foundations of patriarchy, and capitalism. By understanding the fragmentation of culture (Toulouse 1997), one realizes that the ideology of cyber rape is aided by more than a system of lenient laws that serve to protect pornographers but by an aggressive male domination over women deeply imbedded in our cultural value system. Acts of violent degradation and possession (Brownmiller 1975, 389–91) have feminist scholars to draw on the insights of Michel Foucault, urging us to develop "new ways of thinking and speaking" (Hess and Marx Ferree 1989, 519). Rather than focus on only the body of women in these depictions, it is necessary to consider the consciousness or mind of the man (Crowley and Himmelweit 1992, 65). Again, rather than pushing for the legal censorship of pornography alone, which at this juncture is unattainable, a critical critique that fights to control, politicize, and rehumanize culture is long overdue (Daileader 1997).

CONCLUSIONS

Cyber rape commodifies violence against women. Both the class structure of capitalism and the culture of patriarchy privilege men who in turn are encouraged to exploit women on a routine basis. Oppressive power imbalances that are deeply rooted in patriarchal societies and perpetuated by capitalism keep all women in a state of fear (Brownmiller 1975, 5). This horror threatens physically and psychologically the freedoms of women by controlling and distorting their lives (Pitch 1985, 38; Toner 1977). Rape laws, originally linked to property rights and developed out of trespass laws, were designed to protect men's property (Dowdesdell 1986, 43). Rape was seen simply as a form of theft, essentially an offense against male property—an infringement against sole ownership (Clark and Lewis 1977).

Rape pornography does not solely exist in the contexts of sex emporiums, theaters, peep shows, bookstores, and films, but it is well located in many sites of male power in the dominant culture. Likewise, pornography goes beyond the degrading acts of torturing, bonding, mutilating, urinating, defecating, or spitting on women (Longino 1980), to include the routine humiliating subjugation of women—that is, hate literature and practices of hatred against women.

The sociopolitical contexts of control are contests shaped by cultural imperatives that ensure values promoting male privilege. Clearly, fundamental changes at all levels of society and culture are required to liberate women (Hartmann 1979, 231). New ways to alter institutions and deeply held values are long overdue in continuing the assault against patriarchy and capitalism. In this struggle against the anti-feminist agenda, men can no longer remain silent. By unravelling the contradictions, exposing the myths, and by moving beyond the acknowledgment of women's oppression, men are also required to speak loudly and act openly against the tyrannic treatment of women. Rather than retreat into convenient cowardice of virtual reality, men must move beyond recognizing their respective privilege and confront their limited consciousness and, as Valverde (1991, 241) instructs, challenge the organization of basic social categories. In so doing, men will appreciate Luce Irigaray's (1985, 84–85) social indictment:

Women are "products" used and exchanged by men. Their status is that of merchandise, "commodities." . . . Commodities . . . do not take themselves to market on their own. . . . What would become . . . if women, who have been only objects of consumption or exchange . . . were to become "speaking subjects" as well.

Likewise Rowbotham (1989, 281) clarifies:

Consciousness within the revolutionary movement can only become coherent and self-critical when its version of the world becomes clear not simply within itself but when it knows itself in relation to what it has created apart from itself. When we look back at ourselves through cultural creations . . . we begin to integrate a new reality.

By linking the intrapsychic to the intersubjective, "it is important to resist the temptation that law offers, namely the promise of solution" (Smart 1989, 165). Feminist jurisprudence "signals the shift away from a concentration on law reform and adding women into legal considerations to a concern with fundamental issues like legal logic, legal values, justice, neutrality and objectivity" (ibid, 66). The criminal justice system is not a reliable ally. As Snider (1991, 239) argues, "entrusting more power to it means investing it with increased control over women's lives, control that is essentially invisible and unmonitored." The development of cyberspace distanciates its inhabitants from local controls and the physical confines of nationality, sovereignty, and governmentality leading to further the unprecedented and unpredictable dangers unleashed by the vagaries an avaricious "free market."

NOTE

The author wishes to extend to Professor Brenda Spotton Visano his considerable gratitude for the insightful comments regarding the economics of pornography as well as the direction of feminist inquiries. Dr. Debra Kelley's substantive and editorial suggestions were very helpful and supportive. A special acknowledgment is extended to Dragan Spasojevic, who provided a list of Web sites for comparison purposes.

REFERENCES

Akdeniz, Yaman. 1997. *Governance of Pornography and Child Pornography on the Global Internet: A Multi-Layered Approach. Law and the Internet: Regulating Cyberspace*, edited by L. Edwards and C. Waelde. Oxford: Hart Publishing.

Baudrillard, Jean. 1988. *The Ecstasy of Communication.* New York: Semiotext(e).

Baxandall, Rosalyn. 1995. Marxism and Sexuality: The Body as Battleground. In *Marxism in the Postmodern Age: Confronting the New World Order,* pp. 235–245, edited by Antonio Callari, Stephen Cullenberg, and Carole Biewener. New York: Guilford Press.

Beirne, P., and J. Messerschmidt. 1991. *Criminology.* New York: Harcourt, Brace and Jovanovich.

Brownmiller, Susan. 1975. *Against Our Will.* New York: Simon and Schuster.

Check, James. 1984.The Effects of Violent and Nonviolent Pornography. Department of Justice, Ottawa, Canada (June).

Clark, Lauren, and Deborah Lewis. 1977. *Rape.* Toronto: Women's Press.

Crowley, Helen, and Susan Himmelweit. 1992. *Knowing Women.* Cambridge: Polity Press.

Daileader, Celia. 1997. The uses of ambivalence: Pornography and female heterosexual identity. *Women's Studies* 26 (1): 73–88.

Davies, K. 1997. Voluntary exposure to pornography and men's attitudes toward feminism and rape. *The Journal of Sex Research* 34 (2, Spring): 131–38.

Dowdesdell, Jane. 1986. *Women on Rape.* New York: Thompson.

Dworkin, Ronald. 1981. Is there a right to pornography? *Oxford Journal of Legal Studies* 1 (2, Summer): 177–212.

Easton, Susan. 1994. *The Problem of Pornography: Regulation and the Right to Free Speech.* London: Routledge.

Ellis, L. 1989. *Theories of Rape: Inquiries into the Causes of Sexual Aggression.* New York: Hemisphere Publishing.

Falk, Pasi. 1994. *The Consuming Body.* London: Sage.

Gruenwald, Juliana. 1998. Panel again looks to limit Internet porn to children. *Congressional Quarterly Weekly Report* 56 (Feb. 14): 388–89.

Habermas, Jurgen. 1974. *Theory and Practice.* London: Heinemann.

Hartmann, Heidi. 1979. Capitalism, patriarchy and job segregation by sex. In *Capitalist Patriarchy and the Case for Socialist Feminism,* edited by Z. Eisenstein. New York: Monthly Review Press.

Hess, Beth, and Myra Marx Ferree. 1989. *Analyzing Gender.* Newbury Park: Sage.

Irigaray, Luce. 1985. *This Sex Is Not One*. Ithaca: Cornell University Press.

Johnson, Kirsten. 1995. *Undressing the Canadian State: The Politics of Pornography*. Halifax: Fernwood.

Koerner, Brendan. 2000 (March 27). A lust for profits. *U.S. News & World Report* 128(12): 36.

Kristol, Irving. 1999. Liberal censorship and the common culture. *Society* 36 (6[242], Sept-Oct): 5–10.

Lacombe, Dany. 1994. *Blue Politics: Pornography and the Law in the Age of Feminism*. Toronto: University of Toronto Press.

Lamb, Michael. 1998. Cybersex: Research Notes on the Characteristics of the Visitors to Online Chat Rooms. *Deviant Behavior* 19 (2, April–June): 121–35.

Longino, H. 1980. Pornography, oppression, and freedom: A closer look. In *Take Back the Night*, edited by L. Lederer. New York: William Morrow and Company.

MacKinnon, Catharine. 1984. Not a Moral Issue. *Yale Law Policy Review* 2:321–45.

——— . 1985. Pornography, civil rights, and speech. *Harvard Civil Rights—Civil Liberties Law Review* 20:1–70.

——— . 1993. *Only Words*. Cambridge: Harvard University Press.

MacKinnon, Richard. 1997. The social construction of rape in virtual reality. In *Network and Netplay: Virtual Groups on the Internet*, edited by F. Sudweeks, M. McLaughlin, and S. Rafaeli. Menlo Park: AAAI/MIT Press.

Makin, Kirk. 2001. Top Court Rules 9–0: Child Porn Law Stays. *Toronto Star*. Saturday, January 27, A1.

O'Neill, John. 1985. *Five Bodies*. Ithaca: Cornell University Press.

Pally, Marcia. 1985. Ban sexism, not pornography. *The National* 240: 794–98.

Pitch, T. 1985. Critical criminology: The construction of social problems and the question of rape. *International Journal of the Sociology of Law* 13:35–46.

Postman, Neil. 1992. *Technopoly: The Surrender of Culture to Technology*. New York: Alfred A. Knopf.

Report of the Attorney General's Commission on Pornography. 1986. Edited by Michael McManus. Nashville: Rutledge Hill Press.

Rimm, Marty. 1995. Marketing pornography on the information superhighway. *Georgetown Law Journal* 83 (June): 1849–1934.

Rowbotham, Sheila. 1989. Women's consciousness, men's world. In *An Anthology of Western Marxism*, edited by Roger Gottlieb. New York: Oxford University Press.

Samoriski, Jan, John Huffman, and Denise Trauth. 1997. The V-chip and cyber cops: Technology vs. regulation. *Communication Law and Policy* 7 (2, 1 [winter]): 143–64.

Schlosser, E. 1997. The business of pornography: Most of the outsize profits being generated by pornography today are being earned by businesses not traditionally associated with the sex industry. *U.S. News & World Report* (February 10) 122 (5): 42–51.

Schwartz, Martin, and Walter DeKeseredy. 1998. Pornography and the Abuse of Canadian Women in Dating Relationships. *Humanity and Society* 22 (2).

Scott, J.E., and S.J. Cuvelier. 1993. Violence and sexual violence in pornography: Is it really increasing? *Archives of Sexual Behavior* 22 (4 [August]): 357–72.

Simon, Glenn. 1998. Cyberporn and censorship: Constitutional barriers to preventing access to internet pornography by minors. Reno v. ACLU, 117 S. Ct. 2329 (1997). *The Journal of Criminal Law and Criminology* 88 (3, Spring): 1015–48.

Smart, Carol. 1989. *Feminism and the Power of Law*. London: Routledge.

Snider, Laureen. 1991. The potential of the criminal justice system to promote feminist concerns. In *The Social Basis of Law*, edited by Elizabeth Comack and Stephen Brickey. Halifax: Garamond.

Stanko, E. 1985. Would you believe this woman? In *Judge, Lawyer, Victim, Thief*, edited by N. Hahn Raffer and E. Stanko. Boston: Northeastern University Press.

Stewart, Douglas. 1977. Pornography, obscenity, and capitalism. *Antioch Review* 35 (4 [fall]):389–98.

Strehovec, Janez. 1997. The Web as an instrument of power and a realm of freedom. *Ctheory* (26 June).

Tatalovich, Raymond, and Byron Daynes. 1988. *Social Regulatory Policy: Moral Controversies in American Politics*. Boulder: Westview Press.

Toner, B. 1977. *Facts about Rape*. London: Hutchenson.

Toulouse, Chris. 1997. Introduction. *New Political Science* 41–42 (fall): 1–16.

Valverde, Mariana. 1991. Feminist Perspectives on Criminal Cases. In *Criminology*, edited by Jane Gladstone, Richard Ericson, and Clifford Shearing. Toronto: Center of Criminology.

Visano, Livy. 1998. *Crime and Culture*. Toronto: Canadian Scholars.

Walters, Suzanna. 1999. Sex, Text, and Context: (In) Between Feminism and Cultural Studies. In *Revisioning Gender*, pp. 222–57, edited by Myra Marx Ferree, Judith Lorber, and Beth Hess. Thousand Oaks: Sage.

Willis, Clyde. 1997. The Phenomenology of Pornography: A Comment on Catharine MacKinnon's *Only Words*. *Law and Philosophy* 16 (2 [April]): 177–99.

Case law

ACLU et al. v. Janet Reno, 929 F Supp 824 (1996)

Miller v. California, 413 U.S. 15 (1973)

R. v. Butler, [1992] 1 S.C.R. 452, 89 D.L.R. (4th) 449–499

5

Sexual Assault behind Bars: The Forgotten Victims

Charles Crawford

INTRODUCTION

Perhaps one of the most disturbing consequences of the recent imprisonment binge is the act of forcible rape of men and boys behind the walls of our nation's prisons and jails. When a serious examination of this problem is undertaken, the public and even some correctional officials react with a mixture of horror, disgust, and sometimes denial. The administrative response has been tepid at best. According to the Bureau of Justice Statistics (2000), as of midyear 1999, there were roughly 1.2 million men under state and federal correctional custody, with an additional 537,800 men in county jails across the United States. With so many lives at stake, prison rape is a disturbing cold reality for far too many of our nation's inmates.

Most of the public finds it difficult to imagine the rape of males, and to many it simply does not exist. For those who are willing to believe that such a thing exists, there are numerous misconceptions about male rape. For example, "real" men cannot be raped, and males who rape are homosexual. Of particular importance for this discussion is the misconception that once raped, a man is no longer a true "man." Steven Donaldson points out in his chapter in the 1990 text *The Encyclopedia of Homosexuality,* historically, in some societies the rape of the losing warrior was considered essential and a part of being the victor in battle. Once raped, a man could no longer be a leader or warrior in any capacity.

Because of these beliefs many of the victims simply choose not to expose the violence perpetrated against them.

Rape is most often conceptualized as a male-on-female sexual assault. This view is often correct outside of custodial institutions. This conceptualization is reflected in most accepted definitions of rape that were sparked by the work of concerned women and feminists of the 1970s. As Diana Scully (1995) points out, rape was "discovered" during the decade of the 1970s. Most often, feminist theory categorizes rape as a power relationship between men and women, one that is characterized by violence. This violence for many has become part of the fabric of life and has lead to a host of varied explanations for this criminal act that range from rape as a disease in which the offender is unable to control his sex drive, to rape as a learned and rewarding behavior[1] (Scully 1995).

Although the numbers of male-on-male rape in the community are smaller than those for male on female, it does in fact occur, and is perhaps more prevalent than one might imagine. Porter (1986) claims that based on research conducted in the 1980s, boys and girls have an *equal* chance of being sexually assaulted up until their early teens. In 1994, 32,900[2] men and boys over the age of twelve reported having been a victim of sexual assault in the National Crime Victim Survey (Bureau of Justice Statistics 1997). Because of the intense personal nature of rape, the incidence of male rape in the community is difficult to measure due to underreporting and the stigma attached to being a sexual assault victim of another male. Nonetheless, if sexual assault in the community is a concern for men and boys, its prevalence and threat is many times greater behind the walls of prison.

PRISON RAPE—THE RESEARCH

The traditional view of prison rape was that it was one of the "pains of imprisonment" (Sykes 1958). Essentially, it was viewed as simply being a part of the denial of a heterosexual lifestyle and therefore a part of the punishment process. Based on this assumption, society turns a blind eye to victimization behind bars. Prison sexuality, including prison rape, has drawn the attention of researchers and popular writers, most notably Donaldson (1990), Tewksbury (1989), Wooden and Parker (1982), Bowker (1980), and Scacco (1975). Rape in prison has become an institutionalized tradition, in which the battle is over manhood and controlling one's body. Assessing the number of men and boys raped in our nation's prisons is difficult; official crime measures fail to come to terms with the number of victims that are abused in state custody. The Bureau of Justice Statistics does not include prisoners in its measures of victimization, nor are there reporting centers to help us define the nature and extent of rape in prison.

The male prison subculture[3] is defined by a rigid class system with race as a key element. In prison terminology, one who is a "man" is defined by his masculinity and heterosexual status. These inmates define themselves as heterosexual and lead heterosexual lives after prison, and many are aggressors in sexual assaults or join in assaults on weaker inmates. Within the subculture of male prisons, it is the penetration of another male that helps to reinforce and establish their dominance as "men." However, as Donaldson (1990) points out, manhood in prison is tenuous at best, and even the strongest inmates can be overpowered and have this desired status stripped away in a flash of violence.

Furthermore, the demand for sexual partners is difficult to meet, increasing the chance that some inmates will become victims of sexual assault and "claimed" as property of another inmate. It is a curious blend of a need for sexual outlet, power, and establishing dominance in the name of status and manhood. Inmates can and do abstain from this test of manhood and violence, but their claims to the status of "man" may be questioned and in some cases challenged by others.

Sexual Roles in Prison

Inmates have a clearly defined subculture with a distinct set of norms and roles. Although it is difficult to classify all inmates based on sexual behavior and preference, different roles do exist in prison based on the status of manhood. The role of "man" as defined in the preceding section, is one who is the active participant in a same-sex encounter. The role is defined by aggressive sexual activity, and at the pinnacle of this role is to "possess" a sexually receptive, weaker inmate, thus validating and reinforcing the status of manhood. In a sense, the sexual deprivation of prison life creates a situation where some men feel they must seek out the opportunity to define themselves. It must be noted that not all men engage in aggressive patterns of sex, some opt to remain abstinent during their incarceration, particularly older inmates. There are "men" who seek out a companion in order to do their time in a relationship, often a powerful and emotional one.

"Queens" in prison terminology are inmates who are known homosexuals, and by definition they are second-class citizens. They are effeminate in behavior and dress, and their actions in prison are not that different from their activity on the street. In addition, because of their known receptive sexual status, they are not seen as "men" nor are they given the same respect or status in prison life. Interestingly, discovered homosexuals who do not subscribe to the role of "queen"—that is, one that takes on the feminine role—are seen as threats. This can be realized in the question, how can one be a "man" and be a sexual receptive partner to "real" men? These discovered homosexuals are often pressured into assuming a more feminine role and mannerism and sometimes names. The pressures on these inmates can be so great to adopt a new role that, according to Donaldson (1990), there is little room for a self-affirming independent homosexual—their choices are to try and pass as a heterosexual, be forced into the queen role, or face combat, time and time again.

The lowest class of inmates and most relevant for the discussion of this chapter are "punks." These are usually young men who define themselves are heterosexual but have been forced into the sexually receptive role, or in prison terminology they have been "turned out"—referring to the inversion of their gender (Donaldson 1990). This is most often accomplished through the threat of rape or actual gang rape. The life of a "punk" is usually one of terror behind bars, as one is marked as weaker and subject to sexual harassment and sexual attack. Trying to escape this role is nearly impossible, as the reputation tends to follow the inmate from cellblock to cellblock, even institution to institution. These young men are frequent targets of rape; they tend to be the youngest, least violent of inmates and often first time offenders.

THE PREVALENCE OF RAPE BEHIND BARS

As Donaldson (1990) points out, rape is probably the most dreaded prison and jailhouse experience. Although it is similar in nature to the rape of males outside of prisons, the chief difference is that rape behind bars is an accepted and often protected activity. A prison for far too many young men becomes a testing ground, not a place of reform, reflection, or even punishment. These young men are tested to see if they are true "men." Many inmates delight in the variety of ways that they can seduce, force, or con a younger less knowledgeable inmate into the role of a punk.

Measuring the extent or rape behind bars is difficult. For inmates to admit that they have been sexually assaulted is the same as admitting that they are not men, and cannot control access to the one possession they own—their bodies. It can be humbling to say the least. Nonetheless several researchers have attempted to extrapolate the number of sexual assaults that take place behind bars.

Jails

One the earliest attempts to capture the number of rape victims in jails comes from a 1968 survey of the Philadelphia jails by Chief Assistant District Attorney Alan J. Davis with the help of the police department. Davis found that 3.3 percent of all males who were incarcerated in Philadelphia's jails were sexually assaulted. Furthermore, the official records only captured 3.2 percent of these rapes. Working with these numbers, Donaldson (1995) extrapolates the incidents nationally based on the number of adult males in the 3,300 jails in the country. He estimates that in 1994 there were 14,300 victims in the jails at any time and that 290,000 males were victimized in jail every year, 192,000 of them penetrated, with a repeat rate *very conservatively* estimated at every other day;

counting gang-rapes as a single incident, this gives at least 7,150 sexual victim-izations a day in jails.

Prisons

The picture of sexual assault in prison is a bit clearer as more research atten-tion has been focused on these long-term facilities. Cindy Struckman-Johnson et al. (1996), reported that of the 452 male respondents in three prisons in Ne-braska, 101 or 22 percent indicated that they had been pressured or forced to have sexual contact against their will. Sexual assaults tend to happen more in the medium/maximum prisons at a rate estimated to be two to three times the rate at the minimum-security prison. Although the opportunity may be some-what reduced in a medium and maximum security prison, the inmates tend to have more extensive criminal histories and pose both a security and escape threat—indicating that they would be more aggressive and have more pressure to become involved in the "macho" game of rape.

Prior to the study by Struckman-Johnson et al. (1996), Wayne Wooden and Jay Parker (1982) conducted a survey in 1979–80 of a medium-security Cali-fornia prison, reported in *Men behind Bars* (1982). They reported that 14 per-cent of all prisoners had been pressured into having sex against their will. A study by Daniel Lockwood (1980) of six New York State prisons between the years 1974 and 1975, found that 28 percent of the prisoners (half the whites and a fifth of blacks and Hispanics) had been targets of sexual aggressors. Based on these figures, Donaldson (1995) estimates the number of men raped in our na-tion's prisons by applying a victimization rate based on the Struckman-Johnson et al. (1996) study (23 percent) and the Wooden-Parker figure (14 percent, which did not include attempts) for a total of 197,000 adult male victims in prison (119,900 penetrated).

To date there has been no published survey of rape in juvenile facilities. Nonetheless, Bartollas and Sieverdes (1989) in a study of six coeducational training schools reported that almost 10 percent of the residents are identified as sexual victims on site. Furthermore, the authors note that most of the victims were fourteen to fifteen years old, and were essentially in a youth "gladiator" school learning to fight for and take others' manhood. Based on these previous studies, Donaldson (1995) gives conservative estimates that over 300,000 males are sexually assaulted behind bars every year.

THE CONSEQUENCES OF RAPE

The repercussions of a rape in prison are devastating. A single rape incident is rare. Typically when an inmate is raped, he is subject to further attacks or forced in the submissive role in prison. Even facing an attempted sexual attack can be a traumatic experience and can lead to serious stress and defensiveness.

Fending off such attacks can take a serious physical toll as well as cause serious injury. These victims have few choices in the ways they will serve the remainder of their time—they can fight constantly to retain their manhood, submit to a stronger inmate in what is known as a protective coupling, or become a daily rape victim. The only official salvation for most is if they are removed immediately upon discovery of the rape incident and placed into protective custody. It should be noted that becoming the submissive partner in a protective coupling does not imply full consent. This is a decision made under duress. It is a survival strategy, one that violates most official rules in prison. So if the victim is discovered, he is further punished for breaking prison rules of conduct. Essentially, sexual assault is an ongoing process behind bars with limited options for relief for the victims.

The possibility of contracting HIV through rape in prison is both a real and deadly consequence. As previously mentioned, most of the victims are first-time, nonviolent offenders. In jails they are some of the poorest offenders in the system and cannot afford bail; in juvenile facilities they are noncriminal status offenders. So their punishment for being in this position can turn into a death sentence through gang rape and unprotected forced sex. This makes the choice of fighting against an attempted rape a true life-and-death struggle. One of the bleak alternatives is to cooperate with the assailant and try accommodating him through means other than anal rape.

The vast majority of victims go untreated and undetected, suffering from what has been termed Rape Trauma Syndrome. Rape Trauma Syndrome (RTS) is a specific form of posttraumatic stress syndrome—a disorder most often associated with combat veterans. RTS is typically linked with female victims, however the stages and psychological impact are not restricted by gender. Without treatment RTS sufferers suffer from feelings of helplessness, extreme vulnerability, shame, nightmares, self-blame, suppressed rage, and violent behavior. These feelings and emotions may not be universal for all sufferers, but they do appear to be common. These are intense and deep psychological issues. The thought that there may be thousands of men and boys suffering in silence from a disorder that cries out for treatment if there is to be any hope of regaining their humanity is frightening.[4]

RECOGNIZING THE PROBLEM AND STEPS TOWARDS CHANGE

One of the most troubling issues of sexual assault behind bars is that it is both predictable and preventable. Many times the official response is simply to look away. For many administrators it is a public relations nightmare to even admit that such behavior and problems exist in their institutions. To admit that sexual assault among inmates is a problem, is to admit that the staff and administration are not in control of their prisons. Most state and federal prisons lack training for staff, orientation for new inmates to the dangers they may face, and care for those who have become victims of sexual assault.

An inmate's demographic makeup is the easiest predictor of his possible victimization. The key factors are youth, small frame size, race, seriousness of offense, sexual orientation, and being new to prison life. Davis (1968) found in his study that the average age of jail-rape victims was twenty-one, of rapists twenty-four, the average weight of victims was 141 pounds, of rapists 157 pounds; 38 percent of victims were charged with serious felonies, as compared to 68 percent of rapists; interracial rapes were 56 percent of the total.

Race has been a much discussed aspect in power and sexual assault in prisons. Whichever racial group dominates the prison power structure will be the most likely aggressors. These facts allow administrators to classify inmates based on their need for protection and risk of assault. Many of these potential victims are aware of their precarious status and know that rape is a palpable threat wherever guards are not watching.

There are wide ranges of responses to prison rape by administrators. Although most prisons have regulations against sexual contact between inmates, there are many discrepancies between official policy and implementation by line-level officers. Unfortunately, there are numerous examples of prison employees who turn a blind eye to an inmate's violation. Some perhaps feel that it is a fitting punishment for the crimes, others may believe in the roles of masculinity and sexuality demonstrated in prison. There are also incidents in which staff simply claim that the victim was a willing participant and therefore no rape occurred.

One of the most important decisions in the issue of prison rape came from the Supreme Court in the case of *Farmer v. Brennan* (1994). The court examined the case of Dee Farmer, a preoperative transsexual with feminine characteristics who had been incarcerated with other males in the federal prison system. Farmer was sometimes in the general prison population but more often in segregation. Farmer claimed to have been beaten and raped by another inmate after being transferred by federal prison officials from a correctional institute to a penitentiary (a higher-security facility with more high-risk inmates placed in its general population). Striking a major blow for inmate rights, the court held that not only can prison officials be held liable under the Eighth Amendment for acting with "deliberate indifference" to an inmate's health and well-being, but prison officials also had a duty to provide safe and humane conditions for confinement.

A second influential case involving prison rape is *Blucker v. Washington et al.*, 95C50110, U.S. District Court, Northern District of Illinois. According to a 1997 CNN report, while serving a ten-year sentence for burglary and auto theft at Illinois' Menard Correctional Center, Micheal Blucker was raped within days of arrival from a medium-security prison in April 1993 by two gang members. He was forced to become a sex slave to a third prisoner who forced him into sexual service to a whole gang. On June 10, 1993, six months after his initial incarceration, Blucker told a nurse that he had been raped, and was tested for HIV. He was negative. Blucker continued to complain, but also continued to be subjected to sexual coercion, with complicity of guards who helped move him around to his assignments. On August 22 he was gang-raped by fifteen prisoners in the shower. His cellmate in "protective custody" also raped him. On March 29, 1994, he was again tested; this time he was HIV+, infected with the AIDS virus. The possibility of a lawsuit and admission of responsibility on the part of the prison officials were seen as a possible breakthrough in bringing attention to the plight of sexual assault victims in prison.

In 1997 Blucker filed a federal lawsuit seeking $1.5 million against seven staff members of the Corrections Center, including three correctional officers, a teacher, a psychiatrist, a social worker, and an investigator. The lawyer for the Correctional Center argued that Blucker was not a credible witness and lied about his experience in prison, and if they did occur, Blucker did not report them to staff. Blucker countered that the reason he did not report the incidents is that he was afraid for his life. A jury found five of the defendants not liable, and they deadlocked on the remaining two with a retrial expected to take place. Since Blucker's lawsuit, Illinois state legislator Cal Skinner says that he has been contacted by more than thirty inmates claiming to have been raped. Blucker now lives with his wife in a Chicago suburb.

In a separate case, Justice Blackmun of the U.S. Supreme Court summarized the findings of researchers and governmental agencies in this area as follows:

A youthful inmate can expect to be subjected to homosexual gang rape his first night in jail, or, it has been said, even in the van on the way to jail. Weaker inmates become the property of stronger prisoners or gangs, who sell the sexual services of the victim. Prison officials either are disinterested in stopping abuse of prisoners by other prisoners or are incapable of doing so, given the limited resources society allocates to the prison system. Prison officials often are merely indifferent to serious health and safety needs of prisoners as well. (*United States v. Bailey*, 444 US 394, 421–22 [1980; Blackmun, J., dissenting]).

For most administrators the common response to a prison rape victim is to place him in protective custody, which is essentially a twenty-three-hour lockdown and segregation from the general population. However, this is not a long-term strategy to protecting the inmate or reducing sexual violence in the prison. This solution merely punishes the victim again; in fact there are numerous stories of inmates who have been raped while in protective custody, and others have been stigmatized for having been placed in protective custody. Perhaps the first step in dealing with this issue is for administrators to admit that a problem does exist in their prisons and that it deserves their full attention. Prosecution of the aggressor is difficult; as most administrators cannot guarantee the victim's safety. Also few inmates wish to be labeled an informer or snitch, further increasing their chances of assault.

One major step that needs to be taken is to define the rape of males behind bars as heterosexual rape is defined—an issue of power. Through this view of rape, it is not simply a response to the pains of imprisonment but an act of violence perpetrated to dominate and exert some form of control in an institution that offers little individuality or autonomy. Without a clear understanding of the root causes of prison rape, policy cannot succeed in protecting the victims. There are numerous suggestions for reforms available to prison administrators and staff who are willing to deal with such a difficult topic. Administrative policy can have a major impact on the prevalence of prison rape. Most prisons do have some form of intake evaluation in which inmates are often graded on security risk and potential for violence. This is important but it will not solve the problem of prison rape because it does not address the issue of sexual victimization directly.

There are prisons that take inmate sexual assault seriously. The Department of Corrections in Massachusetts has an action plan in place that specifically states that DOC employees and contract employees shall handle sexual assault issues professionally and will be held accountable for their actions in these cases. The federal government has also begun to deal with this troubling issue in our nation's federal prisons. In 1995 the U.S. Department of Justice issued a program that detailed its strategy for dealing with inmate sexual assault. The federal Bureau of Prisons program has several objectives: to develop effective procedures to prevent sexually assaultive behavior; to meet the medical, psychological, safety, and social needs of victims; to promptly investigate allegations of sexual assault; and to ensure that assailants are controlled, disciplined, and prosecuted.

Essentially, most prisons need to develop some type of rape crisis intervention that can meet the needs of survivors of sexual assault—physically, mentally, and spiritually. For those who seek out a protective pairing, condoms should be made available. Most prisons list condoms as contraband, although a few are beginning to ignore this rule or are actually making them available to inmates. One suggestion that is often overlooked is to listen to the inmates themselves. They are in a position in which peer pressure can reduce the incidents of sexual assault as well as to understand the ways that administrators can reduce the threat of sexual assault.

Perhaps one of the most innovative and direct approaches to prison rape is the Prison Rape Education Project by Stephen Donaldson.[5] Donaldson was a prison-rape survivor who has become a crusader in educating the public and officials on the consequences of rape behind bars.[6] The Prison Rape Education Project is published by the Safer Society Press and was funded by a grant from the Aaron Diamond foundation. The project was designed to be a realistic education and information package on rape in prisons and jails. The kit consists of two audiotapes that are designed for prisoners and a forty-six-page overview manual that is designed to be a part of a prisoner orientation program. The first audiotape is twenty-seven minutes and emphasizes tactics to avoid sexual assault; the second tape is ninety minutes and emphasizes survival tactics for victims and potential victims, as well as a forty-six-page overview manual. The manual is designed to provide administrators with information and proactive techniques to minimize the disruption and frequency of sexual assault, and establish more effective policies and procedures for handling known victims.

CONCLUSION

The rape of males is often an overlooked and uncomfortable topic for many professionals and researchers to discuss. It is a taboo subject that is based on ancient notions of the male victim losing his virility and masculinity. However, rape, no matter how prevalent or accepted in prison life, is not a part of the punishment process, nor is it deserved. There is a long and disturbing history of violence in prison. Sexual assault has always been an element as the strong continually prey upon the weak and naïve. The crisis of sexual assault behind bars will not end until the public and correctional officials are willing to take a critical look at the prisons of our nation.

Based on the estimate of victimization of sexual assault behind bars, there are nearly half a million adult male victims in our nation's prisons and jails every year. The spiraling cost of imprisonment along with the seemingly endless supply of inmates is cause for great alarm in light of the violent conditions some will face. Only when prison rape is seen as an issue worthy of serious intervention can society begin to address some of the possible solutions outlined in the text and by advocacy groups listed in the Web Resources section. Administrative policy needs to be at the forefront. Administrative policy needs to be based on the reality of prison life and provide screening and protection for potential victims of rape, as well as punishment for the aggressors.

The results of sexual assault in prison are devastating. The victims of rape are often singled out and labeled as individuals who cannot protect themselves and are considered weak. This often leads to repeat episodes of sexual violence and bleak existence with few alternatives. For some, the threat of AIDS weighs heavily, and a first-time prison sentence can result in a death warrant. The practice of punishing the victim in prison needs to end, and realistic handling of these traumatized victims needs to begin. Staff and counselors need to be made available to provide immediate assistance when a victim is discovered.

Making our nations prisons and jails safe cannot begin until the silence that surrounds sexual assault behind bars is broken. Feminist and various other activists may recall the action taken in bringing the issue of heterosexual rape to the forefront of society and the criminal justice system. This same level of dedication is needed if we are to break the cycle of prison rape, victimization, and test of masculinity for our imprisoned young men and boys.

NOTES

1. For a more detailed discussion of the feminist perspective on rape and the varied explanations of male on female sexual violence, please see Bart 1979; Brownmiller 1975; MacKinnon 1983; and Scully 1995.

2. According to the 1997 National Crime Victim Survey, the number of women reporting being victims of sexual assault was more than thirteen times that of males. This is not to deny the emotional trauma suffered by either group. These statistics are presented to illustrate that fact that men in the community are, and can be, victims of sexual assault.

3. The subculture for incarcerated females is remarkably different than that of males. In response to confinement, many women form pseudofamilies as a means of support and adaptation. Sexual assault in women's prisons, though not unheard of, is extremely rare, as most sex in women's prisons tends to be consensual.

4. For a more detailed discussion of Rape Trauma Syndrome involving male victims please visit the Stop Prison Rape Web site at http://www.spr.org/.

5. Project materials may be ordered from the Safer Society Press at PO Box 340, Brandon, VT 05733. The full kit costs $25. Prisoners who have survived sexual assault can obtain free copies of the second tape by writing to SPR, PO Box 2713, Manhattanville Stn., New York, NY 10027–8817. Tapes can be sent c/o chaplains or psychologists for prisoners who are not allowed to receive tapes directly.

6. For more information on Stephen Donaldson and his campaign against prison rape, please visit the Stop Prison Rape Web site.

REFERENCES

Bart, Pauline B. 1979. Rape as a paradigm of sexism in society—victimization and its discontents. *Women's Studies International Quarterly* 2: 347–57.

Bartollas, Clemens, and Christopher Sieverdes. 1983. The sexual victim in a coeducational juvenile correctional institution. *The Prison Journal* 58(1): 80–90

Bowker, Lee. 1980. *Prison Victimization.* New York: Elsevier North Holland.

Brownmiller, Susan. 1975. *Against Our Will: Men, Women and Rape.* New York: Simon and Schuster.

CNN. 1997. Five employees found not liable in prison rape suit. http://cnn.com/US/9708/29/prison.rape/.

Davis, Alan. 1968. Sexual assault in the Philadelphia prison system. *TransAction* 6: 8–17.

Donaldson, Steven. 1990. Rape of Males. In *The Encyclopedia of Homosexuality*, edited by Wayne R. Dynes. Garland Publications.

Donaldson, Stephen. 1995. Can we put an end to inmate rape? *USA Today: The Magazine of the American Scene*, Vol. 123, no. 2600, May: 40–42.

Farmer v. Brennan (92–7247), 511 U.S. 825 (1994).

Lockwood, Daniel. 1980. *Prison Sexual Violence.* New York: Elsevier.

MacKinnon, Catherine A. 1983. Feminism, Marxism, method and the State: Toward feminist jurisprudence. *Signs* 2: 635–59.

Porter, Eugene. 1986. *Treating the Young Male Victim of Sexual Assault.* Syracuse, NY: Safer Society Press.

Scacco, Anthony. 1975. *Rape in Prison.* Springfield, IL.: Charles C. Thomas.

Scacco, Anthony M., Jr., ed. 1982. *Male Rape: A Casebook of Sexual Aggressions.* New York: AMS.

Scully, Diana. 1995. Rape is the problem. In *The Criminal Justice System and Women: Offenders, Victims, and Workers* 2ed., pp. 197–215, edited by Barbara Raffel Price and Natalie J. Sokoloff. New York: McGraw-Hill Inc.

Struckman-Johnson, Cindy, David Struckman-Johnson, Lila Rucker, Kurt Bumby, and Stephen Donaldson. 1996. Sexual coercion reported by men and women in prison. *Journal of Sex Research* 33 (1): 67–76.

Sykes, Gresham M. 1958. *The Society of Captives: A Study of a Maximum Security Prison.* Princeton, NJ: Princeton University Press.

Tewksbury, Richard. 1989. Measures of sexual behavior in an Ohio prison. *SSR* 74(1): 34–39.

U.S. Department of Justice. 1997. *Sex Differences in Violent Victimization, 1994.* Washington DC: Bureau of Justice Statistics, Bulletin NCJ-164508.

U.S. Department of Justice. 2000. *Prison and Jail Inmates at Midyear 1999.* Washington DC: Bureau of Justice Statistics, Bulletin NCJ-181643.

United States v. Bailey, 444 U.S. 394 (1980).

Wooden, Wayne S. and Jay Parker. 1982. *Men behind Bars: Sexual Exploitation in Prison.* New York: Plenum Press.

6

Rape Law Reform

Frances P. Bernat

INTRODUCTION

The common law in the United States defined rape as the carnal knowledge of a female, not one's spouse, by force and against her will (Connerton 1997; Kennan 1998; Murphy 1996; Spohn 1999). Feminists and criminal law reformers have criticized these traditional elements of rape because the law's application placed an undue burden upon victims and severely limited the types of forced sexual violation that were recognized as criminal. Since the late 1970s, states began legal reforms to address the inadequacies that existed in the common law's definition of rape and in its application. A second wave of legal reform began in the mid-1980s in order to further address concerns that rape laws continued to place undue emphasis on the behavior of victims rather than on that of the offender. This chapter examines rape law reform in the United States and the legal issues that still remain with state definitions of the crime of rape.

THE LEGAL ELEMENTS OF RAPE

The "Carnal Knowledge" and "Of a Female, Not One's Spouse" Elements

The common law of rape focused on a particular sex act between particular individuals. The carnal knowledge element in common law rape defined the prohibited sex act as the sexual penetration of a female by a male, no matter how slight (Langston 1998). To establish this element, sexual penetration between the male sex organ and female vagina (sexual intercourse) had to be proven, but the vagina did not have to be completely entered or the hymen ruptured (Langston 1998). It was not necessary to prove that the sex act resulted in ejaculation. With the sex act limited to sexual intercourse between a male and female, the common law presupposed that only females could be victims and males perpetrators of the crime. In addition, the common law crime of rape did not proscribe sex acts other than sexual intercourse (e.g., cunnilingus, fellatio, anal intercourse, or acts committed with an object). The law also carved out an exception for husbands by exempting forced, nonconsensual sex within marriage (Adamo 1989; O'Donovan 1995; Ryan 1995).

Common law rape was imbued with social and cultural attitudes about sex and sex role responsibilities of men and women (Langston 1998). Historically, a woman was lauded for her chastity, but if she was unchaste, then it was presumed that she consented to the sex act (Kasubhai 1996). In 1671, Sir Matthew Hale articulated the social, cultural, and legal view of rape when he said that rape is an accusation that is easy to make, difficult to prove, and harder yet to disprove by men even though they might be innocent (Edwards 1996; Scalo 1995). His view lasted well into the twentieth century. Women who said that they were raped were mistrusted by the courts and legal system because they were believed to be legally inferior to men (Trucano 1993), thought to be vindictive and revengeful when spurned by a lover (Edwards 1996), or liars who wanted to protect their reputations (Edwards 1996). The common law's marital rape exemption also exemplified the lack of legal and social standing of women. The exemption in rape law excused husbands under a variety of theories pertaining to the legal relationship between husbands and wives (Siegel 1995). One theory posited that married women became the property of their husbands under the doctrine of coverture. Another theory posited that once married, husbands are entitled to have sex with their wives. A third theory suggested that marriage implied a woman's consent to the sex act. Additionally, it was posited that once married, the couple became one legal person and consequently a man could not rape himself (Connerton 1997; Siegel 1995).

Changes in the legal definition of the sex act were among the first areas of rape law reform in the United States in the 1970s. Reformers sought to remove the focus that was placed on the rape victim's behavior and character and to focus on the victim's sexual violation (Edwards 1996; Langston 1998; Murphy 1996; Scalo 1995; Spohn 1999). Rape statutes have been modified to broaden the prohibited sex act. The prohibited sex act includes sexual intercourse, cunnilingus, fellatio, anal intercourse, and acts committed with objects. Following the suggested statutory language in the Model Penal Code, sex acts that do not result in sexual penetration are also criminal. State laws proscribe sexual contact so that the touching of a sexual or intimate body part for the purpose of sexual arousal or gratification is punishable (Langston 1998). Many states modified their "rape" statutes in order to distinguish their "new" laws from common law rape. These statutes use terms such as "sexual assault" or "sexual battery" and reflect the view that rape is a crime of violence and not solely a crime of nonconsensual sexual intercourse. According to Langston (1998, 33), modern rape laws should not focus on unlawful sexual penetration but on the violation of a victim's sexual privacy because victims can be "invaded without being penetrated." In addition, by broadening the sexual act to include other prohibited sex acts, states' sexual assault statutes use gender neutral language. Victims may be either male or female, and principal offenders may be male or female.

The marital exemption to rape also became the subject of state rape law reform. Although the drafters of the Model Penal Code kept the marital rape exemption during their 1960s criminal law reform efforts, by the 1970s, feminists and rape law reformers were able to successfully challenge the legal basis for the exemption (Ryan 1995). Husbands and wives were no longer viewed as "one" in the law, and marriage began to be viewed as impermanent. In addition, by defining rape as a crime of violence rather than sexual release, marital rape was viewed as an unacceptable expression of male domination and the marital veil of privacy was no longer sacrosanct (Ryan 1995). Nonetheless, the marital rape exemption was not significantly changed until the 1980s when each state began to deal statutorily with marital rape (Adamo 1989; Siegel 1995). Some states abolished the marital exemption completely; some states have a partial exemption as they allow for some form of marital exemption or immunity depending upon the living and/or marital status of the couple (e.g., are they legally divorced, separated, or living apart) (Siegel 1995). A number of states have created a new crime of "marital rape" (e.g., Arizona). However, marital rape statutes usually provide for a less severe penalty than other rape law violations. In general, marital rape crimes and modified marital rape exemptions do not provide women with adequate legal recourse that are provided under other rape, sexual assault, or sexual battery statutes (Bernstein 1992).

The "By Force" Element

Historically, English common law rape did not articulate a force element, it proscribed sexual intercourse against a woman's will (no consent). Force was added to the crime of rape under American common law principles and became a key issue in rape cases within the past twenty years (Edwards 1996; Struzzi 1998). At common law, victims had to show that they resisted to the "utmost" of their ability to show that they did not consent. The "utmost" resistance standard required victims to physically resist with all their effort; verbal resistance (saying "No") was not sufficient. The Model Penal Code in its early reformulation of rape law modified the consent element and placed emphasis on the degree of force exerted. The Model Penal Code created three categories of rape depending on the victim-offender relationship and the level of force used to "compel" a victim to submit. Consequently, victim resistance remained an issue as it was juxtaposed against the offender's use of force or threat of force (Edwards 1996). Many states followed the Model Penal Code's rape law reform and emphasize the force element in their statutes and provide for a consent defense to the sex act (Edwards 1996). Some states have sought to eliminate either the consent element or the force element in order to address concerns that too much concern is placed on victim behavior and how much resistance victims have to show to establish forcible compulsion to the sex act (Murphy 1996). Other states have both a consent element and a force element (Anderson 1998).

Although lack of consent and force may be viewed interchangeably, the force element is salient when a victim is deemed incapable of giving consent (e.g., insanity, unconsciousness) or when a victim's level of resistance is in question. At a very basic level, different levels of force are used to grade the severity of rape offenses. If an offender uses a weapon or if a victim sustains serious bodily injury, then the offense is graded as a more serious felony offense than when the crime is committed without these aggravating circumstances. However, state laws vary on how much resistance a victim must exhibit in light of the seriousness of the rape offense charged.

Establishing the legal element of force can be difficult when a victim is conscious but the level of force exerted is no more than that necessary to accomplish the sexual penetration. The legal issues focus on the degree to which a victim expressed, or is able to express, resistance to the sexual aggression, and the level of physical force exerted by the defendant to overcome such resistance. When a defendant does not use "excessive" force as may be typical in acquaintance rape cases, then contradictory legal outcomes occur (Byrnes 1998). The contradictions reverberate the deep-rooted social and cultural clashes that have been at the heart of rape law reform since the 1970s. Reformed rape laws espouse the principle that victims' conduct should not be the focus of rape cases, but in rape cases where serious or grave physical injury or threat is lacking, courts still require the legal element of force to be proven through some measure of resistance. Juries may also place undue emphasis on victims' conduct precipitating a rape. A Florida jury, for example, acquitted a male of rape despite evidence that he used a weapon—the jury foreman indicated that the victim "asked for it" because of the way the victim was dressed (Byrnes 1998). The amount of resistance needed varies from case to case and state to state.

Several cases decided in the 1990s point out the difficulty that exists when a victim's behavior is used to determine whether a defendant in a case of rape exerts force. In one case, the California Supreme Court[1] held that if a victim is placed in immediate fear of bodily injury then the element of force can be established (Fried 1996). Similarly, the Pennsylvania Supreme Court held that a conscious but very intoxicated woman who lacked the capacity to voice her objection to the defendant having sexual intercourse with her was "unconscious."[2] In upholding the defendant's conviction for rape, the court based its ruling on various common law precedents that force is implied when a victim is unconscious and incapable of giving consent (Struzzi 1998). The Pennsylvania Supreme Court, however, also held that if a victim is conscious and capable of giving consent but remains silent during the sexual intercourse, then the victim was not raped.[3] The court stated that some level of victim resistance must be shown in order to establish that the defendant used force (Fried 1996; Murphy 1996; Scalo 1995). An opposite conclusion was reached by at least two other appellate courts. The New Jersey Supreme Court[4] held that the act of sexual penetration constituted enough force to prove rape. The victim indicated that she awoke to find the defendant on top of her. The defendant testified that the victim complained only after the sexual intercourse occurred and he immediately complied when she told him to get off of her (*Harvard Law Review* 1993; Murphy 1996). The Colorado Court of Appeals[5] held that the Pennsylvania court was incorrect and that verbal resistance is enough to show that the defendant had sex against the victim's will (Scalo 1995).

In acquaintance rape cases, the level of force exerted may not be accomplished by explicit threats or actual violence (Edwards 1996). Consequently, many states have laws or evidentiary rules that emphasize victim compliance to establish if force was used. Victim compliance rules focus on victim behavior that does not explicitly show that the victim resisted the sex act rather than behavior that shows that the defendant placed the victim in fear. Such laws may excuse defendants who utilize nonviolent methods of coercion (Byrnes 1998; Murphy 1996). Several cases decided in the 1990s by military courts have shown how the legal and evidentiary standards in acquaintance rape cases can be modified so that courts focus on defendant, and not victim, behavior. By refocusing on defendant behavior, the courts are able to criminalize all acts of unwanted sexual intercourse. The military courts, for example, confirmed convictions of rape when victims have shown some verbal protest (e.g., said "No"), or showed some slight physical resistance (e.g., turned away from a kiss or sexual advance) but did not stop or otherwise physically prevent the act of sexual penetration.[6] These military courts determined that the sexual penetration was committed in a coercive manner and was unwanted. Rather than looking at the victims' ability to resist the sexual advances and sexual intercourse, the military courts analyzed the lack of implied consent in light of defendants' intimidating, coercive behavior that created an atmosphere to compel acquiescence to the sex act (Murphy 1996).

Legal scholars are still debating the degree to which victims must resist to show that force was used to compel compliance to the sex act (Anderson 1998).

On the one hand, if the quintessential aspect of rape is that the sex act occurs without consent, then whether or not physical force was exerted upon a victim becomes irrelevant. Under this view, courts may require that force used against a victim must be greater than that necessary to perform the penetration. Such force may be shown if a victim says "No" but the sex act occurs anyway (Anderson 1998). On the other hand, some courts are finding that an act of penetration is enough force to convict a defendant. The victim's ability to express consent is irrelevant when the totality of the circumstances indicate that there was some form of forcible compulsion used to get the victim to consent to the sex act. Under this view, force is implied if the defendant's conduct places the victim in fear and the victim "freezes" or otherwise cannot express verbal or physical resistance (Fried 1996; Murphy 1996). States are struggling with the degree to which force should be or is an essential element in acquaintance rape cases. The law and legal rules that focus on the sufficiency of victims' ability to resist the sex act should not disadvantage acquaintance rape victims. As Daphne Edwards (1996, 300) stated: "It is the violation, not the violence, that is criminal." Though legal scholars and rape law reformers may agree with this axiom, how to effectively deal with the force element varies from state to state.

The "Without Consent" Element

When the common law modified the definition of rape to include a force element, the legal requirement of consent changed. It changed from an issue of consent at the time of the sex act to an issue as to whether the victim resisted in response to the sex act (Bronitt 1992; Spohn 1999). Most states require that the sex act occur without consent and look for either some form of physical resistance by the victim or some clear evidence that the victim did not consent (Case 1993; Kitrosser 1997; Malm 1996; Spohn 1999). In almost every state, the burden of proving the victim did not consent is on the prosecution (Remick 1993). Rape laws that define rape as "forcible compulsion" analyze consent as a defense (Case 1993). In general, the law presumes that the victim consented to the sex act unless refusal can be proven (Remick 1993). The evidentiary emphasis on victim conduct and the concomitant general distrust of rape victims by the legal system generated procedural rules to protect defendants from "unwarranted" rape allegations (Trucano 1993).

Legal scholars and feminists have challenged the presumption that victims consented unless proven otherwise because it treats the crime of rape differently than other offenses. For example, theft victims do not have to show that they overtly physically resisted the taking of their property but most rape victims must show their lack of consent by means of physical resistance (Malm 1996; Remick 1993). Requiring physical resistance to the crime of rape can disadvantage rape victims. Many rape victims, particularly victims of acquaintance rape, use subtle means of resistance such as words or conduct designed to impose feelings of guilt, like crying behavior. If verbal nonconsent is not sufficient to establish the "without consent" element, then defendants will not be convicted of rape under existing legal rules despite a victim saying "No" (Edwards 1996). This problem is compounded by social rules that teach men that "No" means that a woman is really saying "Yes" to a sex act (Malm 1996).

Legal scholars and reformers offer various viewpoints on how to respond to legal problems associated with consent in rape statutes. Under current laws, confusion about force and consent can result in the net widening or net reduction concerns—that is, the ability to convict defendants who are not guilty (net widening) or acquit defendants who are guilty (net reduction). In some cases, consent may be found to negate rape despite the fact that force was used in the commission of the sex act. In other cases, it may be unclear whether consent was obtained if a victim remains silent and complies with the threatening demands of the defendant. To respond to these problems, rape law reform has attempted to redefine the meaning of consent.

Up until the mid-twentieth century, lack of consent was found if a victim resisted with the "utmost" of her ability, she had corroborating evidence, and promptly reported the rape (Kasubhai 1996). Rape law reforms in the 1970s removed some of the evidentiary rules that placed undue burdens on victims. Rules that women had to promptly report or have corroborating evidence and witnesses to the attack were removed. Resistance standards were modified so that whereas women did not have to resist to the "utmost" of their ability, they had to show "reasonable resistance" or that they were "forcibly" compelled to consent to the sex act.

Rules dealing with resistance as a measure of consent are still troubling to legal scholars and rape law reformers. Some scholars argue that consent should be redefined (Remick 1993). They argue that social and cultural views of what female behavior will be deemed acceptable is inappropriately used as a shorthand method of determining whether a woman consented to a sex act. Women may be found to have consented to sex because they wore particular types of clothing; frequented particular places (e.g., bars); or, engaged in risk-taking behavior (e.g., hitchhiking) despite contrary evidence that shows that the sex act was committed by force (Kasubhai 1996; Malm 1996). Two scholars, Kasubhai (1996) and Remick (1993), argue that the law should require an "affirmative" consent standard. Such a standard would presumably provide women with greater autonomy to decide with whom they wish to have consensual sex. If a man does not receive a verbal assent to the sex act, then the sex act would be rape (Remick 1993). An affirmative consent standard would ensure that sexual partners engaged in a dialogue that enables them to choose how they wish to engage in sex (Kasubhai 1996). Malm (1996) believes that force should be eliminated from the crime of rape, but that actual verbal assent should not be mandated in order to prove consent. Malm (1996, 155) argues that consent should be shown in the negative, "a woman is presumed to have consented unless she has provided a *clear* expression of *dissent*" [emphasis in original].

Some courts still find that verbal nonconsent alone (saying "No") is not enough to convict a person for rape (Kasubhai 1996). The consent element and evidentiary rules designed to determine consent still emphasize victim behavior and statements. A controversial 1994 Pennsylvania Supreme Court ruling held that a victim's "No" statements were insufficient to show that the victim was raped.[7] The court determined that forcible compulsion was not proven because the victim did not physically resist when the defendant pushed her onto a bed. Although she quietly told the defendant "No," she did not scream out. The court found that lack of the victim's verbal consent was irrelevant because the state statute at that time focused on "force" and not lack of consent. The court determined that because the defendant did not use more force than needed to accomplish the sex act, it was not rape (Kasubhai 1996). The ruling resulted in that state's legislature amending their rape statute in order to respond to state and national public outcry by placing greater emphasis on consent than on force, but the legal focus of nonconsent still remains on the victim (Kasubhai 1996).

Other problems of consent are evident in cases when victims ask their assailants to use protection during the sex act. Recent concerns over the transmission of HIV have prompted some rape victims to ask their assailants to use a condom. Courts have to determine if a request for a condom, even though other factors show forcible compulsion (e.g., the offender is a stranger or uses a deadly weapon) constitutes consensual sex (Case 1993). Some courts have found that the woman consented if she asked for or provided a condom, other courts have found that condom usage does not constitute voluntary consent when other factors show forcible compulsion (Case 1993). There is a compelling case for finding lack of consent in condom rape cases. Case (1993) argues that victims should not have their behavior questioned merely because they have the presence of mind to protect themselves from a serious and deadly virus (HIV) and disease (AIDS) when they are raped. The context of the rape (threats, violence, weapon use) should speak louder than the victim's request for or use of a condom.

One procedural rule that has been attacked since the 1970s focuses on the nature and degree to which complainants can be cross-examined on their past sexual history. Under common law principles, a victim's past sexual conduct could be used to impeach her credibility or to show that it was probable that she consented to the sex act. Rape shield laws limit the degree to which victims can be questioned about their sexual history (Boone 1996; Bronitt and McSherry 1997; Hazelton 1991; Spohn and Horney 1991; Trucano 1993). Prior to the enactment of rape shield laws, courts allowed liberal examination of a victim's sexual history as a method to challenge her testimony and character (Trucano

1993). By 1985, all but two states had enacted rape shield statutes (Hazelton 1991). The effectiveness of these laws may depend upon their strength (Hazelton 1991; Spohn and Horney 1991), the degree to which judges have discretion to balance the rights of victims versus the right of the accused to cross-examine the complainant (Bronitt and McSherry 1997), and the degree to which other actors in the criminal justice process such as police officers and jurors determine that the victim's behavior contributed to the rape (Gruber 1997).

Where's the Intent?—The *Mens Rea* Element in Rape Law

The confounding issues of force and consent are intertwined within the *mens rea* (mental state) issue of rape. The criminal law was founded upon a basic principle that the state should not punish persons unless they are "blameworthy." Blameworthiness is grounded in liberal legal philosophy, which posits that one purpose of the criminal law is to punish individuals who choose to commit acts that violate the law (Faulkner 1991). In the nineteenth century, William Blackstone articulated the basic tenets of the English common law by stating that there could be no crime unless there was also a "vicious will" (Kennan 1998). In regard to the crime of rape, the mental state issue is whether a person can intend to have sex with a another person but be mistaken as to whether the act is against the other's will or by forcible compulsion.

Intent can be implied in state rape statutes. At a minimum, the defendant must intend to have sex with the victim. Most states ignore the issue as to whether it must be proven that the defendant intended to have sex without consent and by force. As discussed in the previous sections, the legal focus is placed on the conduct of the victim and whether the defendant had a mistaken belief that the victim consented. In one common law court,[8] for example, the defendants were three men who were told by the victim's husband that the victim wanted to have sex with him. The husband told the men that the victim liked to struggle and fight during sex. The court held that the men had a reasonable, although mistaken, belief that the woman consented despite the fact that the woman fought with the defendants and repeatedly said "No" (Faulkner 1991; Gans 1996).

According to Byrnes (1998), the unique focus that the law places on victim conduct and not on the defendant's *mens rea* can have mistaken and contradictory outcomes. One outcome is net widening; defendants may be convicted of rape although they did not intend to have sex without consent (Byrnes 1998). For example, in date-rape cases it is sometimes difficult to determine if the defendant intended to rape the victim or if there was miscommunication about the issue of consent. Consequently, some legal scholars suggest that victim assent to sex be clear before the sex act occurs (Kasubhai 1996; Remick 1993). The other outcome is net reduction: the acquittal of a defendant who intends to commit rape but the complainant is deemed to be conscious and presumed competent to otherwise have resisted unwanted sexual conduct (Byrnes 1998). For example, in some doctor-patient rape cases, doctors who had sexual intercourse with their patients after misrepresenting the therapeutic value of the sex act and persuading the patients that such treatment is beneficial have been found to be not guilty of rape. In these types of cases, courts look at the connections between the fraud, the defendant's intent and actions, the victim's knowledge and ability to consent before determining whether the doctor should be convicted or acquitted (Falk 1998). The early common law did not consider the defendant's conduct to be rape if he used fraud to obtain a victim's consent to the sex act (Bronnit 1992). This issue about fraud in the inducement to obtain consent to sex may still exist today. One commentor has noted that Michigan continues to utilize the common law definition of rape. Consequently, Michigan courts may be unwilling to recognize a rape by fraud because the victim "consented" to the sex act (*Wayne Law Review* 1999).

Some common law countries and legal scholars have suggested changing the *mens rea* element in rape to reduce these contradictory net widening and net reduction outcomes (Byrnes 1998; Faulkner 1991; Gans 1996; Kennan 1998). Some scholars suggest that the courts should analyze whether the defendant was recklessness or negligent in forming a mistaken belief that the victim consented to the sex act. Such a change would arguably prevent undue attention being placed on victim's state of mind, conduct, and resistance. The defendant could be convicted of rape if the sex act occurs under the unreasonable and mistaken belief that a victim consented (Byrnes 1998). Others suggest that the mental state of the defendant is irrelevant. These legal scholars suggest that rape should become a strict liability crime. Strict liability statutes impose liability on actors for the act alone, no *mens rea* element exists. For rape strict liability offenses, it is argued that the state would be required to prove the sex act, force, and lack of victim consent. Mistaken belief defenses would not be available to the defendant (Kennan 1998). Strict liability in rape laws is not a novel idea as they are most often associated with statutory rape laws—punishing defendants for having sex, even if consensual, with another who is under the age of consent. The mental state element of intent, however, remains implied within the other elements of the crime of rape.

THE VIOLENCE AGAINST WOMEN ACT

Although many aspects of rape law reform have attempted to respond to changing views of women and the crime of rape, deeply engrained social and cultural views of women continue to affect the application of rape laws around the nation (Gaffney 1997). Studies on the impact of rape law reform have shown that statutory changes in rape laws have not had a substantial effect on victim reporting behavior or criminal justice system responses to rape (Bachman and Paternoster 1991; Berger et al. 1991; Bienen 1983). However, the state law reforms did bring a level of awareness to the problem of crimes of violence against women and the ineffective manner that states respond to rape victims (Bienen 1983).

The U.S. Congress sought to respond to the large number of women in the United States who were victims of rape and domestic violence by enacting a statute that might provide for some national uniformity in responding to violence against women (Gaffney 1997). In 1994, Congress enacted the Violence Against Women Act (VAWA).[9] The VAWA was intended to provide women with a civil rights remedy to felonious crimes of violence committed against them that are motivated by gender. Congress based its power to enact this law on the U.S. Constitution's Commerce Clause and Fourteenth Amendment (Gaffney 1997; *U.S. v. Morrison et al.* 2000[10]).

The first case decided under the VAWA involved the rape of a college woman[11] (Gaffney 1997). In 1994, a female student, Brzonkala, filed a complaint under university policy that she was raped by two male students, Morrison and Crawford, within thirty minutes of their meeting at Virginia Polytechnic Institute (Gaffney 1997; *U.S. v. Morrison et al.* 2000). School disciplinary charges were dropped against one of the students, Crawford, for lack of evidence. The university's hearing committee, however, found the other student, Morrison, guilty of sexual assault and suspended him for two semesters. Upon appeal of his suspension, Morrison was granted a new disciplinary hearing because it was determined that the university improperly used a policy that had not been widely circulated to students. A second hearing resulted in Morrison's conviction of a different offense, "using abusive language." The university's senior vice president and provost later set aside Morrison's suspension as being excessive compared to other punishments meted to students who had violated the university's policy. Without notice to Brzonkala, Morrison was readmitted to the university. Bronkala dropped out when she read in a school newspaper about the university's decision to readmit Morrison. The rape traumatized Brzonkala, and she has had to seek professional counseling in its aftermath (Gaffney 1997).

Brzonkala then instituted a federal lawsuit under VAWA against Morrison, Crawford, and the university.[12] The District Court held that under the VAWA, Brzonkala had stated a claim against her assailants Morisson and Crawford. The court determined that Morrison's and Crawford's actions showed "gender animus." The court's decision on this finding is troublesome because it seems to imply that some types of rape show gender animus whereas others do not. Specifically, the court said that one reason gender animus existed was because Brzonkala's rape was more like a gang rape than a one-on-one rape (Gaffney 1997). Most troublesome, however, is the court's final holding. The court invalidated the VAWA. The court held that Congress lacked constitutional authority to enact the VAWA. The U.S. Court of Appeals for the Fourth Circuit affirmed the District Court's holding (*U.S. v. Morrison et al.* 2000).

The constitutional issues involved in the case were so significant that the U.S. Supreme Court took the case on appeal. In May 2000, the Supreme Court agreed with the lower courts and held that the VAWA "cannot be sustained" under either the Commerce Clause or the Fourteenth Amendment.[13] The decision was split, five to four, with Justice Rehnquist being joined in his majority opinion by Justices O'Connor, Scalia, Kennedy, and Thomas. Justice Souter was joined in his dissenting opinion by Justices Stevens, Ginsburg, and Breyer. The Court's majority and dissenting opinions focus on the competing theories that justify judicial review and federalism.

The majority opinion favors a narrow reading of the Constitution. Justice Rehnquist expounds upon the original intent of the Founders of the Constitution in analysis of the Commerce Clause and the original intent underlying the Fourteenth Amendment when it was enacted. Though recognizing that defendant Morrisons's statements about women after the rape were "vulgar remarks that cannot fail to shock and offend," and that rape and crimes of violence against women are serious, the majority opinion finds the VAWA to be unconstitutional. Rehnquist posits that under the Commerce Clause, violent crimes do not have an economic base and therefore cannot be regulated by Congress. In regard to the Fourteenth Amendment, Rehnquist indicates that an *individual person's* violation of the civil rights of another could not be regulated by Congress because the Amendment focuses on limits on *state* conduct that infringes on the due process rights of a person (*U.S. v. Morrison et al.* 2000). Justice Rehnquist's decision evidences a traditional restraintist court on the issue of federalism. In *Morrison*, the court articulates a view that our system of government ought not interfere with states' rights and powers. The court's decision favors a narrow, traditional definition of federalism and states' rights.

Justice Souter's *Morrison* dissent finds that the Commerce Clause can empower Congress to enact statutes like VAWA. Contrary to Rehnquist's majority decision, he argues that Congress does have constitutional authority under the Commerce Clause to enact the VAWA. Souter recognizes that individual actions can affect interstate commerce. He argues that the court majority's static view of the nation, Constitution, and federalism are inadequate to respond to contemporary needs of the nation. He points out that even the states requested federal assistance to deal with the problems states have had in seeking remedies to crimes of violence against women. Accordingly, Souter finds it ironic that the court majority's opinion forces states "to enjoy the new federalism whether they want it or not."

For female victims of violent crime, the *Morrison* decision eliminates a federal avenue for women to redress their victimization as a violation of their federal civil rights. Congress spent four years taking testimony before enacting the

VAWA. The voluminous Congressional record showed that state laws were inadequate to respond to handle tort actions instituted by women to redress gender-based victimization. Justice Souter, in his dissent, indicates that Justice Rehnquist's rationale in *Morrision* is not likely to endure as law; and this assessment is probably, and hopefully, accurate. But, without the VAWA, female victims of violent gender-based crimes must resort to the inadequacy of their state systems to provide them with redress.

CONCLUSION

Rape law has been the subject of reform efforts in the United States since the 1970s. These reforms have sought to eliminate the discriminatory views of rape victims and women that were engendered within the common law of rape. The reforms eliminated the most troubling aspects of rape law statutes and the evidentiary standards required to prove the crime of rape (e.g., corroboration). However, stereotypes about rape victims are still manifested in the views and actions of criminal justice actors (police, judges, and jurors). Victims' words, actions, and characteristics are still used to determine if the elements of "consent," "force," or "intent" are present. In order to provide victims with redress when state legal systems are inadequate to respond to their victimization, Congress passed the Violence Against Women Act in 1994. Despite strong state support for the Act, the U.S. Supreme Court invalidated the Act in May 2000. Without the VAWA, feminists, state rape law reformers and other victims' rights advocates must continue to look to the modification of state legal systems and laws in order to respond to the problems that still exist in rape laws and litigation. Rape victims remain without adequate state and national protections in the law to challenge traditional rape myths and sex role orientations of men and women, and to place the legal onus on rapists.

NOTES

1. *People v. Iniguez*, 872 P.2d 1183 (Cal. 1994).
2. *Commonwealth v. Erney*, 698 A.2d 56 (Pa. 1997).
3. *Commonwealth v. Berkowitz*, 641 A.2d 1161 (Pa. 1994)
4. *State ex rel. M.T.S.*, 609 A.2d 1266 (N.J. 1992).
5. *People v. Schmidt*, 885 P.2d 312 (Colo. Ct. App. 1994).
6. *United States v. Clark*, 35 M.J. 432 (C.M.A. 1992, *cert. Denied*, 113 S.Ct. 1948 (1993); *United States v. Webster*, 40 M.J. 384 (C.M.A. 1994).
7. *Commonwealth v. Berkowitz*, 641 A.2d 1161 (Pa. 1994).
8. *R. v. Morgan*, A.C. 182 (1976).
9. U.S.C. Section 1381.
10. *U.S. v. Morrison et al.*, 449 U.S. 361 (2000); online see: wysiwyg://14/http://caselaw.findlaw.com/c . . . pl?court=US&navby=case& vol=000&invol=99–5

11. *Brzonkala v. Virginia Polytechnic & State University*, 935 F.Supp. 779 (W.D. Va. 1996).

12. *Ibid.*

13. *U.S. v. Morrison et al.*, 449 U.S. 361 (2000).

REFERENCES

Adamo, Sonya A. 1989. The injustice of the marital rape exemption: A survey of common law countries. *American University Journal of International Law and Policy* 4:555–89.

Anderson, Michelle J. 1998. Reviving resistance in rape law. *University of Illinois Law Review* 1998: 953–1011.

Bachman, Ronet, and Raymond Paternoster. 1993. A contemporary look at the effects of rape law reform: How far have we really come? *Journal of Criminal Law and Criminology* 84: 554–74.

Berger, Ronald J., W. Lawrence Neuman, and Patricia Searles. 1991. The social and political context of rape law reform: An aggregate analysis. *Social Science Quarterly* 72: 221–38.

Bernstein, Lisa. 1992. Trends in marital rape laws: Progress or façade? *UCLA Women's Law Journal* 2: 273–74.

Bienen, Leigh. 1983. Rape reform legislation in the United States: A look at some practical effects. *Victimology: An International Journal* 8: 139–51.

Boone, Shacara. 1996. New Jersey rape shield legislation: From past to present—the pros and cons. *Women's Rights Law Reporter* 17: 223–36.

Bronitt, Simon H. 1992. Rape and lack of consent. *Criminal Law Journal* 16: 289–310.

Bronitt, Simon, and Bernadette McSherry. 1997. The use and abuse of counseling records in sexual assault trials: Reconstructing the "rape shield?" *Criminal Law Forum: An International Journal* 8: 259–91.

Byrnes, Craig T. 1998. Putting the focus where it belongs: Mens rea, consent, force, and the crime of rape. *Yale Journal of Law and Feminism* 10: 277–305.

Case, Donna J. 1993. Condom or not, rape is rape: Rape law in the era of AIDS—Does condom use constitute consent? *University of Dayton Law Review* 19: 227–50.

Connerton, Kelly C. 1997. The resurgence of the marital rape exemption: The victimization of teens by their statutory rapists. *Albany Law Review* 61: 237–84.

Edwards, Daphne. 1996 Acquaintance rape and the force element. *Golden Gate University Law Review* 26: 241–300.

Falk, Patricia J. 1998. Rape by fraud and rape by coercion. *Brooklyn Law Review* 64: 39–180.

Faulkner, James. 1991. *Mens rea* in rape: *Morgan* and the inadequacy of subjectivism or why no should not mean yes in the eyes of the law. *Melbourne University Law Review* 18: 60–82.

Fried, Joshua Mark. 1996. Forcing the issue: An analysis of the various standards of forcible compulsion in rape. *Pepperdine Law Review* 23: 1277–315.

Gaffney, Jennifer. 1997. Amending the *Violence Against Women Act*: Creating a rebuttable presumption of gender animus in rape cases. *Journal of Law and Policy* 6: 247–89.

Gans, Jeremy. 1996. When should the jury be directed on the mental element of rape? *Criminal Law Journal* 20: 247–66.

Gruber, Aya. 1997. Pink elephants in the rape trial: The problem of tort-type defenses in the criminal law of rape. *William & Mary Journal of Women and the Law* 4: 203–62.

Harvard Law Review. 1993. Rape law—Lack of affirmative and freely-given permission—New Jersey Supreme Court holds that lack of consent constitutes "physical force." *Harvard Law Review* 106: 969–74.

Hazelton, Peter M. 1991. Rape shield laws: Limits on zealous advocacy. *American Journal of Criminal Law* 19: 35–56.

Kasubhai, Mustafa T. 1996. Destabilizing power in rape: Why consent theory in rape law is turned on its head. *Wisconsin Women's Law Journal* 11: 37–74.

Kennan, Brian. 1998. Evolutionary biology and strict liability for rape. *Law & Psychology Review* 22: 131–177.

Kitrosser, Heidi. 1997. Meaningful consent: Toward a new generation of statutory rape laws. *Virginia Journal of Social Policy & the Law* 4: 287–338.

Langston, Lundy. 1998. No penetration—and it's still rape. *Pepperdine Law Review* 26: 1–36.

Malm, H.M. 1996. The ontological status of consent and its implications for the law on rape. *Legal Theory* 2: 147–64.

Murphy, Timothy W. 1996. A matter of force: The redefinition of rape. *The Air Force Law Review* 19: 19–35.

O'Donovan, Katherine. 1995. Consent to marital rape: Common law oxymoron? *Cardozo Law Review* 2: 91–107.

Remick, Lani Anne. 1993. Read her lips: An argument for a verbal consent standard in rape. *University of Pennsylvania Law Review* 141: 1103–51.

Ryan, Rebecca M. 1995. The sex right: A legal history of the marital rape exemption. *Law and Social Inquiry* 20: 941–1001.

Scalo, Rosemary J. 1995. What does "No" mean in Pennsylvania?—The Pennsylvania Supreme Court's interpretation of rape and the effectiveness of the legislature's response. *Villanova Law Review* 40: 193–232.

Siegel, Lalenya Weintraub. 1995. The marital rape exemption: Evolution to extinction. *Cleveland Law Review* 43: 351–78.

Spohn, Cassia C. 1999. The rape reform movement: The traditional common law and rape law reforms. *Jurimetrics* 39: 119–30.

Spohn, Cassia C., and Julie Horney. 1991. "The law's the law, but fair is fair": Rape shield laws and officials' assessments of sexual history evidence. *Criminology* 29: 137–61.

Struzzi, Melissa A. 1998. *Commonwealth v. Erney*, 698 A.2d 56 (Pa. 1997). *Dusquesne Law Review* 36: 705–14.

Trucano, Jennifer K. 1993. Force, consent and victims' rights: How State of New Jersey in *re M.T.S.* reinterprets rape statutes. *South Dakota Law Review* 38: 203–25.

Wayne Law Review. 1999. Rape by fraud or impersonation: A necessary addition to Michigan's criminal sexual conduct statute. *Wayne Law Review* 44: 1781–1807.

7

Myths of Woman and the Rights of Man: The Politics of Credibility in Canadian Rape Law

Margaret A. Denike

INTRODUCTION

In Western Judeo-Christian countries our criminal courts have long been notorious for their differential and reprehensible treatment of female victims of sexual crimes. Survivors of rape face institutionally sanctioned forms of scrutiny, incredulity, and distrust, which are directed at them in ways that are virtually unknown, if not only exceptionally employed, in the investigation and trial processes of any other criminal offense. The rules of evidence and the judicial procedures that have long granted aggressive cross-examinations of female complainants may well remain unique to this crime as long as "the world generally, and the law specifically, regard us as less worthy of belief than men for the sole reason that we are women" (Mack 1993, 328). This holds particularly true for women who are sexually active, women who have sought counseling or therapy, and women from marginalized groups, such as women of color and women who have been institutionalized. Criminal sexual assault is one domain of law where such a gendered hermeneutics of suspicion and contemptuous incredulity are as explicit as they are definitive of its jurisprudence. It is a crime for which the vast majority (over 80 percent) of victims are women, and the courts have occasion to decipher and assess the "truth" of their confessions and testimonies on the one subject they are, in more ways than one, "loathe to speak." Our law and legal system reflects the extent to which woman is ensnared by a cultural semiotics that, in the discourses of our everyday life, casts woman as the less rational, unreliable, unpredictable, feeble-minded *other* to man. As *the other sex*, she is trapped within the taint of the impropriety and criminality of her sexuality, as her mythical sexual insatiability sustains a presumption of her readiness to prompt and tease seduction, then to lie to protect her "reputation."

Myths ingrained in the rituals and practices of religion, politics, and law have rendered "woman" and "sex" synonymous terms, ambivalently demonizing and idealizing female sexuality while projecting onto woman alone the social guilt and fear of sexual criminality and sexual transgression. The mistrust and suspicion disproportionately applied to women reflects archaic myths that generations of feminist theorists and equality advocates have worked to expose and eradicate: The female sex is as "insatiable" as she is "feeble-minded"; as guilty as she is deceptive; as sexually devious as she is untrustworthy. Her credibility, dignity, and privacy are conditional on the extent to which she deviates from her patriarchally prescribed roles and conduct of possessive chastity, encoded dress and gesture, and normative filial relations with one man. Such restrictive and unrealizable expectations form the context against which her propensities of deceit and desire are formulated and measured. A history of patriarchal jurisprudence and common law rules of evidence in criminal sexual assault cases has performatively enacted such ambivalence toward women's sexuality, sensibility, disposition, and character, and has rendered the legal system a critical domain for defining, controlling, and regulating women. These myths, reflective of the origin myths of Eve, are not mere elements of Western Christian knowledge; rather, they are elemental, fundamental, to the structures of patriarchal societies and their institutions, and they infuse the systems of domination in which sexual violence against women has prevailed.

Examining Canadian criminal sexual assault proceedings, this chapter traces the inscription of such ambivalence in and through the development of criminal jurisprudence and legislative reforms to sexual assault law. The dance of the legislature and the courts, which relies heavily on a sexual politics of truth, has performatively constituted and institutionalized the highly peculiar constructions of the "victims" and "pretenders" to this violation. The *de facto* assumptions about women's lack of credibility and insatiable sexuality are pervasive enough to entail that criminal proceedings for rape have historically, consistently displaced the threat that sexual violence poses to its victims and have attended primarily to the threat that presumed deceivers pose to the rights of the accused. The saga of sexual assault and its reforms tells of a struggle between the courts and the legislature to reconcile myths of woman with the rights of man. Tracing the development of sexual law and its recent reform in Canada, and mapping within them the pervasive ideology of women's culpability and lack of credibility, this chapter summons the perspective of Michel Foucault

(1978, 1980), whose genealogical methodology invites historical and situated analyses of the relations of power implicated in the "production of truth." Feminist analysis enables us to excavate the gendered nature of such "power," and the role of judicial truth games in reinforcing women's sexual subordination to men.

THE SEXUAL POLITICS OF CREDIBILITY

Sanctioned through a tradition of common law rules, employed in various guises by defense counsel, woven into judicial decisions, and inscribed in legislation and procedural guidelines, notions of women's sexual and emotional proclivities have rendered sexual assault trials unique as contests of credibility between the complainant and the accused. Misogynist myths underlie everything from the establishment of the facts of the case; the conditions imposed on reporting it; the determination of the relevance of questionable evidence; the forms and strategies of permissible cross-examination; to the definition and articulation of the rights of the accused. The same myths have entailed that sexual assault trials have primarily concerned themselves with ensuring that the accused's rights be protected, that he be granted a fair trial, and that he be allowed to fully defend himself, with whatever relevant evidence is available, against the misrepresentations, lies, or thwarted fantasies of his seductress. In rape law the sexual politics of credibility has been as blatant as it has been notorious. "The myth of the woman lying," says Susan Estrich (1992, 11), is perhaps the most powerful and most tenacious myth in the tradition of rape law. Though there is no evidence to support the operative assumption that women are more likely than men to lie about sexual activity or anything else (LEAF 1991, 4), this idea has a long legal history and is used to sanction extraordinary evidentiary rules to protect the rights of the accused. As Canadian Supreme Court Madam Justice Claire L'Heureux-Dubé puts it, "Common law has always viewed victims of sexual assault with suspicion and distrust" (*Seaboyer*, in dissent, at 665), just as it has enshrined prevailing mythologies and stereotypes "by formulating rules that made it extremely difficult for the complainant to establish her credibility and fend off inquiry and speculation regarding her 'morality' or 'character' " (*Seaboyer*, at 665). Common law rules of evidence, such as the requirement that a complainant's testimony be corroborated by witnesses, that her complaint be launched immediately after the assault, and that her past sexual history be considered relevant to the issues at trial, are a few of the more notorious constraints applied only in sexual assault cases. We find these rules at play from the first recorded cases of sexual assault in early Canadian courts, which clearly reflect the misogyny of the English precedent from which they were derived. Sir Matthew Hale's 17th century treatise *History of the Pleas of the Crown* (1676) and, a century later, William Blackstone's *Commentaries on the Laws of England* (1769), detailed the steps to be taken "to prevent malicious accusations" of rape complainants, and they both firmly established and reinforced the rule of "recent complaint" (Blackstone 1769, 210). Embracing this tradition, the first criminal law textbook published in Canada in 1835[1] reinscribed Hale's famous dictum that rape "is an accusation easily to be made, and hard to be proved, and even harder to be defended by the party accused, though never so innocent" (Keele 375; cited in MacFarlane 1993, 170). William Conway Keele's textbook went on to outline a variety of reasons, including a complainant's reputation, her lack of evident injury, or errors in describing the attire of the accused, and the time or the location of the alleged rape, which "carry a strong presumption that the testimony is false or feigned" (*Provincial Justice*, 375; cited in MacFarlane 1993, 170). As MacFarlane notes, in the first sexual assault case to be reported in Canada, *R. v. Francis* (1856), the Court of Queen's Bench of Upper Canada found occasion to adopt Hale's and Blackstone's dicta verbatim, noting the "danger in implying force from fraud, and an absence of consent when consent was in fact given." In acquitting the accused, despite what MacFarlane describes as "clear evidence of criminality," the Court entertained that such a case might arise "when a detected adulteress, might, to save herself, accuse her paramour of a capital felony" (*R. v. Francis*, cited in MacFarlane 1993, 170).

Such common law rules have persisted for centuries and have been subjected to extensive critique and legislative reform in the past thirty years, yet we still see new and varied forms that are based on the same fallacies of women and their sexuality. They are evident, for example, in the pathologizing discourses of "false memory syndrome," and even more recently, in the implementation of procedures for disclosing as evidence the counseling and psychiatric records of complainants with the aim of impugning their credibility on the stand. Some observers have suggested that it is no coincidence that such new versions of time-honored ploys have appeared in the wake of a wave of recent reforms to the discriminatory laws passed down through the centuries. As Susan Estrich and Kathy Mack have argued, since men have lost some of unwarranted protection previously afforded by the substantive and procedural law of rape, "the underlying distrust of women and the myth that women lie about rape have reasserted themselves even more forcefully" (Estrich 1992, 5; Mack 1993, 339). Others similarly see the use of personal, psychiatric, and counseling records in sexual assault trials to be "part of the retrenchment movement against equality advances made by women in Canadian society," an "assault on the progress made by women who have been working toward the goal of ending violence against women in Canada" (Sampson 1998, 4). In any case, a consistent trend of invoking women's sexual and emotional proclivities to sustain the disparity in the credibility accorded to men and women enables new misogynist tactics to emerge and thrive in sexual assault law, despite reform initiatives. An analysis of their historical role in sexual assault law requires consideration of the sexual politics of truth's production.

RAPE SHIELD: THE STRUGGLE FOR REFORM

In Canada, the first significant reforms to the longstanding common law doctrine marked the culmination of extensive feminist lobbying to have Parliament acknowledge the prevalence of sexual assault, its impact on the status of women, and the hostility of the justice system toward female complainants. In the mid-1970s, Parliament responded with statuatory amendments to the *Criminal Code*, which included abolishing the corroboration requirement and implementing Canada's first "rape shield" provisions. Introduced in 1976 as a part of this package, section 142 of the *Criminal Code* was designed to protect rape complainants from being subjected to tactics of cross-examination on their sexual history and reputation.[2] But Parliament's objectives were quickly abrogated by courts, who, in *Forsythe v. the Queen* [1980], interpreted the provision in a way that "provided *less* protection to the complainant than that offered at common law [emphasis in original]" (MacFarlane 1993, 173–74; Los 1994, 48). By this judgment, at the insistence of the accused, the complainant was now compelled to attend the *in camera* hearing, and, unlike what had been provided in traditional common law rules, she had no option but to answer questions about her relationships with other men (MacFarlane 1993, 174). Thus, rather than restricting cross-examination, the courts used the provision to broaden its scope, and they further allowed the defense to call witnesses to testify about the complainant's reputation. In effect, as MacFarlane (1993) "credibility was elevated to the status of a material issue" (174). Far from allowing the first rape shield provisions to curb the discriminatory treatment of female complainants, as was intended by a protective Parliament, the courts conversely used them as leverage to exacerbate this very problem.

The demise of the first rape shield reforms attests to the antagonism between the courts and the legislature, and this relationship continues to characterize the next two decades of sexual assault legislation and jurisprudence. Such resistance to progressive statutes, which further re-entrenches a *de facto* presumption of the duplicity and culpability of sexually active rape complainants, is born of the very prejudicial assumptions about women and their sexuality that the legislative reforms have been designed to eradicate from judicial discretion.

In 1982, partly in response to this judicial latitude, Parliament introduced a second package of sweeping reforms to the *Criminal Code*. Implemented under Bill C-127, these included reclassifying rape as sexual assault and ushering in new, restrictive rape shield provisions to limit the cross-examination on a complainant's sexual experience with both the accused and persons other than the accused. Now sections 276 and 277 of the *Criminal Code*,[3] these equality-minded statutes recognized "that the traditional practices and procedures of the criminal courts 'stacked the deck' against the victims of sexual assault in ways that were unique to these offences and ungrounded in reality" (LEAF 1991, 6). They recognized the indignities perpetuated by procedural and evidentiary rules that deterred them from pursuing criminal charges, and denied them the "equal benefit of the criminal law and equal protection within the criminal justice system" (LEAF 1991, 7).

Like the 1976 reforms before them, the 1982 statutes proved equally vulnerable to constitutional challenges, which were sympathetically received by the courts. In each instance, the challenge has been made on the same grounds: by restricting the right of the accused to cross-examine and lead evidence of a complainant's sexual conduct, the provisions infringe on the constitutional rights of the accused to a fair trial (s. 11d of the *Charter*) and violate the "principles of fundamental justice" (s. 7 of the *Charter*)[4] that inform these rights. Specifically, the new rape shield provisions (ss. 276 and 277) came under direct attack with the sexual assault case *R. v. Seaboyer* [1991]. Charged with the sexual assault of a woman with whom he had been drinking at a bar, Mr. Seaboyer, at a preliminary inquiry, sought to cross-examine the complainant about her sexual conduct on other occasions. He contended that other acts of sexual intercourse may have caused the bruising and various injuries that the Crown had put forward as evidence. On appeal to the Supreme Court of Canada, defense counsel tapped into the mythology that has traditionally sustained the *de facto* assumption that women lie about rape, and that evidence about the sexual history of the female complainant is pertinent to assessing the "truth" of the evidence before the court. The new rape shield provisions, Seaboyer argued, imposed a "blanket exclusion" of evidence of critical relevance to the facts of the case, and as such, they violated his rights to a fair trial and to full answer and defense, as guaranteed by sections 7 and 11d of the *Charter of Rights and Freedoms*. The majority of the Supreme Court of Canada (per Lamer, La Forest, Sopinka, Cory, McLachlin, Stevenson, and Iacobucci) agreed and struck down the entirety of s. 276, though it upheld s. 277 (at 616). Finding that the rape shield provisions excluded evidence of "critical relevance" to the facts of the case, they ruled that it is

fundamental to our system of justice that the rules of evidence should permit the judge and jury to get at the truth and properly determine the issues. . . . A law which prevents the trier of fact from getting at the truth by excluding relevant evidence in the absence of a clear ground of policy or law justifying the exclusion runs afoul of our fundamental conceptions of justice and what constitutes a fair trial. (*Seaboyer*, 3)

Though the majority in *Seaboyer* acknowledged that certain myths and stereotypes of women's sexual proclivities may prejudice or distort the determination of facts, this recognition had no bearing on their decision about integrity of the "truth-seeking process." Only in the dissenting reasons of Madam Justice

Claire L'Heureux-Dubé do we find a critical examination of the paradox of this reasoning. As she notes,

It seems odd to recognize the use of stereotype in the 'test for judicial truth' but nevertheless conclude that the test for "truth" is met. If the only thing that renders a determination of relevancy understandable is underlying stereotype, it would seem contradictory to conclude then that 'truth' has been found. (*Seaboyer*, 54)

The sexual history evidence excluded by this provision, she adds, "is either irrelevant or so prejudicial that its minimal probative value is overwhelmed by its distorting effect on the trial process. It operates as a catalyst for the invocation of stereotype about women and about rape" (*Seaboyer*, 54). It would take another five years, however, for her analysis to finally ring true to her colleagues on the bench.

   Seaboyer, like *Forsythe* before it, is a testament to how judicial decisions may effectively distort and evacuate the equality initiatives of the legislative reform process (Sheehy 1991, 450). The majority court did not engage with the abundance of affidavit evidence submitted through the *amicus* interventions of a coalition of equality-seeking groups and the Attorney General of Canada to highlight the gendered nature of sexual assault, their low conviction rates, and the discriminatory treatment of victims within the legal system. Although the equality provisions of the *Charter* clearly invite judicial consideration of the context and impact of the sexual politics at stake in sexual assault claims, as Sheehy argues, decisions such as *Seaboyer* show only a judicial preference "to abstract legal issues from their political and historical contexts," and to treat equality claims as if they are not even legal issues at all, much less ones that could fit within recognized paradigms (Sheehy 1991, 460). Such decontextualization lends itself to the majority Court's exclusive focus on the enshrined, fundamental legal rights of the accused, while minimizing and ignoring the so-called equality interests of complainants to their dignity, security, and privacy.

   Using the *Seaboyer* decision as a case in point, Elizabeth Sheehy notes that a structural obstacle to the Court's basic ability to *hear*, much less incorporate, the equality analysis provided by reform legislation and *amicus* interventions derives from "the exclusion of women from the articulation and design of both criminal law and the *Charter* itself. The fact that complainants do not have party status in criminal trials, "means that we lack language, concepts and precedent for the recognition of rights for women who testify in rape trials" (Sheehy 1991, 461). In this specific criminal context, those who are most vulnerable—survivors of the social injustice of sexual assault and the myths that butress and support it—have not been able to benefit from the constitutionally guaranteed principles of justice. Women consistently lose in the game of balancing competing rights engaged by the Court in its "pursuit of truth." "We might expect that the accused's 'fundamental freedoms' will trump women's rights at every turn" (Sheehy 1991, 461), if indeed, as the high court has stated, "the *Charter* is essentially an instrument for checking the powers of government over the individual" (Justice LaForest, *McKinney* 1990, 261–62). So criminal law may be "impervious" to gender equality, as McInnes and Boyle have argued, because of the underlying assumptions that the only inequality that matters to the courts in a criminal context is that which exists between punitive, aggressive state and the individual/accused: "The need to remedy inequality between the state and the accused is a major premise animating the rights of accused persons in ss. 7–14 of the *Charter*" (McInnes and Boyle 1995, 346). The inequalities inherent to the prevalence of sexual assault are effectively trivialized as a special interest, which palls in the face of the more fundamental rights of the accused. The legal paradigm that hierarchicizes the accused's rights over her mere interests may well appear to be a function of constitutional law in this context; but it happens to mirror the greater symbolic order of patriarchy, the Law of the Father, whose language predisposes the exclusion of women, as it defines the conditions of credible speech.

With respect to rulings by the Supreme Court of Canada on the constitutionality of the rape shield provisions, the closing years of the millennium witnessed a shift in the clear propensity of the courts to evacuate the equality, dignity, and privacy of female complainants. In the year following the *Seaboyer* decision, and in consultation with equality lobbyists, Parliament responded in much the same way as it had to *Forsythe*, introducing yet another rape shield statute (together with a sharpened definition of consent) under Bill C-49. The new provisions (s. 276) categorically prohibited evidence of a complainant's sexual history when it is used to support the inference that she is more likely to have consented, or the inference that she is less credible by virtue of her prior sexual experience, though it allowed evidence of sexual history for other inferences. It provides a procedure for determining the admissibility of such evidence, which requires the defense to file a detailed affidavit on its relevance to be considered by a judge prior to the trial. Following the trend of previous responses to such protective legislation, the new law was quickly subjected to a constitutional challenge, the precedent for which, *R. v. Darrach*, has been very recently decided by the Supreme Court (October 2000).

Charged with assaulting a former employee with whom he had previously had a sexual relationship, Mr. Darrach argued that these provisions violated the principles of fundamental justice and an accused's right to a fair trial, as they raised the threshold for admissibility established in *Seaboyer*, and they imposed "blanket exclusion" of the complainant's sexual history. Releasing its decision in October 2000, the Supreme Court for the first time upheld the constitutionality of the rape shield provisions, adopting the very rationale offered earlier in the dissenting reasons of Justice Claire L'Hereux-Dubé. Unanimously dismissing the accused's appeal, the court acknowledged that the "twin myths" for which sexual history evidence is explicitly excluded under s. 276 do not lend themselves to determining the facts or arriving at the truth of the allegations; rather they risk "severely distorting" the trial process itself. Conceding some of the mythic import in the link between evidence of sexual experience with consent and credibility, it held that the provisions actually "enhance the fairness of the hearing" *because* they exclude "misleading" evidence (*Darrach* 7). By sparing the latest rape shield provision in this way, *R. v. Darrach* marks the first unsuccessful challenge to these aggrieved statutory protections, the first to be applauded by advocates like LEAF, who, as in *Seaboyer*, had again intervened with *amicus* briefs to offer equality analyses to the Court. *Darrach* thus launches the new millenium with the appearance that, at least for the Supreme Court, the principles of justice have come closer to addressing and accommodating the substantive inequalities of criminal sexual assault proceedings by keeping in check some of the myths that actively define and privilege the assumed vulnerablity of the rights of the accused. In this decision, woman's dignity and privacy are treated less as interests and more as rights (that is to say, it considers not only *his*, but *her*, access to fundamental justice, and the privacy rights guaranteed by s. 7 of the *Charter*); as such, it is less consistent with preserving notions of women's sexual accessibility and more with recognizing her autonomy. However, we cannot forget that, for all the equality analysis of this latest rape shield law, we still effectively have in place a formalized scheme and procedure for negotiating the relevance of her sexual history to the facts of a case, while all along the accused remains constitutionally protected from any question of the relevance of his criminal-sexual history, of any previous charges or convictions for assault. The discrepancy presupposes that the greatest threat and vulnerability at stake in sexual assault trials is that of false accusations against a vulnerable accused. The proceduralization of assessing relevance of a sexual past, which is established only for those (complainants) who also happen to lack any party status in criminal trials, nonetheless legitimizes defense counsels' efforts to at least pursue this line of intimidation.

COUNSELING AND PSYCHIATRIC HISTORY

In the context of criminal sexual assault proceedings, myths and stereotypes about women's lack of credibility, their instability, their propensity to beguile and malign their presumptively innocent lovers are not restricted to evidentiary rules pertaining to sexual history. As the protective rape shield statutes afforded somewhat limited restrictions under the 1992 reforms, new defense counsel tactics, deploying these very myths, began to appear as a feature of Canadian criminal sexual assault proceedings. Emerging for the first time in the early 1990s, these involve defense counsel's bid to use as evidence the personal re-

cords of complainants, and particularly, their counseling and psychiatric records, to impugn their credibility on the stand. Aimed at intimidating and
deterring witnesses through "fishing expeditions," the requests for, and use of,
personal records tap into the long-standing patriarchal ideology of the irrational, feeble sex, prone to suggestion and deception, to falsely remember and
misrepresent the "truth" of sex. As Madam Justice L'Heureux-Dubé describes
them, requests for complainant's records are clearly past discriminatory practices in new "guises" (*O'Connor* at 122). The "pernicious" evidentiary rules
that allow them, she says, are not unlike those that permitted "unwarranted inquiries into sexual histories" for they allow "defence to do indirectly what it
cannot do directly" under the amended rape shield provisions (*O'Connor*,
122).

   As is the case with sexual history evidence, the courts have proved receptive
to the idea that a woman's psychological, medical, educational, and employment histories are often pertinent to ensuring that the accused is granted a fair
trial. The British Columbia Court of Appeal (*O'Connor* [1993]) and, in turn,
the Supreme Court of Canada (1995) went so far as to formalize and legitimize
a procedure for disclosing records held by third parties, such as psychiatrists, in
the precedent-setting sexual assault trial of Bishop Hubert O'Connor.[5] As various advocates have pointed out, the use of such private records is restricted almost exclusively to sexual offense trials (Oleskiw and Tellier 1997, 5; Busby
1997, 148–52). Oleskiw and Tellier's Quick Law study of 1997 shows that 120
of the 140 recorded cases involving defense counsel requests for access to
third-party records were cases where the accused was charged with a sexual offense (1997, 5–8). Over the eighteen-month period (November 1993 to May
1995) that followed the BC Court's decision in *O'Connor*, Busby's Quick Law
study captured forty sexual assault cases in which records were requested
(Busby 1997, 149). Though the practice of using personal records was completely unfamiliar to criminal sexual proceedings before the *O'Connor* case, it
has become a standard feature of sexual assault trials and poses an imminent
threat to women who, in wanting not to have such personal information available to the public, much less to their rapist, are deterred from testifying at trial
and essentially forced to choose between counseling and criminal proceedings
to deal with the effects of the assault or to seek protection and redress (Busby
1997, 174).

   Bishop Hubert O'Connor was charged with two counts of rape and two of indecent assault committed in the 1960s against students in the Indian residential
in British Columbia where he worked as a priest and served as a the school's
principal. Prior to his 1993 trial, he obtained a court order, without formal notice to the Crown or the complainants, to acquire and produce records held by
almost anyone who had contact with or information on, the complainants, including therapists, counselors, psychologists and psychiatrists, educators, em-

ployers, and medical doctors (*O'Connor* 445–46). During his first trial, the
court determined that the Crown had not fully complied with the order, and a
stay was issued in the case. On appeal, the BC Court dealt with the issue of records' disclosure by implementing a two-stage procedure for determining their
relevance. Two years later, the procedure was in turn accepted, though slightly
modified, by the Supreme Court of Canada (1995). Acknowledging the prejudicial effect of such records, both courts attempted to devise what they described as a "fair" scheme for balancing the privacy rights of complainants with
the fair trial rights of the accused: At the first stage, prior to any disclosure, the
accused applies to the judge to determine *in camera* whether the records in
question are "likely relevant" to the issues at trial or to the competence of the
complainant to testify; if the records pass this test, they are turned over to the
judge. At this second stage, the judge must balance the competing rights and interests at stake before deciding if the records are to be further disclosed to the
court and to the accused. The majority Court specified that, for the initial relevancy test, "fishing expeditions" conducted in the "mere hope" of finding
something with which to impugn the complainant's credibility were not sufficient grounds to grant an application. Yet they also emphasized that the burden
on the accused at the initial stage of the relevancy test should not be an "onerous" one. At a glance, the court seems attuned to the violation of privacy and
dignity inherent in such fishing expeditions. However, what it does not consider is the extent to which the very suggestion that such records have *any* relevance in the first place rests on a suspicion disproportionately directed toward
female rape complainants, and on certain diffidence toward those who seek
support services, counseling, or therapy. They explicitly rejected the view of
the minority, per L'Heureux-Dubé, that therapeutic records would only be relevant "in rare cases" (*O'Connor* 176); and instead offered various illustrations
as to when they would be.[6] These examples, alone, as Bruce Feldthusen has argued, ensure that the accused will have little difficulty meeting even a "significant onus" (1996, 448) because the only basis for compelling the production of
records is the very rape myths that thrive in judicial discretion.

Subsequent applications under the *O'Connor* guidelines have confirmed
that little, if any, foundation is required to meet the requirements of the initial
"likely relevance" test, and to compel women and their counselors or support
agencies to produce their personal records, diaries, and files to the court. As Karen Busby's study has shown, the test quickly tended to be very literally and
widely applied, such that over the course of the 1990s, records production
could become routine in sexual violence cases (Busby 157; Feldthusen 1996,
passim). Furthermore, interviews conducted in 1999 with five Crown counsel
in British Columbia indicate that, since *O'Connor*, 40 to 50 percent of all their
sexual assault cases now entail either threats or formal requests for the disclosure of third-party records (Denike and Renshaw 1999, 42). According to one

Crown representative who deals with high-profile sexual assault prosecutions, the *O'Connor* guidelines have only acted as a "red flag" for defense counsel to whom it might previously never have occurred to request personal records. The relevancy test has effectively formalized and reinstitutionalized the *de facto* assumption that women lie about rape. Furthermore, *O'Connor* launched a new judicial trend of exploiting the notion that the clients of counselors, psychologists, and analysts are likely to fabricate or to have implanted false memories of sexual abuse and sexual assault. Indeed, the new precedent takes full advantage of the historically pervasive sexual politics that define the differential relation of sex to truth that has long served to protect the rights of man.

R. v. Carosella [1997][7] is a testament to the extent to which, over the course of the 1990s, judicial logic had fortified and normalized the notion that for sexual assault cases, access to the complainant's counseling records bears directly on protecting the constitutional rights of the accused, despite the novelty of this rationale and practice. In this case, a stay of proceedings was issued by the Ontario trial court judge solely on the basis that the sexual assault center (where the complainant had gone in 1992 for advice as to how to lay charges for the alleged sexual abuse) had shredded their file and destroyed the notes taken by a social worker at the interview. Though the file had been shredded prior to the trial and in accordance with the center's policy, the court found that the destroyed notes were relevant material evidence that would have tended to assist the accused, were they available. On appeal, the majority of the Supreme Court of Canada (per Lamer C.J. and Sopinka, Cory, Iacobucci and Major JJ) in turn agreed that a stay of proceedings was the "appropriate remedy" in this case, as the destruction of the notes effectively breached the accused's right to make full answer and defense: It "had seriously prejudiced the accused by depriving him of the opportunity to cross-examine the complainant as to her previous statements relating to the allegations she made" (at 2). This disastrous decision, which implicitly and remarkably finds evidence that is even unavailable or non-existent to be relevant to a case, turns on the presumption of the complainant's presumed lack of credibility. This presumption precipitates profound implications for all support services and record-keeping agencies, whose records are now *always* potentially subject to production and disclosure, at least for anyone who may launch legal proceedings.

As was the case with sexual history evidence, the court's tolerance and legitimization of the new defense tactic for intimidating rape complainants has been widely criticized by equality advocates, therapists, and support providers. With substantial input from women's equality organizations, Parliament responded by introducing corrective legislation (Bill C-46 [1997]; now section 278 of the *Criminal Code*) to compensate for the negative impact of the disclosure rulings of *O'Connor* and to offer additional protections to complainants by expanding on the grounds that are insufficient for determining the relevance of their records. The new legislation reiterates and builds upon the guiding principles of the 1992 (Bill C-49) reforms, acknowledging the detrimental effects on the victims of sexual abuse and on those who work with them, emphasizing society's interest in having crime reported, and requiring further recognition of the complainant's equality and privacy rights at each stage of the relevancy test. However, as was the case with the rape shield reforms, these additional protections introduced under Bill C-46 were immediately subjected to a constitutional challenge, which two provincial courts (Ontario and Alberta) were quick to sympathetically receive.[8] In the name of fundamental justice, neither the Ontario nor the Alberta court hesitated to strike down the entirety of the new law, s. 278 of the *Code*. In *R. v. Mills* (1997), Alberta Queens Bench Judge Belzil found most objectionable s. 278.5, the additional requirement that, in determining whether to order the production of a record, courts were to consider factors such as the complainant's dignity, society's interest in having women report sexual offenses and/or obtain counseling, and the integrity of the trial process itself. At issue was whether such societal interests, when added to the *O'Connor* guidelines, significantly altered the balance struck by the *O'Connor* majority such that these "interests of justice" placed an additional and onerous burden on the accused for establishing the relevance of record.[9] In a decision that enabled the lower courts of Alberta to return to the very low threshold for records production endorsed by the majority in *O'Connor*, Judge Belzil simply railroaded the equality analysis introduced through Bill C-46. He held that the majority in *O'Connor* had already determined a proper balance between the competing rights and interests of the accused and complainant: "In my view," he wrote, "Bill C-46 is not a proportional response and does not constitute a minimal impairment of rights but rather constitutes a substantial impairment of the fundamental right to a fair trial" (at 71–72). Such reasoning captures the palpable judicial resistance to substantive equality reforms, and the tendency to permit fundamental freedoms to be procedurally interpreted and granted only to the accused—not to women, individually or collectively. It displaces concern about vulnerability from the complainant to the accused, erasing any consideration of the social threat posed by sexual violence and reinscribing the mythic threat posed by devious and deceptive women.

When *Mills* was further appealed by the Crown, the Supreme Court of Canada had occasion to revisit their records disclosure guidelines and assess their impact in the five-year period following *O'Connor*. Their remarkable decision, rendered in November 1999, signals a considerable development in the majority's critical analysis of the myth-driven strategies used to impugn women's credibility. Compared to preceding judgments in the area of sexual assault, *Mills* is particularly striking for its efforts to incorporate equality analysis into its consideration of the truth-seeking objectives of judicial process, and to look to the discrimination against female complainants proffered through invasions to their privacy, dignity, and security of the person. To this end, the judgment critically engages with the logic applied by the majority in all previous challenges to legislative reforms to rape law, and finds room to further address the constitutional rights of complainants and the collective rights of women. The court ruled that the principles of fundamental justice that inform the accused's right to "full answer and defense," including the "pursuit of truth," should "embrace interests and perspectives beyond those of the accused" (3), and these include the mental integrity and dignity of the complainant and the societal interests in seeing rape reported. Information contained in the therapeutic records of the complainant, which were sought by the accused, would only "serve to distort the search for truth" as the determination of the relevance depends on little more than myth, and they introduce "discriminatory biases and beliefs into the fact-finding process" (*Mills,* 4). Thus the Supreme Court upheld the constitutionality of the revised guidelines and overturned Belzil's earlier ruling.

New to *Mills* is an analysis of the sexual politics and equality implications of the truth-seeking objectives of "justice." Though these arguments have been formulated by equality advocates and intervenors and inscribed in legislative reforms, it has taken until the close of the second millenium for them to begin to shape the rationale of the majority court in assessing and balancing the competing rights and interests that are presumably at stake in sexual assault trials. The novelty of situating women's equality, dignity, and privacy within the "interests of justice" and embracing the principles of parliament's protective statutes, however, betrays their tenuousness. After all, the lower courts continue to operate under a new regime that has essentially formalized the disclosure and production of third-party records, and it remains the case that the determination of their relevance and of the extent to which their disclosure is deemed "in the interest of justice" rises and falls on judicial discretion. A cursory glance at distant and recent history of sexual assault cases, including the hundreds of cases of the past decade where the relevance of this new evidence has been weighed and assessed, leaves little doubt that it is in judicial discretion that myths and assumptions about women's sexual and emotional proclivities are able to thrive.

CONCLUSION

In Canada, the struggle between the legislature and the courts to seek justice in sexual assault trials, and to settle on fair rules and procedures for doing so, reflects the challenge of negotiating between truth and lies, facts and fantasies, certitudes and fictions in a domain of knowledge and practice already skewed with layers of prejudice and bias. It tells of the deep ambivalence toward women that imbues social and institutional relations of Western Judeo-Christian culture. The struggle of the past twenty-five years has witnessed the tireless efforts of equality advocates and legislators to counter the conservatism of the courts with a consideration of women's dignity, autonomy, privacy, and their vulnerability as victims of sexual violence. On the other hand, it has witnessed the judicial propensity to cast aspersion on rape complainants and to presume women's lack of credibility, their propensity to deceive, misrepresent facts, and malign men to protect their own reputations. Until this past year at least, the struggle betrays the Canadian Supreme Court's willingness to vacate these equality reforms, and to render judgments that rely on and reinforce a view that the sexual and emotional proclivities of women pose a perpetual threat to the "rights of man." These truth games tap into the cultural readiness to find fault in the female seductress for man's transgressions, to privilege and protect his fundamental rights at the expense of her interests.

The story of this struggle can perhaps be written as a chapter in what Michel Foucault describes as a "history of truth," a "history of the politics of truth," which is to say a history of the relations of power and subjection, domination and subordination, that are implicated in the institutionalized production of truth (Foucault 1978, 60). Indeed, the truth games played with sex do capture the spirit of how power operates in late modernity's legal institutions, and a genealogy may help to bring their complexity to light: As feminist scholars have been saying for a good two centuries before Foucault, power relations, in all their complexity, multiplicity, and mobility, work insidiously, invisibly, and performatively through the production and circulation of knowledge. Truth games of sex have operated within patriarchy to create and sustain gendered relations of domination and subordination through a myth-driven determination of want counts as truth, of who gets to speak it, and under which circumstances. The politics of truth service the modes of patriarchal domination invested in recirculating notions of women's insatiability, culpability, irrationality, and deceptiveness, as they ensure that "the truth of sex" can be spoken legitimately by one sex alone. Legislating and institutionalizing systemic suspicion against the testimony of women, the sexual politics of credibility has lent itself to reinforcing their sexual accessibility at the expense of their dignity and autonomy, sanctioning the silencing of women and endorsing the male control of female sexuality. It has worked to strengthen the "rights of man" in the face of mythic threat posed by woman. It has been used in the context of sexual assault and sexual abuse, such that much of what is practiced as sex is "intrinsically inaccessible to history" (MacKinnon 1992, 120), as its victims "have no way of telling you what happened to them," and "the silence of the silenced is filled by the speech of those who have it" (121).

NOTES

1. William Conway Keele, *Provincial Justice*. Toronto: U.C. Gazette's Office, 1835, 375. See Bruce A. MacFarlane, *Historical Development of the Offence of Rape.*

2. According to the 1975–1976 amendments, s. 142 of the *Criminal Code of Canada,* "No question shall be asked as to the sexual conduct of the complainant with a person other than the accused" unless written notice is first made to the prosecutor and a hearing *in camera* concluded that the exclusion would prevent a just determination of fact, including the credibility of the complainant.

3. According to section 276, "No evidence shall be adduced by or on behalf of the accused concerning the sexual activity of the complainant with any person other than the accused"; and to section 277, "Evidence of sexual reputation, whether general or specific, is not admissible for the purpose of challenging or supporting the credibility of the complainant" (1983, c. 125, s. 19; R.S. 1985, c. 19 [3d Supp.], ss. 12–13).

4. Section 7 of the *Canadian Charter of Rights and Freedoms* provides: "Everyone has the right to life, liberty and security of the person and the right not to be deprived thereof except in accordance with the principles of fundamental justice."

5. In his reasons in *R. v. Stromner* (1997), Judge Patterson noted, "Prior to the *O'Connor* decision there was no way for the accused person to compel disclosure of records in the hands of third parties. *O'Connor* provided a means to overcome this situation. This procedure provided a pathway through the common-law barrier. (*Stromner* [1997] at 53).

6. The majority gave the following examples of situations that may be sufficient grounds for establishing the relevance of records: (1) They may contain information concerning the unfolding of events underlying the criminal complaint; (2) they may reveal the use of a therapy that influences the complainant's memory of the alleged events; (3) they may contain information that bears on the complainant's credibility, including testimonial factors such as the quality of their perception of events at the time of the offense, and their memory since; and (4) there is a possibility of materiality where there is a "reasonably close temporal connection between" the creation of the records and the date of the alleged commission of the offense . . . or in cases of historical events, as in this case, a close temporal connection between the creation of the records and the decision to bring charges against the accused (*O'Connor*, at 176).

7. *R. v. Carosella* [1997] 1 S.C.R. 80.

8. *R. v. Lee* [(Q.L) 1997 O.J. No. 3796] Ont. C.A. Gen Div. (September 23, 1997); *R. v. Mills* (1997), 12 C.R. (5th) 138 and 163 (Alta Q.B.).

9. Section. 278.5 of the *Criminal Code* now requires that the judge order the person in possession or control of the records to produce them for review by the judge if after an *in camera* hearing,

a. the judge is satisfied that the application was made in accordance with ss. 278.3(2) to (6);
b. the accused has established that the record is likely relevant to an issue at trial or to the competence of a witness to testify; and
c. the production of the record is necessary in the interests of justice.

Under Bill C-46, section 278.5 added to the *O'Connor* guidelines the "likely relevant" standard for judges to order the production of records, as well as the further requirement that the production be "necessary in the interests of justice."

REFERENCES

Blackstone, Sir William. 1769. *Commentaries on the Laws of England*, Book IV. Oxford: Clarendon Press.

Busby, Karen. 1997. Discriminatory uses of personal records in sexual violence cases: Notes for sexual assault counselors on the Supreme Court decisions in *R. v. O'Connor* and *L.L.A. v A.B. Canadian Journal of Women and the Law* 9: 148–77.

Denike, Margaret, and Sal Renshaw. 1999. *Legislating Unreasonable Doubt: Bill C-46, Personal Records Disclosure and Sexual Equality.* Vancouver: Feminist Research, Education, Development and Action Center.

Estrich, Susan. 1992. Palm Beach stories. *Law and Philosophy* 11: 5–33.

Feldthusen, Bruce. 1996. Access to the private therapeutic records of sexual assault complainants. *The Canadian Bar Review* 75 : 536–63.

Foucault, Michel. 1978. *The History of Sexuality.* Translated by Robert Hurley. New York: Penguin.

———. 1980. *Power/Knowledge: Selected Interviews and other Writings.* Edited by Colin Gordon. Translated by Colin Gordon, Leo Marshall, John Mepham, and Kate Soper. New York: Pantheon.

Hale, Sir Matthew. 1736. *A History of the Pleas of the Crown.* London: Nutt and Gosling. Reprinted, London: Professional Books, 1971.

LEAF (Women's Legal Education and Action Fund). 1991. *Factum of the Interveners: R. v. Seaboyer.* Toronto.

Los, Maria. 1994. The struggle to redefine rape. In *Confronting Sexual Assault: A Decade of Legal and Social Change*, pp. 20–56, edited by Julian Roberts and Renate Mohr. Toronto: University of Toronto Press.

MacFarlane, B. 1993. Historical development of the defence of rape. In *100 Years of the Criminal Code in Canada*, pp. 111–188, edited by the Honorable Josiah Wood and Richard C. C. Peck. Ottawa: Canadian Bar Association.

Mack, Kathy. 1993. Continuing barriers to women's credibility: A feminist perspective on the proof of process. *Criminal Law Forum* 4: 327–53.

MacKinnon, Catharine. 1992. Does Sexuality Have a History? In *Discourses of Sexuality*, pp. 117–138, edited by Domna Stanton. Ann Arbor: University of Michigan Press.

McInnes, John, and Christine Boyle. 1995. Judging sexual assault law against a standard of equality. *University of British Columbia Law Review* 29: 341–81.

Oleskiw, D., and N. Tellier. 1997. *Submissions to the Standing Committee on Bill C-46, An Act to Amend the Criminal Code in Respect of Production of Records in Sexual Offence Proceedings.* Ottawa: National Association of Women and the Law.

Sampson, Fiona. 1998. The production and disclosure of complainant's personal records in sexual assault trials. In *METRAC Conference Proceedings: Can Confidentiality Survive?* Toronto: METRAC: 3–6.

Sheehy, Elizabeth. 1991. Feminist argumentation before the Supreme Court in *R. v. Seaboyer; R. v. Gayme:* The sound of one hand clapping. *Melbourne University Law Review* 18: 450–68.

Cases Cited

R. v. Darrach (2000) S.C.C. 46.

Forsythe v. The Queen (1980) 2 S.C.R. 268.

R. v. Lee [(Q.L) 1997 O.J. No. 3796] Ont. C.A. Gen Div. (September 23, 1997)

R. v. Mills (1997), 12 C.R. (5th) 138 and 163 (Alta Q.B.).

R. v. O'Connor (1995) 4 S.C.R. 411.

R. v. Seaboyer and R. v. Gayme (1991) 2 S.C.R 577.

R. v Strommer (1997) 205 A.R. 385.

8

Psychological Evidence in Sexual Assault Court Cases: The Use of Expert Testimony and Third-Party Records by Trial Court Judges

Giannetta Del Bove and
Lana Stermac

INTRODUCTION

The legal and theoretical literature on the relevance of psychological evidence in judicial proceedings, to date, has not examined the actual practice and effects of introducing this type of evidence in sexual assault cases. The present research attempts to address this gap by examining the use of two types of psychological evidence in sexual assault trials. Specifically, this study investigated how trial judges are using expert testimony evidence and third-party personal records in their court decisions. Results highlight the potential consequences of introducing psychological evidence on trial outcome, the impact of judges' decisions on rape law reform, and the contribution to social constructions of women.

HISTORICAL CONTEXT OF RAPE LAW DEVELOPMENT

The way in which psychological evidence is employed in the courtroom is shaped by the historical development of rape laws. An analysis of rape law reform shows that the Canadian Criminal Code contained the offenses of rape, attempted rape, and indecent assault as recently as 1983, defining rape as a purely sex-specific offense necessitating penile penetration without consent (Boyle 1985). Evidentiary rules existing at the time suggested that women, particularly those of "unchaste" character, were lying or fantasizing about rape (Boyle 1985; Stuart 1993). Evidence that a woman had disclosed soon after a rape was often used to show that the complaint had not been fabricated (Boyle 1985; Gelsthorpe and Morris 1990). Also, corroboration rules at the time required judges to warn juries that it was unwise to convict solely on the word of the complainant.

Social justice initiatives criticized the legal system for "blatantly" protecting the interests of men. This spurred the Canadian Parliament to repeal the old rape laws and introduce a three-tier structure of sexual assault offenses with the goal of equalizing the legal process (Stuart 1993; Boyle 1985; Kelly 1997). These reforms, specifically, Bill C-127, included (1) abolishing spousal immunity and the notion that a sexual attack required penetration, (2) repealing corroboration requirements, (3) restricting cross-examination of the primary witness as to her previous sexual history, and (4) abrogating the doctrine of recent complaint (Stuart 1993; Gelsthorpe and Morris 1990).

However, in 1991 the Supreme Court of Canada in *R. v. Seaboyer* resumed the historical undermining of women's equality rights by striking down section 276 of the Criminal Code, which limited the questioning of victims regarding their sexual history. The Supreme Court held that restricting the use of a complainant's sexual past with anyone other than the accused was an unconstitutional violation of an accused's right to a fair trial (Metropolitan Action Committee on Violence Against Women and Children [METRAC] 1998; Roberts and Mohr 1994). Moreover, it was argued that the provision excluded evidence without permitting a judge to engage in a determination of whether the possible prejudicial effect of the evidence would outweigh its probative value (Stuart 1993). This ruling allowed the decision of whether to admit or exclude evidence of past sexual behavior to be within the discretion of individual trial judges (Roberts and Mohr 1994).

Public outrage at the *Seaboyer* decision mobilized the involvement of national and regional women's groups and resulted in the Canadian Parliament introducing new "rape shield" legislation in 1992 through Bill C-49 (METRAC 1998). Bill C-49 provided the legal parameters for determining the admissibility of a victim's past sexual history as evidence in sexual assault trials (Roberts and Mohr 1994). It also provided, for the first time, a definition of the concept of "consent" and restricted the defense of "mistaken belief" as it concerns sexual assault (Roberts and Mohr 1994). These legislative changes represented an attempt to address the *legal* bias against victims of sexual assault; however, the *social* bias inherent in attitudes and behaviors of criminal justice remained largely unexamined.

COURTROOM CONSTRUCTION OF SEXUAL ASSAULT

The modification of the structure of sexual assault laws is only one force determining the scope and practice of evidentiary presentation. The ideological and cultural assumptions of patriarchy and women's sexuality have also played a role in shaping the legal construction of rape and determining the victim's experiences within the courtroom.

Social Mythology Regarding Women and Sexuality

Research examining the relationship between attitudes toward women, sex, sex roles, violence, and rape indicates that many people, including members of the judiciary and potential jurors, attribute responsibility for rape to women (Tetreault 1989). These stereotypes of sexual assault, victims, and perpetrators assist in discrediting women by reinforcing social myths about women and sexual assault. For example, various victim characteristics are known to influence the processing of sexual assault complaints within the criminal justice system (Du Mont 1999). Women with a psychiatric history, multiple sexual experiences, and low social status are less likely to see their complaints processed because these characteristics are not seen as socially desirable or normative. As well, rape victims are viewed as more likely to make false accusations of sexual assault (Bond 1993). Together, these notions form a basis for discrediting complaints of sexual assault and promote views of women and their sexuality that work to discriminate against women.

The Victim's Experience in Court

The institutional response to the sexual assault complainant and the sexual assault trial has been characterized as a "second rape" and highlights historical and current perceptions regarding the crime of sexual assault (Bond 1993). Despite recent changes in sexual assault law, rape remains a gendered crime (Bond 1993, 417; Fuller 1995). There is an inherent power imbalance that is reproduced in sexual assault trials, most notably, when the complainant rather than the defendant becomes the focus of the trial (Bond 1993; Temkin 1987; Thomas 1994). A common defense tactic is to undermine the credibility of the complainant in an attempt to harass and intimidate the victim (Bond 1993). Although the introduction of the woman's sexual history has been restricted by the enactment of rape shield laws, studies have found that defense attorneys continue to investigate the complainant's background, attempting to shift the focus from sexual history to general character and reputation (Bond 1993; Temkin 1987). As Holstrom and Burgess (1978) suggest, anything other than completely "proper and respectable" behavior can be used to discredit the rape victim's general character—for instance, the use of food stamps, a psychiatric history, alcohol use, absence from school, religious views, and vague innuendoes (Bond 1993).

The Judicial Construction of Sexual Assault

Empirical literature supports the influence of social stereotypes regarding women involved in trial proceedings for sexual assault. However, to date, only one study has explored the social construction of rape in the context of judges' opinions in sexual assault court cases (Fuller 1995). Through the analysis of judges' decisions in the 1970s and 1980s, Fuller (1995) found that definitions of rape were limited to a narrow category of incidence that assumed that rape was a sexual act. Furthermore, Fuller reported that women's account of the sexual assault was discredited by (1) suggesting that the victim was sexually promiscuous, (2) by focusing on the woman's responsibility and the man's interpretation of her behavior as indicating consent, and (3) by implying that women enjoy violent sex.

LITERATURE REVIEW: PSYCHOLOGICAL EVIDENCE IN SEXUAL ASSAULT TRIALS

Legislative reforms have attempted to shift the focus of sexual assault from a sexually based crime to a violence-driven offense. However, there are still significant issues open for judicial interpretation (Roberts and Mohr 1994). Given the significant impact trial court judges' discretionary power can have on how victims are viewed and treated in the courtroom, it is perplexing that research literature examining the phenomenon is scant. This section overviews the limited literature regarding the use of psychological evidence, specifically the use of expert testimony and third-party records. In addition, the inherent conundrum in presenting such evidence during the sexual assault trial is detailed.

Expert Testimony

The introduction of psychological evidence, often obtained through expert testimony, has become increasingly more common as medical evidence provides, at best, ambiguous information on one of the most important issues in a sexual assault trial—consent (Feldberg 1997). In determining admissibility of expert testimony, a judge must first evaluate the evidence in terms of relevancy and expert testimony standards, and then balance the probative value of the evidence against its potentially prejudicial effect (Wilk 1984). These legal issues create numerous arguments for both the inclusion and exclusion of expert psychological testimony in court. Though most of the literature has focused on rape trauma evidence, several arguments also apply to the use of other kinds of psychological information.

An Argument for the Use of Psychological Expert Testimony. Prosecutors use psychological evidence in court in an attempt to increase the chance of conviction (Stefan 1994). As lack of consent is critical to effective prosecution, the means of establishing such proof becomes integral to the case. Expert testimony about the traumatizing impact of rape is used in trials to bolster complaint credibility that a rape actually occurred when consent is at issue. Although legislative reforms have made the uncorroborated word of the victim legally sufficient to support a rape conviction, commentators assert that in practice corroboration is necessary (Wilk 1984). Research studies have revealed that without corroboration, jurors tend to view the testimony of rape complainants with skepticism, particularly if the victim and defendant were acquainted (Wilk 1984). Evidence of rape trauma syndrome (RTS) or post-traumatic stress disorder (PTSD) refutes the inference of consent and thereby counters the prejudicial effect of a prior consensual sexual relationship between the victim and the defendant (Wilk 1984).

Introducing expert psychological evidence in court also serves an educative function. It provides the judge and jury with information about the behavioral sequelae of rape victims that may initially appear counterintuitive (Tetreault 1989). It has been argued that unless it is explicitly stated for the jury that rape victims psychologically respond to the violent nature of the assault, as opposed to its sexual aspect, the victim's actions will likely be interpreted as consent (Ross 1982–1983). Moreover, victims of sexual assault exhibit reactions that would appear unreasonable to judges and jurors, such as delaying in reporting the incident, an inability to consistently identify the defendant, or a calm demeanor (Dwyer 1988). Research results suggest that psychological information provided to judges and jurors is both helpful in demystifying these behaviors and necessary in informing nonexperts on significant rape-related issues that influence the perceived credibility of the complainant (Tetreault 1989). Finally, expert testimony also provides judges and jurors with information on the hostile social framework confronting complainants, notably the likelihood that they will not be believed, the widespread social stigma, and the courage needed to report a sexual assault.

An Argument Against the Use of Psychological Expert Testimony. Scholars have also outlined several pervasive and negative consequences of introducing expert psychological testimony in sexual assault trials (Stefan 1994; Bond 1993). In general, focusing on RTS in a criminal trial shifts attention from the defendant's actions to the victims' reactions. These reactions inherently posit causality between present symptoms and past events. As such, a woman's past history, including traumatic sexual experiences, may become relevant evidence (Wilk 1984). Most importantly, the use of RTS evidence threatens the demise of past legal reforms by reintroducing psychiatric examinations of the rape victim, evidence of the victim's past sexual activities, and even corroboration requirements, through permitting the defendant's access to the woman's medical and psychiatric records (Stefan 1994). Also, the use of psychological theories to explain "counterintuitive" reactions such as a delay in reporting, suggests the notion of psychopathology and fails to explain these reactions as sensible behavior in the context of pervasive male violence against women (Stefan 1994).

Disclosure of Personal Records

The production and disclosure of a sexual assault complainant's personal records comprises a second form of psychological/psychiatric evidence that has been increasing in use since the 1992 introduction of Bill C-49 (Busby 1997). The efforts of defense counsel to access third-party records of victims in sexual assault trials has been characterized as a backlash against equality advances made by women in Canadian society (METRAC 1998). As part of this backlash, defense counsel practice has turned away from discrediting sexual assault complainants through exposing their prior sexual history, and turned to using their personal records to advance discriminatory myths and stereotypes. Specifically, defendants have sought access to psychiatric and psychotherapy records, files from abortion clinics, child welfare agencies, residential and public schools, drug and alcohol recovery centers, and personal diaries (Busby 1997; Cameron 1996). Moreover, because in the majority of cases the defendant and victim know each other, the accused may know not only of the contents of such records but also which records are likely to contain sensitive information. In fact, in some cases, the accused has been involved in creating the record. In *R. v. O'Connor*, the accused, Bishop O'Connor, was charged with sexually assaulting several Aboriginal women at a residential school where he was both the principal and priest. Defense counsel for *O'Connor* requested the complainants' medical, therapeutic, education, and employment records; records that the accused himself had generated (Busby 1997; METRAC 1998). The Supreme Court of Canada (1995) in a majority decision, concluded that the accused (*O'Connor*) need only satisfy a very "low threshold of relevancy" before a judge must examine any records sought by the defense. Moreover, the accused is not required to demonstrate the specific use of the information as it is not possible to do more than speculate about what personal records may contain. The result of the Supreme Court *O'Connor* case was that a victim's records were almost always considered "relevant" in sexual assault trials and the practice of third-party production and disclosure has subsequently increased.

It is significant to note that, in theory, defense counsel in any criminal case can seek personal records. However, in reality, they have almost exclusively been requested in sexual assault cases (Busby 1997; METRAC 1998). Advocacy groups suggest that this tactic is used to intimidate complainants into abandoning their allegations through the threat of exposing the victim's most personal and private details (METRAC 1998). Disclosure of records has been permitted in the hope of finding an inconsistency between what the complainant reported about the assault in supportive therapy and official statements made to the police or in court (Busby 1997). Consequently, the justice system's use of counseling records in this manner represents a deviation from their intended purpose. Specifically, it fails to recognize the dynamic nature of therapy and the importance of the therapeutic alliance and concomitantly supports societal mythologies about women and sexual assault.

Researchers have documented the detrimental impact of disclosing personal and psychiatric records in sexual assault trials. First, this tactic adversely affects and decreases women's support systems as counselors, crisis workers, and medical personnel are used against them (Kelly 1997; Busby 1997; METRAC 1998). This has created an environment where psychotherapists now tell clients that their records could be subpoenaed if criminal charges are laid. In addition, some victim assistance programs discourage women from referring to the actual assault in counseling scenarios and are limited to offering only general support to victims (Busby 1997; Kelly 1997). Second, the threat of disclosing personal records discourages women from invoking the criminal justice system and reporting their victimization. The majority in *O'Connor* found that "the extent to which production of the records would frustrate society's interest in encouraging the reporting of sexual offences could be dealt with through other avenues" and was not of "paramount consideration" when determining whether information should be disclosed to the accused (Busby 1997, 174). Consequently, as Busby (1997) argues, the majority created a new inequality: Specifically, women who have been sexually assaulted will have to choose to either seek counseling to deal with their violation or rely on the justice system for protection and redress. Finally, with the production of complainants' records, women can be constructed as "lacking credibility" or "rapeable" as the focus of sexual assault trials continues to be on the victim, her behavior, and her mental health, versus on the accused.

In an attempt to counteract the lack of equality inherent in the Supreme Court's *O'Connor* decision, new production and disclosure laws were introduced by the Canadian Parliament in May of 1997 through Bill C-46 (METRAC 1998). The purpose of this bill was to raise the threshold for disclosure of records by making it more difficult to obtain judicial consent for examination. The onus was on the accused to present specific details as to how the records were likely to be relevant. Through the preference for many women was for a law that prohibited any disclosure of personal records, this law does provide recognition of a complainant's privacy rights and recognition that a defense counsel's applications for a victim's records are based often on discriminatory beliefs about women (METRAC 1998).

This new legislation has not yet allowed sufficient research regarding the actual practice of disclosing third-party records, the type and extent of victim history evidence that is disclosed, and how it is used to emerge. The only study that has looked at the use of complainants' personal and therapy records in sexual assault trials was conducted prior to the passage of Bill C-46. In that investigation, Kelly (1997) interviewed police officers, defense and crown attorneys, judges, and victim workers to obtain information concerning the kinds of records sought, when they are accessible, the frequency of their use, and the rationale for their use. Research findings showed that personal and mental health records were used by defense counsels to attack complainants' credibility and to shrink margins of who is rapeable by reflecting patriarchal myths of rape.

Additional research focusing on the nature of complainants' records, how they are produced, and the reasons for, and impact of, their introduction following the 1997 legislative reforms is suggested.

PURPOSE OF CURRENT STUDY

Research literature indicates that psychological information in the form of expert testimony and the disclosure of complainants' personal records has a significant impact on whether legal reforms are appropriately protecting the victims of sexual assault. However, studies examining how and why psychological evidence is actually used by trial judges is lacking. The present study attempts to address this gap in knowledge through a qualitative investigation of the use of psychological evidence in sexual assault trials. The study is guided by the following research questions:

1. Has access to personal/therapy records been restricted since the introduction of Bill C-46?
2. How are expert psychological testimony and personal/therapy records being used in sexual assault cases? What effect does their use have on trial outcomes?
3. What is the purpose of introducing expert psychological testimony and personal/therapy records in sexual assault cases?
4. What is the potential impact of utilizing psychological evidence on rape law reforms?

METHOD

Sample

The sample was comprised of Court cases heard following the passages of Bill C-49 and Bill C-46, during the period June 1997 to December 1999. Cases for analysis were selected through a survey of the Quicklaw Database System, accessing Dominion Law Reports, Canadian Journals Databases, and Ontario Reports. Two keyword searches were used: "sexual assault 1997–1999 and records" and "sexual assault 1997–1999 and expert testimony" and produced a sample of 184 cases. Inclusion criteria required that (1) complainants involved females aged fourteen years or older, (2) sexual assaults were committed by a male other than an immediate family member (i.e., father, stepfather, brother), and (3) sufficient information on how expert testimony evidence and disclosure of third-party records were used by judges in their decisions was available (34 cases did not have enough information). Court cases involving child victims ($N = 50$) and/or incest ($N = 36$) were excluded because the nature of these offenses is frequently different as are evidentiary standards for reliability and credibility. Also, cases involving expert testimony on only the accused

($N = 6$) and/or applications for solely the accused's third-party records ($N = 8$) were also excluded, as well as cases with male victims ($N = 14$) and female perpetrators ($N = 2$). A number of other cases were eliminated from the analysis for not having a sexual assault charge ($N = 10$), not being a criminal case ($N = 6$), or using other types of records, e.g., videos ($N = 4$). The final sample included 14 Ontario Provincial Court cases.

Data Analysis

Research questions were addressed through an analysis of judges' court case decisions using Glaser and Strauss's (1967) constant comparison method for qualitative data. This process of analysis attempts to identify the similarities and differences that exist between instances, cases, and concepts, allowing the full diversity and complexity of the data to be explored (Hayes 1997). Analysis of judges' decisions began by coding all incidents of psychological evidence used into as many constructs of analysis as possible while simultaneously comparing them with the previous incidents in the same and different categories and across court cases. As the coding continued, related categories and their properties were integrated, allowing themes of how and why psychological information is introduced, and the impact of its use, to emerge. In particular, the constant comparison method involves comparing incidents applicable to each category and integrating categories and their properties (Glaser and Strauss 1967). A unique feature of this method is the notion of a "continuous growth process," meaning that previous stages remain in operation throughout the analysis and provide a seamless development of the following stage until the analysis is terminated (Glaser and Strauss 1967; Flick 1998).

RESULTS

Case Characteristics

A quantitative breakdown of cases ($N=14$) illustrating (1) the characteristics included in applications for third-party records, (2) types of records sought, (3) judges' decisions regarding the applications, and (4) types of expert testimony used in the cases is presented in Tables 8-1 to 8-4. As seen in the tables, the majority of third-party records applications were initiated by defence counsel and contained medical or psychiatric information that was disclosed to the applicant. In addition, the most frequently used expert testimony evidence was psychiatric or medical.

Table 8.1 Third Party Record Applications

N	Particulars
6	Defense applies for records
2	Defense questions complainant about her records
1	Defense applies to have Bill C-46 deemed unconstitutional
5	Case contains no information regarding use of records
14	Total

Table 8.2 Types of Records Sought by Defense

N	Particulars
8	Psychiatric/Therapeutic
4	Medical
2	Personal diaries
1	Sexual Assault Care Clinic (SACC)
1	Drug and Alcohol Services
16	Total

Note: N does not total 14 as defense counsel requested multiple types of records

N	Particulars
	Table 8. 3 Judge's Decisions Regarding Defense Application for Third Party Records
N	Particulars
5	Judge discloses complainant's records to defense
2	Judge allows questioning of complainant regarding her records
1	Judge finds Bill C-46 to be unconstitutional
1	Judge denies disclosure of records to defense
9	Total

Note: Of the 14 cases reviewed, 5 cases had no application for 3rd party records.

N	Particulars
	Table 8.4 Types of Expert Testimony Evidence Introduced in Cases
N	Particulars
3	Psychiatric (e.g., incest, rape trauma, PTSD, borderline personality disorder, false memory syndrome, schizophrenia)
2	Medical (e.g., general practitioner, medical staff from SACC)
1	School mental health (e.g., youth worker, guidance counselor)
1	Street Kids (no credentials specified)
7	Total

Themes

The qualitative data analysis of judges' court decisions resulted in the emergence of four separate themes. These are organized around the central research questions and presented next.

But first some discussion about the accessibility of complainants' records. In general, it was found that the courts failed to be guided by Bill C-46 and easy access to complainants' records was evident. Of the nine cases involving defense applications for third-party records (refer to Table 8-3), all nine are represented by this category. Specifically, the standards for determining the "relevancy" of complainants' records were very low. The relevancy requirement is easily fulfilled by information acquired through a preliminary hearing wherein defense counsel may conduct a thorough examination into the existence of personal records and their relevancy to court proceedings. This is illustrated by the rendering of one judge who stated that the complainant of a sexual assault had "no expectation of privacy in a matter which is the subject in chief" nor should "the judge's ability to review the records be affected by the complainant's privacy rights." Also, the mental health act provision that prohibits the production of records if it threatens the complainant's emotional health was of "secondary importance" over the accused's rights of "full answer and defense."

Victims' personal records were also disclosed to defense counsels for such reasons as (1) unsubstantiated comments made about the complainant's mental health, (2) a close temporal connection between the creation of the record and the allegations, and (3) where personal diaries contained information about the accused. Results showed that judges dismissed arguments involving the potential usefulness of Bill C-46 as unreliable and argued that the cross-examination of complainants regarding their records was allowed because questioning did not fall under the scope of Bill C-46. In contrast, judges turned to the common law, citing the 1995 Supreme Court of Canada *O'Connor* decision, which concluded that the accused need only satisfy a very low threshold of relevancy before a judge must examine any records sought by the defense.

Use of Psychological Evidence against Complainant. Results showed that a wide scope of records were deemed relevant by the courts and were used to question complainants' credibility and identify inconsistencies. Of the nine cases involving defense applications for records (refer to Table 8-2), six are represented by this category. Relevant records included psychiatric histories, medications taken, past medical exams, therapy narratives, and personal journals. Trial judges reasoned that third-party records were relevant if the complainant had a mental illness or personality disorder and credibility was an issue, or to look for psychiatric disorders that had not already been diagnosed. Once personal records were deemed relevant, complainants could be extensively cross-examined on their emotional/psychiatric history. This theme is exemplified by one judge's statement that "although the information in therapeutic records reflected primarily treatment issues, they were still deemed relevant since they could shed light on the complainant's credibility, consistency, memory, and whether or not the therapist used recovered memory techniques."

Expert Testimony. Expert testimony was also used to discredit the complainant or was disregarded if introduced to provide context and explanation of the complainants' actions. Of the eight cases involving expert testimony (refer to Table 8-4), seven are represented by this category. In particular, expert psychological testimony was employed by defense counsel as a strategy to undermine complainant's credibility. Defense experts discredited women's stories (1) by arguing that memories of the sexual assault were false because they were recovered during therapy, or (2) by arguing that the women's accounts of the details were inconsistent, and (3) by disputing the women's ability to identify their attackers. Analysis revealed that if the complainant experienced increased anxiety, expert witnesses testified that this was a reason to believe that the complainant was lying. Other defense experts used complainants' psychiatric and medical records to "diagnose borderline personality disorder on the basis of victim's history of childhood sexual abuse," or to reconstruct the attack so that the complainant was viewed to have consented. In contrast, when the Crown introduced expert testimony to explain a complainant's actions, the judges disregarded it as either having "no foundation" or "not necessary since they could assess the complainant on their own."

Rationale for the Introduction of Psychological Evidence. Analysis of the judges' decisions revealed that psychological evidence was used often to focus on the complainant and discredit her. Six of the fourteen cases are represented by this category. This category includes judicial judgments such as the need for independent confirmatory evidence (e.g., physical injuries, eyewitnesses) when the complainant had a psychiatric history, personality disorder, or a "tendency to lie." Similarly, judges noted complainants' alcohol use, sexual history, social calendar, motives to fabricate, degree of resistance, manner of testifying, and whether or not the complainant expressed anger or sadness following the assault. Results suggest that according to judges, if the complainant drank too much alcohol, did not resist enough, failed to testify in a clear and calm manner, or did not seem angry at the accused after the assault, she was less likely to be believed. This is highlighted by one judge who, while noting that the fourteen-year-old complainant is physically larger than the thirty-five-year-old accused states that "maybe a show of strength would have solved the problem."

Recognition of the Evidentiary and Equality Rights of Complainants. Seven of the fourteen cases are represented by this category. In contrast to the findings discussed here, judges in seven of the cases did recognize the fact that the accused should not be permitted to "fish" for the complainant's third-party records. This category is exemplified by the acknowledgment of judges that if the rate of records produced increased, the number of complainants to come forward following a sexual assault would decrease.

CONCLUSION

The present study examined the role and application of psychological evidence in the prosecution of sexual assault offenses in fourteen Ontario Provincial Court cases. Results suggest that the introduction of new Canadian production legislation in May of 1997, attempting to increase the standard for determining the "relevancy" of complainants' records, has not deterred defense counsels from successfully accessing third-party records in the majority of disclosure applications. The results also suggest that even though some judges are verbally acknowledging the complainant's equality rights by stating that defense applications for the disclosure of records need to include specific reasons for how the records will likely be relevant, this specification does not appear to restrict access. In particular, some trial court judges are using their discretion to disregard the new legislation and instead follow case precedent (i.e., the *O'Connor* decision). Moreover, they are also allowing defense arguments that include unsubstantiated innuendoes directed at the victim's mental health as valid rationale for the production of personal records. Consequently, women are discouraged from reporting their assaults. As well, the quality of therapeutic services and support systems diminishes under the threat of documenting information on the sexual assault.

This investigation also suggests that the majority of expert psychological evidence introduced in court assists in discrediting the complainant. Specifically, the victim's mental health and substance use histories are raised by experts to undermine credibility, even when no question of competency arises, and to identify the woman as "deviant" and outside the law's protection. A woman's experience of any prior abuse is used against her as reason to diagnose a psychiatric disorder or to suggest that she indeed consented to the sexual act. In addition, the judiciary fails to recognize the nature of therapy and therapeutic relationships when the testimony of a complainant's personal therapist is used to suggest that her allegations are either inconsistent or fabricated.

In contrast to the argument that psychological information would bolster complainants' credibility, provide corroboration, and educate judges and jurors, the present findings suggest that judges tend to ignore expert testimony introduced by the Crown to help explain the victims' behavior and emotions. Unfortunately, the prosecution's introduction of psychological evidence allows the defense to examine the complainant with their own expert thereby reintroducing the psychiatric examination of the victim, corroboration requirements, and allowing access to women's personal records.

The final conclusion to have emerged from the present study is consistent with the findings of much of the past research. In essence, the power imbalance within society is often reproduced in a sexual assault trial because the complainant rather than the defendant is on trial. Although legal reforms have abolished corroboration requirements, restricted cross-examination on sexual history, and abrogated the doctrine of recent complaint, judicial discretion continues to focus its attention on complainants' character and credibility thereby illustrating its ideological and cultural assumptions of patriarchy and women's sexuality. This general discrediting and focusing on the complainant by the judiciary has potentially negative consequences even for those women whose records are not disclosed to the accused. A judge's review of the records may, in itself, have a detrimental impact on the judge's perceptions of the complainant and how she makes evidentiary decisions later on in the trial.

Limitations of the Study

The current findings need to be considered in the context of the investigation's limitations. First, cases used for analysis were chosen from the Quicklaw Database System, a database that selects cases for inclusion based on whether or not the trial involves a particularly noteworthy legal issue. As a result, cases included in the Quicklaw database may not be representative of sexual assault cases heard in court. Similarly, the present sample includes a small number of cases heard only in the province of Ontario, and how these findings generalize within Canada or worldwide needs to be examined. Third, the transcripts used were of judges' decisions and not actual court transcripts. Consequently, the information available for analysis lacked specific details regarding expert testimony and the nature of the information included in the third-party records. Finally, this investigation was conducted prior to the Supreme Court of Canada's 1999 ruling in *R. v. Mills*. In that decision, the court upheld Bill C-46 as constitutional and raised the requirement standards for relevancy, but still left it to individual trial judges to determine whether an accused will be able to examine the complainant's records. Future research on the practice, nature, and impact of disclosing third-party records and introducing psychological evidence needs to include the examination of actual court transcripts following the 1999 decision by the Supreme Court to uphold Bill C-46.

REFERENCES

Bond, S. 1993. Psychiatric evidence of sexual assault victims: The need for fundamental change in the determination of relevance. *The Dalhousie Law Journal* 16: 416–47.

Boyle, C. 1985. Sexual assault and the feminist judge. *Canadian Journal of Women and the Law* 1: 93–107.

Busby, K. 1997. Discriminatory uses of personal records in sexual violence cases. *Canadian Journal of Women and the Law* 9: 148–77.

Cameron, J. 1996. *The Charter's Impact on the Criminal Justice System.* Toronto: Carswell.

Du Mont, J. 1999. So few convictions: The role of victim related characteristics in the legal processing of sexual assault cases. Unpublished doctoral dissertation. University of Toronto.

Dwyer, D.A. 1988. Expert testimony on rape trauma syndrome: An argument for limited admissibility. *Washington Law Review* 63: 1063–86.

Feldberg, G. 1997. Defining the facts of rape: The uses of medical evidence in sexual assault trials. *Canadian Journal of Women and the Law* 9: 89–114.

Flick, U. 1998. *An Introduction to Qualitative Research.* Thousand Oaks, CA: Sage Publications.

Fuller, P. 1995. The social construction of rape in appeal court cases. *Feminism and Psychology* 5: 154–61.

Gelsthorpe, L., and A. Morris. 1990. *Feminist Perspectives in Criminology.* Philadelphia: Open University Press.

Glaser, B.G, and A.L. Strauss. 1967. *The Discovery of Grounded Theory: Strategies for Qualitative Research.* Chicago: Aldine Publishing Company.

Hayes, N. 1997. *Doing Qualitative Analysis in Psychology.* Erlbaum (United Kingdom): Psychology Press.

Holmstrom, Lynda Lytle, and Ann Wolbert Burgess. 1978. *The Victim of Rape: Institutional Responses.* New York: John Wiley & Sons.

Kelly, K.D. 1997. "You must be crazy if you think you were raped": Reflections on the use of complainants' personal and therapy records in sexual assault trials. *Canadian Journal of Women and the Law* 9: 178–95.

Metropolitan Action Committee on Violence Against Women and Children (METRAC). 1998. *Can confidentiality survive? A day of study on disclosure of personal records in sexual assault cases.* Post Conference Package.

Roberts, J.V., and R.M. Mohr. 1994. *Confronting Sexual Assault: A Decade of Legal and Social Change.* Toronto: University of Toronto Press.

Ross, J.L. 1982–1983. The overlooked expert in rape prosecutions. *University of Toledo Law Review* 14: 707–34.

Stefan, S. 1994. The protection racket: Rape trauma syndrome, psychiatric labeling, and law. *Northwestern University Law Review* 88: 1271–345.

Stuart, D. 1993. Sexual assault: Substantive issues before and after bill C-49. *Criminal Law Quarterly* 35: 241–63.

Temkin, J. 1987. *Rape and the Legal Process.* London: Sweet and Maxwell.

Tetreault, P.A. 1989. Rape myth acceptance: A case for providing educational expert testimony in rape jury trials. *Behavioral Sciences and the Law* 7: 243–257.

Thomas, E.W. 1994. Was Eve merely framed; or was she forsaken? *The New Zealand Law Journal* 14: 91–96.

Wilk, P.A. 1984. Expert testimony on rape trauma syndrome: Admissibility and effective use in criminal rape prosecution. *The American University Law Review* 33: 417–62.

9

Reconceptualizing Sexual Assault from an Intractable Social Problem to a Manageable Process of Social Change

K. Edward Renner

INTRODUCTION

Over the past three decades there has been a gradual evolution in how adult sexual assault and child sexual abuse have been defined by the law, and how they are seen professionally and by the general public. As a result of these changes in awareness, there is now a growing consensus that male sexual violence is a social problem of considerable magnitude. Despite this awareness, however, effective reform and social change have been hard to accomplish.

Law Reform in Canada

In the late 1960s the women's movement called attention to the high frequency of male sexual violence and the low proportion of arrests, prosecutions, and convictions. In Canada, this social movement was exemplified by the publication of *Rape: The Price of Coercive Sexuality* (Clark and Lewis 1977), effectively documenting that under the existing rape law, women were treated as "property," and that rape was a form of assault, not a "sexual" act. In 1983 Canada modified its criminal code, replacing the crime of rape with that of sexual assault (Department of Justice Canada 1983).

Under the impact of the new legislation, more women started to report sexual assaults, but the response of the criminal justice system remained virtually unchanged. A large proportion of the cases were still classified as unfounded by the police, were not charged by the prosecution, and were not convicted by the courts (Department of Justice Canada 1990; Roberts 1990b). Clearly, the old problems remained despite the new legislation. Over the intervening years several "rape shield" laws were passed making it more difficult for the defense to raise questions about victims' past sexual history or gain access to their counseling records. These reforms were all challenged and their applications limited by the Supreme Court.

Thus, after nearly four decades of reform efforts, male sexual violence continues to remain largely outside of the effective jurisdiction of the criminal justice process. What has changed, however, is the level of awareness of the problem and a sense of urgency over the need for a solution. What is lacking is a conceptualization of what specific changes are required and how to accomplish them.

An Action-Research Program

My research program on sexual assault began in 1983 in Halifax, Nova Scotia, when a sexual assault service for the city grew out of my community psychology class (Renner and Keith 1985). In the early years, the research focus was on the nature of the victim's experience and how best to provide support. Later, the focus shifted to the social, medical, and legal context, which often seemed to hinder rather than help. The goal of the program was always "action-research" with the dual objectives of having policy and theory inform practice to provide the most useful service, and to have the practice inform policy and theory to have the best possible conceptualization (Renner 1995).

Back in 1983, I was among those who suspected that changing the terminology from "rape" to "sexual assault" would not make any difference to how victims were treated (Renner and Sahjpaul 1986; Sahjpaul and Renner 1988). The problem is not with the statutory definition of the offense but rather with a fundamental flaw in the legal process. I believe the courts themselves are direct contributors to the very problem for which they are the intended solution. This redefinition of the issues points less to the need for legislative law reform and more to the need to reform the way the existing laws are administered—that is, the precedents and common law practices that form the "legal doctrine." As a result of our redefinition of the central issue, we have now called for a National Social Action Program. The justification for this perspective, based on the results of fifteen years of action-research, is described in the sections that follow.

THE LEGAL DOCTRINE

Although the focus of this chapter is on the legal system, it is important to keep in mind that sexual assault and abuse are primarily "social problems" with legal aspects. An issue becomes a social problem when it becomes so pervasive as to undermine the integrity of the political process. When this happens, the effect of the issue is felt by everyone, even those not directly involved in any specific manifestation. As a result, any treatment of the issue must accommodate psychological, social, and political ramifications, and no simple "solution" is possible. Many changes must occur across the entire spectrum of the quality of civic life (Renner 2000).

A Social Justice Perspective

Social justice is a conceptual ideal of our democracy. Laws and legal procedures are intentionally created tools (means) to achieve social ideals (ends). Social science evaluation research is one of the methods available for measuring actual outcomes and for contrasting them with a theoretical ideal, to see if there are statistically "significant" differences. If there are, then some adjustments are needed either to the theory or to the practice to achieve greater concordance. In a less than perfectly understood world, with less than perfect practices, there will be differences. Once differences are clearly identified, modifications to theory or practice can be tried and the outcome reassessed. Such is the reiterative process of social progress, and the role of social science in social change (Renner 1995). This is the philosophy of science on which action-research is based.

"Selectivity" and "Disparity" within the Criminal Justice Process

Our initial research was based on two sets of data collected in Halifax, Nova Scotia, from 1983 through 1992. The first was from the case records kept by the sexual assault service that grew out of my community psychology class. The case data file included 2,533 consecutive cases responded to by the sexual assault service. (For methodological details, see Renner and Wackett, 1987; Renner, Wackett and Ganderton 1988; Renner, Alksnis, and Park 1997.) This descriptive information defined the actual nature of sexual assault and sexual abuse as a social reality.

The second set of data was obtained between 1989 and 1992 from the court records and included 1,074 consecutive court cases tried in the Halifax Law Courts. This data was composed of cases of sexual assault ($n=354$), and, for comparative purposes, cases of physical assault ($n=513$) and robbery ($n=207$). (For methodological details see Yurchesyn, Keith, and Renner 1992; Renner and Yurchesyn 1994; Renner et al. 1977.) This information defined the consequences of these offenses as a legal reality.

Selectivity. In 1993, Statistics Canada conducted a large national victimization survey and found that 94 percent of women who were sexually assaulted did not report the incidents to authorities. Of the 6 percent reported, only 40 percent resulted in charges being laid. Of those cases where charges were laid, two-thirds resulted in convictions, but only one-half of those convicted received a jail term. This final .008 of the assailants who received a jail term represent an exceedingly small proportion of the cases, given the seriousness of the offense and the fact that in 85 percent or more of the cases the offender is known to the victim and thus easily identifiable (Gregory and Lees 1994; Roberts and Grossman 1994; Yurchesyn, Keith, and Renner 1992).

The case data file from the sexual assault service when compared to the court records provided an extraordinary opportunity to evaluate what accounts for the small proportion of highly selected cases that pass through the criminal justice process.

In adult cases, those with violence and injury are disproportionately selected into the criminal justice process. According to the records of the crisis center, in more than 90 percent of the cases the typical offender is a known acquaintance, and the assault involves the use of physical restraint without a weapon. In these instances, women submit to the physical force and the demand for sex, choosing not to be otherwise harmed or injured. However, in the cases that appeared before the courts, the opposite was true; only 18 percent of the cases were similar to the typical case from the sexual assault service in which there was neither injury, the use of a weapon, nor serious harm. In 82 percent of the court cases at least one of these features was present. Clearly, the "typical" incident of sexual assault does not receive an equal frequency of legal redress.

In cases of sexual abuse against children, the records of the sexual assault service indicate that 77 percent of the abuse is perpetrated by a family member and that in 80 percent of the cases the abuse takes place in the child's own home. Yet, in the court cases, it is cases of abuse by strangers (5 percent) and acquaintances such as family friends and caretakers (58 percent) that disproportionately find their way into the criminal process, with the most frequent location outside the victim's own home (64 percent).

Only the cases officially reported receive media coverage. For child cases, this has the effect of minimizing public awareness of the overwhelming degree to which children are mostly at risk of sexual abuse in their own home by their own family members. For adult cases, it contributes to the myth that a "real" sexual assault involves violence and physical injury to the victim. As a result, many adult women who choose not to resist in order to avoid injury in a sexual assault feel self-blame and guilt and are blamed by others (Renner, Wackett, and Ganderton 1988).

Disparity. Disparity refers to the differential ways cases are treated once they are selected into the criminal justice system. A fundamental assumption of the justice system is that punishment should be proportional to the seriousness of the offense (Canadian Sentencing Commission 1987). It is in the severity of the sentence given to those deemed to be guilty where the disparity between different types of sexual assault and between sexual assault and other types of crimes can be evaluated to discover the implicit rationale of the courts (Roberts 1990b). (For a detailed account of the statistical comparisons used to evaluate disparity see Yurchesyn, Keith, and Renner 1992; Renner, Parriag, and Park 1997.)

Men convicted of sexual abuse against children received lighter sentences than men convicted of sexual assault against adult women. At the harsh end of the severity scale, only 13 percent of child offenders received a sentence of two years or more in contrast to 30 percent of offenders of sexual assault against an adult woman. At the lenient end of the scale, 61 percent of those convicted of child sexual abuse received less than one year in jail compared to 44 percent of those convicted for adult sexual assault.

For adult sexual assault cases, high levels of violence were related to both trial outcome and to the severity of the sentence. When verbal threats or physical force alone was used, there was a 50 percent rate of conviction, and only 8 percent of those convicted received sentences of two years or more. In those cases where injury occurred or a weapon was used, the conviction rate increased to 66 percent and 35 percent received sentences of two years or more. These figures increased to 92 percent and 40 percent when the woman's life was endangered or serious physical harm resulted.

When comparing the outcome of sexual assault cases with other types of crimes, perpetrators of sexual assault are usually sentenced less severely than those convicted of robbery, even though there are similar amounts of violence and victim injury in both types of cases. At the lenient end of the scale, 80 percent of the sexual assault offenders received a sentence of less than two years in contrast to 47 percent of those convicted of robbery. However, those found guilty of sexual assault are generally sentenced more severely than are those found guilty of physical assault, where 96 percent of the offenders received a sentence of less than two years. This more lenient sentence is despite the fact that in physical assault cases there was a greater incidence of violence, more victim injury, and more frequent use of weapons.

"Discounting" the Severity of Male Sexual Violence

The selectivity and disparity found in our data form a pattern that reveals the implicit philosophy used by the court to assess the relative severity of male sexual violence. The pattern can be accounted for by three factors. The courts are most lenient when (1) there is a relationship between the victim and the offender, (2) there are no visible physical injuries, and (3) the offender is not otherwise criminally dangerous (Renner, Parriag, and Park 1997).

Relationship. Whenever there is a relationship between the victim and the accused, some of the responsibility is shifted to the victim who is seen as the author of his or her own misfortune. This explains why physical assaults, most common between two men trying to assert domination, are punished the least. Robbery, on the other hand, is most likely at the hands of a stranger, and the court is very severe on what looks like random acts of violence, including physical assaults by a stranger. This explains why sexual assaults at the hands of strangers, and child abuse from outside the family circle (the atypical cases), are selected into the system, and once in, are treated harshly. However, the majority of actual incidents of sexual assault and child sexual abuse are at the hands of those to whom the adult has willingly exposed herself, usually in a social setting, and on whom the child is primarily dependent. These are the typical sexual assault and abuse cases, and yet these are the ones that have least credibility before the criminal justice system.

Harm. Whenever there is a lack of visible physical harm, or lack of a clear threat of physical harm, the court is more lenient. In cases of physical assault, any resulting small injuries are taken as self-evident proof that a simple assault took place (the typical case), and the court holds both individuals accountable to some degree. However, if the victim is severely beaten, after domination has been established, the courts are harsh in their judgments (the atypical case). Likewise, armed robbery is treated very seriously and is seen as physically threatening to the victim. In contrast, in most sexual assaults the woman or child is seldom visibly injured. Most women, similar to robbery victims, choose not to be physically injured as well as sexually violated, and most children trust and obey the adult upon whom they are dependent. However, because of the analogy created between sexual and physical assault, the lack of visible physical harm is taken as evidence that no sexual assault took place (the typical case). Thus, if a victim of sexual assault acts like a robbery victim (take something but don't hurt me), she is treated like a victim of physical assault (held partially accountable), but only if she acts like a victim of physical assault (is beaten up) will the court treat her like a robbery victim (deal harshly with the offender). The simple reality is that a woman must be prepared to be physically harmed (which should never be required) if her case is to be treated as "serious" by the courts (Renner and Yurchesyn 1994).

Danger. When the offender is not otherwise criminally dangerous, the courts will be most lenient. Most robberies are an economic crime committed by "punks" who are seen as dangerous to the community. In contrast, in most sexual crimes, the offender is an "ordinary" man, one to whom an adult woman willingly exposed herself, such as a date or an acquaintance, and on whom the child is dependent, such as Uncle Joe. The primary factors accounting for discrepancies between child and adult cases is that the child abuse offender often has a better reputation (e.g., a teacher, soccer coach) than the men charged with sexually assaulting women. Again, the effect is twofold, first acting to select which cases go to trial, and then playing an important role in the disposition of those already highly selected cases (Renner, Parriag, and Park 1997).

Social Justice, Equality, and the Legal Doctrine

The combined effects of "relationship," "harm," and danger" are to introduce two fundamental failures of social justice into the legal doctrine. Both discriminate against women and children and are forms of injustice.

Discounting Severity through Confounding. The net effect of these three factors is to discount the severity with which male sexual violence is treated. The legal system has confounded the criterion for leniency with the defining circumstances and situations in which women and children find themselves with respect to the men who sexually assault and abuse them: The existence of a relationship, the lack of visible physical harm, and the fact that the offender is not otherwise criminally dangerous are both the criterion for leniency and a description of the social position of women and children with respect to the men who abuse them. The legal doctrine, by definition, has established sexual offenses as "not serious." These two concepts do not need to be hopelessly confounded as they now are. But, until they are separated, women and children will experience selectivity and disparity at the hands of the legal process.

Denial of Women's and Children's Reality. Because the courts do not deal with sexual assault as it exists in reality, the cases that do reach the courtroom are unrepresentative and misleading. When the legal process that is intended to protect women and children from sexual assault and abuse does not do so through restricted access to justice and unequal treatment, the equity provisions of the Canadian Charter of Rights and Freedom and guarantees of due process and equal protection of the law in the United States are violated. The reluctance of women and children to use the system, revealed by the victimization survey cited previously and the experience of sexual assault services, documents a serious breakdown in our democratic process at an extreme civic price. The legal doctrine itself contributes to a huge social problem, affecting as many as one of every two women and one in four children by the time they are age sixteen as being largely outside the jurisdiction of the legal process (Statistics Canada 1993).

THE DYNAMICS OF DISCOUNTING

My colleagues and I wanted to go beyond the sterile portrait of the issues that came from working with the statistical data from the court records and the sexual assault service. We wished to see how, in terms of the actual practices within the courtroom, male sexual violence was excused when there was a relationship, when there was not visible physical injury, and when the offender was not otherwise dangerous. How could the courts confound the typical experiences of women and children with the standard for leniency? This was our motivation for obtaining a random subsample of 105 transcripts from the same data source that was used for the analysis of the court records.

Categorization of Courtroom Dynamics

The first step was to gain a qualitative insight by reading the material. For the students who were working with me this became, personally and psychologically, the most difficult task of the entire project because of the feelings of moral outrage and indignation aroused over what was happening. I personally came to understand more deeply the simply devastating emotional reaction to the criminal prosecution of their cases that I had seen in some of the women in working with the sexual assault center. We were not prepared for the fact that these were not just a few isolated exceptions but a consistent pattern across all the court cases for both women and children.

It was our belief that the pattern we saw in the courtroom was no coincidence. We suspected that there were a finite number of strategies and tactics being used. Our approach was to look for "runs of questions" that formed coherent "scenarios" and to transcribe each of them. For example, a run of questions about how soon the victim told someone about the assault was named "Recency of Complaint." In this way we were able to group scenarios that were similar into categories.

What we discovered was extraordinarily simple. Only twenty-four categories were required to describe what both the prosecuting and defense attorneys did in the course of a trial as shown in Table 9.1 (Park and Renner 1998; Parriag and Renner 1998). Each case could be divided into a collection of scenarios, like the one in Table 9.2, which fit neatly into one of the sixteen categories of content, or one of eight categories of social influence tactics. The 105 cases yielded approximately 3,500 scenarios that captured the content of sexual assault trials and allowed us to count the frequency with which each occurred. The complete list of categories and definitions have been incorporated into a coding manual for both research use (Renner, Parriag, and Park 1997) and for applied use by local community groups (NSAP 1998). The courtroom dynamics that we discovered were slightly different, however, for both the content and the tactics, in terms of how they were used in the child and adult cases.

Content

Holding Children Responsible for Sexuality. Counting the frequency with which the prosecution and the defense used each of the content categories made it possible to statistically describe what each lawyer did in comparison to the other. We discovered that they acted in a "complementary" way. Whenever the facts of the case permitted, the prosecution would emphasize the good adjustment of the child before the abuse and the bad adjustment after the abuse, that the accused removed the child's clothing, that the child resisted, was of good character, reported the abuse quickly, and did not initiate contact with the ac-

Table 9.1 Categorization Scheme

The questions asked of victims of sexual assault by the prosecution and the defense can be classified into two broad types of Content and Tactics. Each of the two types can be further subdivided into a total of 24 specific categories into which the examples can be categorized.

Content		
History	Previous Sexual History
	Previous Nonsexual History
	Previous Relationship with the Accused
Psychological	Adjustment Before
	Adjustment After
	Feeling at the Time
Themes	Injury
	Resistance
	Removed or Torn Clothing
	Violence/Intimidation
	Place/Situation
	Culpability/Character
	Recency of Complaint
	Initiation
	Honest Misunderstanding
	Communication of Consent
Tactics of Social Influence	Word Pictures
	Impeachment
	Overgeneralization
	Implied Fabrication
	Tactics/Style
	Credibility of Witness/Victim
	Credibility of Accused
	Objections

cused. However, whenever possible, the defense would emphasize the opposite. Using chi-square statistics to evaluate these differences in emphasis between the prosecution and defense, all were statistically significant at p <.001(Park and Renner 1998). The net effect is to hold children responsible for their sexuality, when legally the exact opposite is the case. In fact, full and complete responsibility rests with the adult to refrain from all sexual activity with a child. Yet, overwhelmingly, both the prosecution and the defense introduce myths about the nature of adult sexuality that effectively hold children responsible for preventing their own sexual abuse from taking place (Park and Renner 1998; Renner and Park 1997).

Table 9.2 Sample Scenario and Data Sheet for an Adult Case of Sexual Assault				
Type	**Lawyer**	**Category**	**Case ID**	**Victim Age**
Theme	Defense	Removed or Torn Clothing	10088	Adult

Defense: But your coat wasn't torn!
Witness: No, it wasn't torn.
Defense: These are your bra and panties you were wearing, correct!
Witness: Yes
Defense: Your bra and panties, they were not damaged?
Witness: No

Distorting the Reality of Sexual Assault. Many authors (e.g., Burt 1980; Lonsway and Fitzgerald 1994) over the past two decades have written about the commonly held "myths and stereotypes" about sexual assault—for example, if the clothing was not torn, if the complaint was not recent, or if there was no physical harm, then it is not seen as a sexual assault. Our research has documented that a standard list of sixteen such content items are consistently introduced into sexual assault trials by both the prosecution and the defense, depending on the circumstance of the case, as was illustrated in Table 9.2. Similarly, if the woman needs counseling after the assault, the prosecution introduces this as evidence; if she does not, the defense claims the absence of the rape trauma syndrome is evidence against a sexual assault. The lawyers act out a script in a complementary fashion based on a common set of sixteen stereotypes (Parriag and Renner 1998), which we have reduced to the three broad issues of relationship, harm, and danger (Renner, Parriag, and Park 1997). To be a credible victim, the woman must be a physical and emotional wreck, and show it.

But, the reality of women's experience is distorted even more through "word pictures" created by using the language of consensual sex of which the myths and stereotypes are composed. Both the prosecution and the defense use "sanitized" language in the courtroom that bears little resemblance to the fact that the woman's testimony and experience are about an assault. For example, the defense will string together a chronology of events, ending with "and *that* is when you performed oral sex! Correct?" The emphasis on the word "that" refers to the chronology, but the victim's simple answer of "yes" implies a consensual sexual activity. Lost in the sanitized account for public consumption in the courtroom is her actual experience of "that is when he lifted my head up by my hair and forced his penis into my mouth. He said suck my cock or I will scar your face." Unfortunately, the prosecution seldom creates a situation where the victim's account, as she experienced it, gets communicated in clear and unequivocal language (Bavelas and Coates 2001; Coates, Bavelas, and Gibson 1994; Matoesian 1993).

Tactics

Developmental Level. An even more serious problem than holding children accountable for their "sexuality" is the strategy of using developmentally inappropriate questions that require mental skills not yet acquired by the child. Children are perfectly capable of remembering important events and giving accurate information about them, when asked age appropriate questions (e.g., Schuman, Bala, and Lee 1999; Walker 1999). Children cannot answer questions they do not understand or that require mental capacities they have not yet developed. A skilled defense attorney will ask a series of seemingly reasonable, yet developmentally inappropriate questions at the preliminary hearing and at the trial to encourage conflicting or inaccurate responses. Usually, these involve questions based on numerical values and facts about time and distance that require a cognitive level of development the child has not yet acquired. Any discrepancies will be noted, and used to question the credibility of the child as illustrated in Table 9.3.

The issue in this example is not one of the child "lying" or of children not being able to remember significant events that happened to them. Children have good memories, but they cannot describe them using higher order concepts of time and computation that they have not yet mastered. Young children do not expect to be misled or manipulated by adults. However, they will comply with requests from adults to give answers to such questions (Walker 1999). This courtroom strategy is itself a form of child abuse that serves to make the child appear to be an unreliable witness in the eyes of the court, when in fact it is the questions that are developmentally inappropriate.

Table 9.3 Sample Scenario and Data Sheet for a Case of Child Sexual Abuse				
Type	**Lawyer**	**Category**	**Case ID**	**Victim Age**
Strategy	Defense	Developmental Level (Tactic)	11562	Age 8

Defense: And what can you tell us about how often these events happened?

Child: How often did this happen? I can tell you that the last time when I was at the preliminary hearing I said it was about five times that he made me put my mouth on his penis, but it was really about 25 times.

Defense: Well, which one is right? Did you lie at the preliminary or are you lying now?

Beyond Reason. As we have just seen for children, their developmental level provides an absolute standard for evaluating whether the questions asked were appropriate or not. What would provide a similar absolute standard for the questions asked of adults? How are defense lawyers able to systematically undermine the credibility of adult witness so that the courts discount the seriousness of the offense?

What is absolutely true about myths and stereotypes is that they are false beliefs that have no place in factual rational discussion. Yet, they constitute the bulk of the content of the trials, finding their way into the reasons lawyers use to argue their case. But, the standard of logic requires that rational arguments follow the rules of reasoning, and that they must be based on true, not false, statements (i.e., premises).

Because the false beliefs of myths and stereotypes are commonly mistaken as true, arguments based on such false premises may not always be easy to recognize. It is rare that the false premise is as obvious as it is in the following example:

> All horses in this barn can be considered cows.
> As we all know, cows give milk.
> Thus, any particular horse in this barn can be milked.

No one would be misled by this argument. Clearly, the conclusion that a horse in the barn can be milked is false, even though the argument conforms to a correct formal structure dictated by the rules of logic:

> All As are Bs.
> C is an A.
> Therefore, C is a B.

However, propaganda, advertising, and deliberate distortions of communication frequently incorporate false premises within arguments having a correct formal structure, which gives the appearance of a logical conclusion. In sexual assault trials, the false assumptions are based on myths and stereotypes about the nature of sexual assault that are incorporated into lawyers' arguments. For example, the assumption is frequently made that all women at a bar who are drinking and dancing are available for sex. When a sexual assault victim reports that she was drinking and dancing at a bar, she is seen as having consented to sex. This point can be illustrated by substituting "women" for "horse," "sexually available" for "cow" and "consent" for "milk" in our original example:

> All women in this bar can be considered sexually available.
> As we all know, sexually available women consent to sex.
> Thus, this particular woman consented to sex.

The argument hinges on the assumption that a woman who goes to a bar to drink, meet men, and dance is sexually available and has implicitly consented to sex with any man from the nightspot she continues to be with after leaving the bar. (For additional examples of using the standard of logic as a criterion, see Alksnis 2001; Renner, Alksnis, and Parriag 1999). So prevalent are these basic logical errors regarding implied consent that in 1992, legislation (Bill C-49) was passed in Canada to make consent to sexual activity an explicit requirement rather than an implied default based on some situational circumstance such as drinking and dancing. This change in the law was required because judicial decisions frequently cited the stereotyped belief that consent could be reasonably (although sometimes mistakenly) assumed in many situations if there was no evidence of nonconsent (Sheehy 1996).

The Failure of Social Justice

The failures of social justice that have been described are not due to a lack of clarity of the law: Sex between adults requires consent, and any sexual contact with a child is absolutely prohibited. Instead, the system fails due to the influence of the social context on the legal doctrine. The myths, misconceptions, stereotypes, and male prerogatives that result in the wide spread occurrence of sexual assault in the social world are also reflected in the deliberations of judges, lawyers, and members of juries when they bring with them into the courtroom the same beliefs and attitudes. Thus, the popular culture becomes entwined in the legal doctrine in five ways that deny women and children due process and equal protection of the law in the United States, and violate the equity provisions of the Charter of Rights and Freedom in Canada (see Table 9.4).

Both women and children are denied the full protection of the law when the criterion used for leniency is *confounded* with circumstances that define the normal social situations in which they are exposed to male sexual violence.

In addition to re-victimizing children by *holding them responsible for their sexuality*, the court allows the defense lawyer to do the very thing from which the trial is intended to protect the child—namely, for an adult to use his or her superior mental ability to exploit or take advantage of a child. The use of *developmentally inappropriate questions* has the effect of destroying good evidence children are otherwise capable of providing. In this way the legal process becomes an accessory after the fact to crime it is judging, which is itself a criminal offense (Renner and Park 1999). Yet, by asking simple, age appropriate questions, it is possible to separate information the child does not know or cannot recall from failures to answer because the child did not understand the question.

Table 9.4 Social Justice Issues Requiring a Redefinition of the Legal Doctrine

1. Confounding

The defining characteristic of the relationship of women and children to the men who sexually assault them are identical to the criterion for excusing offenders.

2. Re-victimization of Children

In cases of child sexual abuse, the court fails to respect the special legal status of children by holding them accountably for their sexuality.

3. A Developmental Standard

Adult agents of the court use their superior mental ability and authority to ask children developmentally inappropriate questions, thus becoming an accessory after the fact to the original abuse by knowingly destroying good evidence.

4. Denial of the Reality of Women Experience

In cases of adult sexual assault, the issues of relationship, harm, and danger operate through selectivity and disparity to place male sexual violence effectively beyond the range of legal recourse.

5. The Standard of Logic

The courts treat the unreasonable as though it were reasonable and the illogical as if it were logical, thus re-victimizing women.

For adult women, selectivity and disparity based on misconceptions about the true nature of sexual assault, and the use of inappropriate "sanitized" language, deny justice by the *denial of the reality of women's experience*. To compound the issue even more, the distortion of the rules of reason introduced into the legal process *re-victimizes women*, thus failing the standard of fairness and justice. These two conditions give an unprecedented new meaning to catch-22: Women who have been sexually assaulted are denied equal access to a justice system that fails to provide justice, and are then blamed for the injustice by not making use of the justice system.

The failure of the legal remedy for male sexual violence is part of the problem for which it is the intended solution. These considerations require us to redefine the legal precedents and common law practices, corrupted by popular misconceptions, that form the current legal doctrine.

REFORMING THE LEGAL DOCTRINE

Principles of Equity

When legal precedents and common law practices directly contribute to the problem for which they are the intended solution, there is a serious issue requiring legal reform. When the official treatment under the law differentially affects women and children to their disadvantage, there is a constitutional issue of inequality that requires interpretative clarification by the courts (L'Heureux-Dubé 2001). There is no excuse for delay, nor any need to wait for legislative law reform. The route is the appeal process that will set new precedents for future cases.

By redefining the central legal issues as a failure in the application of the law, the need for legislative changes are minimal, such as requiring by statute that questions asked of children to be developmental appropriate. One step in this direction is to end the competency examination for child testimony, a reform currently under consideration in Canada (Department of Justice 1990). As we have argued (Park and Renner 1998), it does not make any sense to place a competency threshold on the child, which does nothing to ensure reliable testimony. Rather, the threshold must be placed on the questions asked of the child, which will ensure that the information the child is capable of providing can be taken into account by the court. A second area requiring legislative action is to explicitly separate the criterion for defining the severity of sexual assault and abuse from the defining circumstances under which male sexual violence occurs.

Not a Conflict of Rights

The primary effect of the redefinition of the legal issues is to avoid a false dilemma of viewing law reform as an issue of victim rights versus offender rights. Offender rights are no different for sexual offenses than for any other offense, including the right to a fair trial and a full defense. However, this basic right of the accused does not extend to the abuse of children by the very legal processes provided for the protection of children from abuse, nor to the denial of access to justice for women. The ideal is to achieve fairness and social justice.

A NATIONAL SOCIAL ACTION PROGRAM

The question is How can the legal doctrine be redefined? Unfortunately, social change is not simply an academic exercise, and seldom is it achieved through the publication of research papers. The findings must somehow engage the social, political, and psychological mechanisms of change.

With this in mind, we proposed a threefold national social action program available through the Internet (NSAP 1998). The grass-roots program can be carried out at minimal costs, does not require extensive national coordination, and should quickly gain the serious attention of the judicial process. The goal is to use the simple five-point summary of the legal issues (Table 9.4) to create a new vocabulary for redefining the central problem as a failure of social justice. A single, yet simple, conceptual framework unites the social, political, and psychological aspects of male sexual violence.

Document the Outrageous

At the social level, the primary issue is one of consciousness raising. When enough people are outraged over a social issue, change is possible. One of the difficulties in raising public awareness is getting sustained media coverage of a conceptual issue. Only occasionally does a sensational case capture national attention. When it does, the focus is on the sordid details of the case or some unreasonable statements by an individual judge, thus particularizing the story; seldom is the short-lived coverage on systemic legal issues. On the other hand, local cases get extensive coverage by local papers. Our coding system offers local human rights groups a framework for observing these cases, documenting the outrageous processes that we have identified, and talking to the local media about these issues in the context of local cases. The coverage should be locally extensive, building a common conceptual frame of reference about a failure of social justice in many communities: Do not confound the criterion for leniency with the social status of women and children, respect the developmental level of children, and provide women equal access to justice.

These are very specific and reasonable requests with clear and measurable behavioral expectations. In these instances, it is specific people, who have names and who hold local offices of public trust, who can have their judgment processes respectfully questioned and who can be called upon to do better. This is the power of local actions; they need not wait for legislation nor the Supreme Court, they can start tomorrow with as few as one person siting in the local courtroom with a clipboard.

Challenge the Legal System

At the political level, local community groups have good potential access to the local prosecuting attorney's office. Local pressure can be effective to have a single prosecutor specialize in sexual assault cases (which some have already done), who will raise formal objections during the trial based on the research described here and who will appeal the case if the objections are not sustained. If the objections are sustained, then the defense will probably appeal. In either case, a wave of similar appeals should start to appear in many appeal districts across the country. This will have the immediate effect of arousing the interest of the judicial system because individual judges do not wish to have their decisions overturned. The use of the appeal process will attract the attention of legal scholars, who will need to sort out what to do about these failures of social justice. Last, but by no means least, a number of cases in the appeal process will prolong the media coverage and give reporters something more substantial to write about than the usual details of the case, which has only served to reinforce the myths and stereotypes.

Challenging the legal system should raise the level of the debate to the interpretative process of the law, where it properly belongs as a serious challenge to the current legal doctrine based on the equity requirements of social justice. One should not, however, underestimate the difficulty of this task. The office of the prosecution is overworked, not sensitive to the issues of sexual assault and abuse (Konradi 1997, 2001), and resistive to assume the role of protection of the legal rights of victims, whose primary role is a witness for the state (Murphy 2001). However, the office of the prosecution is sensitive to social pressure, in particularly local media coverage, so that the public documentation of the issues will actively support legal challenges, while the challenges will reinforce media coverage of the appropriate issue of social justice and the legal doctrine.

Support Victims

Psychologically, most victim-witnesses are unprepared for what will happen to them when they take their cases to court (Konradi 1997). In our work with the sexual assault service, many women were devastated by their experience, which is what made us focus our attention on the legal process. As we discovered, most sexual assault and child sexual abuse cases are scripts waiting to be played out in court and can be readily anticipated in terms of only twenty-four categories. There are very few surprises. Victims in general can be better prepared for what will happen. In individual cases, this will enable prosecuting attorneys to better protect women and children in general against the common traps. And, in test cases selected to become center pieces for legal appeal, the category system will help to ensure that the specific instances selected are strong examples of the issues to be legally challenged. Although this is not much satisfaction for many individuals, it is better than, as one of our victim-witnesses put it, feeling "like meat on a rack." For those who choose to fight, there is a plan around which third-party legal support can rally (Murphy 2001).

CONCLUSION

Our entire effort has been dictated by what is known as action-research. This is a very specific philosophy of science that argues "To understand, do, and to do, understand" (Renner 1995). It puts equal responsibility on practice to be well informed by up-to-date policy and theory, and that policy and theory should constantly be accountable for its consequences and outcomes. Within such a framework of philosophy of knowledge, the failures of social justice we have documented need not be the occasion for defensive blaming and efforts to dilute responsibility by pointing to another level as primarily responsible. Rather, any identified shortcomings are opportunities for progress. Complex social problems, by definition, have multiple aspects and require intervention across many levels. Fixing the legal doctrine will not end male sexual violence, but it is an essential step in progress toward that end.

REFERENCES

Alksnis, C. 2001. Fundamental justice is the issue: Extending full equality of the law to women and children. *Journal of Social Distress and the Homeless* 10: 69–86.

Bavelas, J., and L. Coates. 2001. Is it sex or assault? Erotic vs. violent language in sexual assault trial judgements. *Journal of Social Distress and the Homeless* 10: 29–40.

Burt, M. 1980. Cultural myths and support for rape. *Journal of Personality and Social Psychology* 38: 217–30.

Canadian Sentencing Commission. 1987. *Sentencing Reform: A Canadian Approach.* Ottawa: Department of Justice Canada.

Clark, L., and D.J. Lewis. 1977. *Rape: The Price of Coercive Sexuality.* Toronto: The Women's Press.

Coates, L., J. Bavelas, and J. Gibson, 1994. Anomalous language in sexual assault trial judgements. *Discourse and Society* 5: 189–206.

Department of Justice Canada. 1983. *Sexual Assault: The New Law.* Ottawa: Author.

———. 1990. *Sexual Assault Legislation in Canada: An Evaluation, Report No. 5.* Ottawa: Author.

Gregory, J., and S. Lees. 1994. In search of gender justice: Sexual assault and the criminal justice system. *Feminist Review* 48: 80–93.

Konradi, A. 1997. Too little, too late: Prosecutor's pre-court preparation of rape survivors. *Law and Society* 22: 1101–54.

———. 2001. Pulling strings doesn't work in court: Moving beyond puppetry in the relationship between prosecutors and sexual assault survivors. *Journal of Social Distress and the Homeless* 10: 5–28.

L'Heureux-Dubé, C. 2001. Beyond the myths: equality, impartiality and justice. *Journal of Social Distress and the Homeless* 10: 87–104.

Lonsway, K.A., and L.F. Fitzgerald. 1994. Rape myths: In review. *Psychology of Women Quarterly* 18: 133–164.

Matoesian, G. 1993. *Reproducing Rape: Domination through Talk in the Courtroom.* Chicago: University of Chicago Press.

Murphy, W. 2001. The victim advocacy and research group: Serving a growing need to provide crime victims and other third-parties with personal legal representation in criminal cases. *Journal of Social Distress and the Homeless* 10: 123–138.

NSAP. 1998. National Social Action Program. http://www.carleton.ca /~erenner/nsap.html.

Park, L., and K.E. Renner. 1998. The failure to acknowledge differences in developmental capabilities leads to unjust outcomes for child witnesses in sexual abuse cases. *Canadian Journal of Community Mental Health* 17: 5–19.

Parriag, A., and K.E. Renner. 1998. Do current criminal justice practices lead to unjust outcomes for adult victims of sexual assault? http://www.carleton.ca/ ~erenner/nsap.html

Renner, K.E. 1995. To understand, do—and to do, understand: The scholarship of community psychology. *The Nova Scotia Psychologist* 10: (4): 7–8.

————. 2001. The civic price of sexual assault and sexual abuse. *Journal of Social Distress and the Homeless* 10: 1–4.

Renner, K.E., C. Alksnis, and L. Park. 1997. The standard of social justice as a research process. *Canadian Psychology* 38: 91–102.

Renner, K.E., C. Alksnis, and A. Parriag. 1999. Is logic optional in the courtroom? An examination of adult sexual assault trials. http://www.carleton.ca/~erenner/nsap.html.

Renner, K.E., and A. Keith. 1985. The establishment of a crisis intervention service for victims of sexual assault. *Canadian Journal of Community Mental Health* 4: 113–23.

Renner, K.E., and L. Park. 1997. "Discounting" the seriousness of child sexual abuse by the courts. *Viva Voce: A National Newsletter About Child Victims and Witnesses* 2 (September): 1–2.

————. 1999. Contradictions in the Legal Doctrine concerning Child Sexual Abuse. http://www.carleton.ca/~erenner/nsap.html

Renner, K.E., A. Parriag, and L. Park. 1997. *Manual for the Categorization of Courtroom Dynamics*. (Free electronic copy available from authors.) Ottawa: Department of Psychology, Carleton University.

Renner, K.E., and S. Sahjpaul. 1986. The new sexual assault law: What has been its effect? *Canadian Journal of Criminology* 28: 407–13.

Renner, K.E., and C. Wackett. 1987. Sexual assault: Social and stranger rape. *Canadian Journal of Community Mental Health* 6: 49–56.

Renner, K.E., C. Wackett, and S. Ganderton. 1988. The social nature of sexual assault. *Canadian Psychology* 29: 163–354.

Renner, K.E., and K. Yurchesyn. 1994. Sexual robbery: The missing concept in the search for an appropriate legal metaphor for sexual aggression. *Canadian Journal of Behavioural Science* 26: 41–51.

Roberts, J. 1990a. *Sexual Assault Legislation in Canada: Sentencing Patterns in Cases of Sexual Assault, Report No. 3*. Ottawa: Department of Justice Canada.

————. 1990b. *Sexual Assault Legislation in Canada: An Analysis of National Statistics, Report No. 4*. Ottawa: Department of Justice Canada.

Roberts, J.V., and M.G. Grossman. 1994. *Criminal Justice Processing of Sexual Assault Cases*. Ottawa: Canadian Center for Justice Statistics.

Sahjpaul, S., and K.E. Renner. 1988. The new sexual assault law: The victim's experience in court. *American Journal of Community Psychology* 16: 503–13.

Schuman, J.P., N. Bala, and K. Lee. 1999. Developmentally appropriate questions for child witnesses. *Queen's Law Journal* 25: 251–302.

Sheehy, E. 1996. Legalising justice for all women: Canadian women's struggle for democratic rape law reforms. *The Australian Feminist Law Journal* 6: 87–113.

Statistics Canada. 1993. *The Violence Against Women Survey*. Ottawa: Author.

Walker, A.G. 1999. *Handbook on Questioning Children: A Linguistic Perspective*, 2nd ed. Washington, DC: American Bar Association.

Yurchesyn, K., A. Keith, and K.E. Renner. 1992. Contrasting perspectives on the nature of sexual assault provided by a service for sexual assault victims and by the law courts. *Canadian Journal of Behavioural Science* 24: 71–85.

10

Law Enforcement's Response to Sexual Assault: A Comparative Study of Nine Counties in North Carolina

Vivian B. Lord and
Gary Rassel

INTRODUCTION

Investigation and prosecution of the crime of rape has been one of the more controversial issues in criminal justice in the United States. The nature of the evidence and the response of the victim required for a successful prosecution are different from any other crime, making it less likely that police will aggressively investigate or that prosecutors will bring charges. Feminists argue that female sexual assault victims receive adverse treatment, including a reluctance by criminal justice personnel to pursue the investigation and prosecution of rape cases (Atkins 1996).

Responding to the rapid increase in official rates of sexual assaults between 1960 and 1975 and to pressure from the women's rights movement, all fifty states revised their sexual assault statutes in order that rape cases would receive more attention from the judicial system and the community. The goals of these reforms were recognition of the crime as one of violence, more effective administration of criminal justice for rape victims, and increased capability of the law to act as a deterrent (Bourque 1989; LaFree 1989; Searles and Berger 1987). Changes included (1) reform of rape laws to include all types of sexual penetration, the elimination of requirements for physical resistance, and protection of the victim's sexual history; (2) development of medical protocols that met legal requirements for evidence collection; (3) emergence of rape crisis centers to provide emotional support to the victims and education programs for the public; and (4) the creation of special prosecution units.

Although these efforts were successful, there is little evidence that changes in rape laws have affected the disposition of rape cases (Bourque 1989; Horney and Spohn 1991). Proponents of rape law reform predicted that the statutory changes would produce a number of results. Their expectations may have been unrealistic. Evidence still suggests that victim credibility continues to be doubted and that this doubt prejudices sexual assault processing (Caringella-Macdonald 1988). To become a court case, a rape complaint must first be accepted for investigation, be investigated, and then be given to the district attorney, who makes the decision whether or not to prosecute. Bourque notes that the extent to which law reforms changed this process is unknown. She emphasizes the need for studies to examine the process by which police decide to initiate an investigation, carry out the investigation, and then close it or give it to the district attorney. Frazier and Haney (1996) reiterate Bourque's appeal for the evaluation of law enforcement's investigative procedures of sexual assault cases. Horney and Spohn (1991) assessed the impact of rape law reform in six urban jurisdictions. They tested reformers' expectations that reforms would result in increases in the reporting of rapes to the police, the indictment of rape cases by prosecutors, and the conviction of offenders. Their results indicate that the reforms had little effect on reports of rape or the processing of rape cases.

Another contribution of the women's rights movement to the criminal justice system's response to rape is the emergence of rape crisis volunteers and centers (Koss and Harvey 1991). Martin et al. (1992), Ullman (1996), and Schmitt and Martin (1999) report various ways in which the feminist approach to combating rape has been transformed and has changed the response of mainstream service organizations whose mission is to serve rape victims. The volunteers' emotional support of the victims provides an indirect benefit to law enforcement's investigations. Police report an increase in victims' willingness to cooperate with investigations (Martin et al. 1992) and higher reporting rates (Harvey 1985). However, Ullman's (1996) finding of mixed social reactions of victims who reported to rape crisis advocates was thought to be related to the dual reporting of victims to police and advocates. Rape crisis centers' activities surrounding education programs for the public now often include training for local police (Martin et al. 1992). Harvey's study of exemplary rape crisis centers recorded more responsive services from local medical, mental health, and law enforcement agencies after the inclusion of police training in the centers' activities. Martin et al. (1992) described a rape crisis center that incorporated into its domain of influence mainstream organizations that are often suspicious of, if not hostile toward, them. This hostility was attributed to the previous strident stand of feminist organizers of early rape crisis centers.

Horney and Spohn (1991) found a rape crisis center in each of the six jurisdictions studied; however, in Detroit the rape crisis center was run through the Police Department. The authors noted that this close association gave the crisis center earlier and greater access to victims than in many cities and potentially greater influence in encouraging reporting and in pressing for prosecution. Schmitt and Martin (1999) discuss such institutionalization in their description of a rape crisis center housed in a hospital. Though noting some constraints, the authors argue that institutionalized social movement organizations influence the communities in which they operate; they assure an ongoing presence of anti-rape advocates, provide resources for mobilizing, and possess legitimacy and the voice to speak out about rape. In addition, institutionalization allows the center to perform functions for other mainstream institutions such as law enforcement. However, Byington et al. (1991) found significant differences in effectiveness among rape crisis centers with different affiliations. They found freestanding rape crisis centers to be among the most effective ones.

Rape crisis advocates in North Carolina were helped in their struggle to support sexual assault victims beginning in 1981. Although the state had revised laws to provide more protection to rape victims, rape crisis centers were operated totally by volunteers. In 1981, the state legislators approved funding for rape crisis centers. This funding was expanded with additional federal funds through the Violence Against Women Act of 1984. Relatively stable funding has increased the voice of the rape crisis centers in North Carolina and could be providing some influence on the investigation procedures of North Carolina law enforcement departments.

Law enforcement officers are the most important criminal justice officials involved in sexual assault cases (Frazier and Haney 1996; LaFree 1989). As the victim's first contact with the criminal justice system, the police usually determine whether the victim's complaint can be considered a sexual assault, whether an arrest will be made, and the severity of the charge. The initial actions of the police will influence whether or not the victim decides to press charges and testify. Despite this important role, little research has examined law enforcement officers' decisions to investigate sexual assault complaints or has evaluated officers' investigative procedures (Bourque 1989; Frazier and Haney 1996).

Although Bourque found little evidence that rape law reforms have impacted the criminal justice system, other researchers report evidence of improved outcomes. Largen (1988), in a study of rape law reforms in three states, concluded that victims' experiences with the criminal justice system improved after law reforms. The change most frequently cited by victim advocates is a greater sensitivity on the part of the police in dealing with complainants. Police themselves frequently cite law reforms concerning evidentiary matters as facilitating their investigations and enhancing their credibility with victims.

Organizational Context of Investigating Sexual Assaults

Frohmann, in a 1991 study of the prosecutor's screening of sexual assault cases, outlines the organizational context of the district attorneys' offices by which it prosecutes sexual assault cases. Features such as vertical prosecution (handled by the same district attorney throughout the court process) appear to be related to the priority given to sexual assault cases.

Berger, Searles, and Neuman (1988) conclude that criminal justice personnel in many locations continue to operate on the basis of traditional assumptions about rape and do not always comply with the statutes. They note that the reforms do not greatly affect the formal operations of the criminal justice system.

Epstein and Langenbahn (1994) examine the organizational arrangements in law enforcement departments regarding the investigation of sexual assault cases. Special organizational features could reflect the priority law enforcement departments give sexual assault victims and cases. In a report to the National Institute of Justice, Epstein and Langenbahn outline the reforms they assess as key to effective investigation of sexual assault. They obtained information from the National District Attorneys' Association, American Prosecutors' Research Institute, Police Foundation, International Association of the Chiefs of Police, Police Executive Research Forum, Harvard's Kennedy School of Government, National Center for State Courts, National Victim Center, Center for Women's Policy Studies, and National Coalition against Sexual Assault in order to compile a list of reforms considered key to effective investigation, prosecution, and treatment of rape cases and victims (telephone interview with Stacia Langenbahn, November 14, 1996). Epstein and Langenbahn then examined four police departments with "national reputations for successful approaches to investigation and prosecution of sexual assault and for successful coordination among criminal justice agencies, hospitals, and rape crisis centers" (Epstein and Langenbahn 1994, 2).

The key law enforcement reforms Epstein and Langenbahn found are in the following areas: specialized sex crime units, victim assistance officers and in-house victim/witness advocates, procedures for working with victims, and the specific recruitment and training of law enforcement officers for sexual assault investigation. The following sections describe these reforms.

Specialized Sex Crime Units

Creating specialized sex crime units is considered an approach of developing the expertise of individual investigators. It is also seen as a means of sending a message to the community that a department is deeply committed to solving sex crime cases. Epstein and Langenbahn (1994) acknowledge that small departments whose annual sexual assault cases are few in number will not need a separate sex crime investigation unit; however, they note that effective small departments develop the expertise of individual investigators.

In-House Victim/Witness Advocates

In-house victim/witness advocates free detectives to focus on investigations. These advocates review all sexual assault reports, personally contact each victim, and often provide community education programs on rape prevention. They may attend the first interview between the victim and detective to offer support and orient the victim to the criminal justice process. Acting as a link between the prosecution and the investigation phase, in-house advocates provide continuity throughout the entire criminal justice process for the victim and the agencies.

Working with Sexual Assault Victims

Epstein and Langenbahn (1994) describe three major procedures for working with sexual assault victims that contribute to effective investigations: reporting, interviewing, and ensuring privacy.

Reporting. Because of the vast underreporting of rape, especially in instances of acquaintance rape, offering rape victims different options for reporting the offense appears to encourage victims to press charges. These options include third-party reports to the police from rape crisis centers without identifying the victim, information-only reports indicating the victim's wish not to pursue prosecution (blind reporting), and standard reports for those willing to prosecute. The first two types of reports describe the suspect, the suspect's mode of operation, and location of the assault.

Interviewing. Specific interviewing protocols stressing the importance of developing rapport with the victim and interviewing her at different periods of time (multiple interviews) are important to retain the victim's willingness to cooperate with the police and the prosecutor. It is particularly important to give the victim a day to rest before conducting an in-depth interview. Investigating officers are also trained to address questions related to the standard rape defenses used by defense lawyers. In order to circumvent the consent issue, the victim is asked to address questions dealing with resistance.

Ensuring privacy. Victims have the right to confidentiality with respect to both their identity and the information surrounding the offense. One of a victim's greatest fears is the discovery by others of the rape. Law enforcement's ability to conceal the information from the public and media alleviates some of the victim's fears of discovery.

Training

Training is the fourth criteria Epstein and Langenbahn describe. Because patrol officers usually receive the complaint first, they, as well as the investigators, must be trained. Basic training for patrol officers usually is limited to teaching sensitivity toward crime victims, including victims of rape. Additional in-service training is often provided by rape crisis volunteers and is focused specifically on the needs of the rape victim immediately after the assault.

Specialized training for investigators includes interviewing techniques for victims and suspects, collection of physical evidence unique to rape cases, and coordination with rape crisis centers, medical personnel, and prosecutors. This training is often cross-disciplinary, utilizing trainers from other agencies, including rape crisis centers, who address related areas. Those departments deemed most effective assign new sex offense investigators to work with experienced investigators even if they previously have extensive general investigative experience and training.

Recruitment

The last criteria surround the issue of selection of sex crime investigators. Departments effective in investigating sexual assaults look for officers who have good interviewing skills, who can be sensitive to victims, and who will be able to obtain the information they require from victims, witnesses, and suspects. Epstein and Langenbahn also list abilities to process crime scenes, handle suspects productively, be familiar with offender typologies, and understand short- and long-term effects of sexual assault on victims as criteria important for the selection of sex crime investigators.

Departments identified as effective by Epstein and Langenbahn noted the need for female and male investigators in the sexual assault unit. In some departments few female officers have reached the rank required for sexual assault investigator, so these departments staff the unit with female officers rather than male detectives or sergeants. Sex crime investigation is considered a positive career move for most of the departments Epstein and Langenbahn studied; however, because of burnout, few officers remain for more than two years.

If applied nationally, these reforms could increase the percent of rapes reported, the percent of complaints investigated thoroughly and prosecuted, and the number of cases in which a conviction is obtained. Epstein and Langenbahn identify departments in only four government jurisdictions. They do not discuss how well the practices of law enforcement departments in these jurisdictions represent those of most departments in the nation nor do they indicate the extent to which these reforms have been implemented by law enforcement agencies nationwide.

METHOD

The current study was conducted (1) to compare the processes used by several North Carolina law enforcement departments in the investigation of sexual assault cases with a set of effective procedures identified by Epstein and Langenbahn (1994) and (2) to examine the influence of agencies' variables and relationships with rape crisis centers on the departments' methods of investigating sexual assaults.

Sample

Counties with autonomous sexual assault centers were selected for this study. The purposes of these centers were to serve sexual assault victims and educate the community about rape and rape prevention. Counties with autonomous sexual assault centers provided more independent measures unencumbered by formal contracts with other services. As noted previously, Byington et al. (1991) found freestanding rape crisis centers to provide certain types of services and to be more effective than those with other affiliations.

Investigators from all nine sheriff's departments and the police departments of twenty-five towns and cities in these nine counties in North Carolina were interviewed for this study. The communities, the law enforcement departments, the overall crime numbers, and the reported sexual assault rates of the sample counties and municipalities are described in Table 10.1 (*State of North Carolina Uniform Crime Report*, 1994).

Because reports of sexual assaults did not necessarily reflect the actual number of assaults and were dependent on the law enforcement agency's definition of sexual assault (Kerstetter and Van Winkle 1990), we could not assume that the reported numbers of sexual assault are accurate.

Procedures

This study was based on on-site visits and follow-up telephone interviews with law enforcement investigators from these thirty-four departments. The interview protocol was developed to ascertain the departments' use of procedures based on Epstein and Langenbahn's model of agency effectiveness (1994). Where possible, supporting documents such as organizational charts, written investigative procedures, and report forms were obtained.

Each agency's history of interagency cooperation was also examined. Of particular interest was the relationship with the rape crisis center in the county. To reduce the subjectivity of the investigators, the law enforcement department's relationship with the county's rape crisis center was operationalized as (1) the point at which the law enforcement department allowed the rape crisis center volunteers to be involved with the victim in the investigation, (2) the use of third-party reports from rape crisis centers, and (3) the use of cross-training between rape crisis centers and the law enforcement departments.

County/Department	Population Coverage	Total Crime	Reported Sex Crimes/10,000	Sworn Officers	Total Personnel
Alamance					
County Sheriff	46,083	1,297	2	68	109
Burlington	41,916	2,154	1	88	117
Elon College	4,912	123	10	9	10
Graham	11,047	716	2	20	22
Mebane	5,145	279	0	12	15
Buncomb					
County Sheriff	102,337	2,240	1	133	242
Asheville	64,920	5,808	6	162	200
Black Mountain	7,181	81	0	14	18
Woodfin	2,819	30	0	7	7
Catawba					
County Sheriff	67,816	1,742	3	100	106
Hickory	29,206	3,271	9	86	111
Conover	6,143	488	2	18	19
Newton	11,589	771	3	33	42
Craven					
County Sheriff	35,515	1,514	3	50	93
Havelock	17,062	607	2	21	31
New Bern	21,106	2,406	8	67	87
Cumberland					
County Sheriff	170,002	10,812	6	325	403
Fayetteville	87,526	10,482	10	247	321
Hope Mills	9,040	850	3	14	21
Spring Lake	8,290	1,378	7	17	24
Durham					
County Sheriff	44,559	1,022	.5	96	314
Durham	138,055	15,550	6	341	400
Henderson					
County Sheriff	63,966	928	2	71	95
Hendersonville	7,913	898	10	36	49
Laurel Park	1,474	26	0	4	4
Orange					
County Sheriff	41,509	1,336	1	77	92
Chapel Hill	33,838	2,734	3	78	97
Hillsborough	4,888	582	2	18	19
Carrboro	13,052	951	6	28	30
Robeson					
County Sheriff	73.706	1,471	1	67	82
Lumberton	19,238	2,348	4	65	75
Maxton	2,657	180	0	9	11
Red Springs	3,876	369	12	14	18
Pembroke	2,411	322	10	10	14

RESULTS

Procedures for Investigating Sexual Assault Cases

As indicated by Table 10.2, the departments in these nine counties compared favorably on Epstein and Langenbahn's procedures in some areas and less favorably in others. A majority of departments accepted third-party reports from rape crisis centers (73.5 percent) and blind reports from victims (82 percent), obtained multiple interviews from victims (91 percent), maintained victims'

Table 10.2 Law Enforcement Responses to Measures of Sexual Assault Effectiveness

Factor		Total	Percentage
Specialized Unit		16	47.1%
In-house Victim Advocate		6	17.6
Reporting	3rd Party	25	73.5
	Blind Reports	28	82.4
	Standard	34	100.0
Interviewing	Written Procedures	15	44.1
	Multiple Interviews	31	91.2
	Polygraph	18	52.9
Confidentiality		34	100.0
Training	Interviewing	25	73.5
	Collecting Evidence	24	70.6
	Coordinating Agencies	29	85.3
	Patrol Trained	11	32.4
Selection		0	0.0

confidentiality (100 percent), and provided sexual assault training in all three major areas for their investigators (73.5 percent, 71 percent, and 85 percent, respectively).

Third-party reports usually were received from the rape crisis centers. Therefore, the relationship between the rape crisis center and the police department appeared to be a relevant factor in the use of these types of reports as well as in the degree of cooperation between the two agencies during the entire investigation. As noted by one investigator, "They [rape crisis advocates] do a lot to educate the public. I think . . . it's gone toward reporting, as well, to let people know: 'There is someone you can go to report this and it's a friendly environment.' So it's encouraged reporting." The departments varied in the actions taken on blind reports received from victims themselves. Even though a victim might not plan to go to trial, some investigators asked permission of the victim to continue the investigation in order to identify the suspect. Other departments only filed the reports. Those who attempted to continue the investigation normally communicated the information from the report to their rape crisis centers. Third-party and blind reports were good vehicles of two-way communications between law enforcement and rape crisis centers.

Multiple interviews were defined as more than one interview of the victim. For a few departments, multiple interviews might mean an interview by patrol and one done by investigation. The majority of investigators noted that they interviewed the victim more than once.

Without exception, departments did not actively release information about the victim to the media; however, some departments made a concerted effort to keep victims' names and addresses from the media. This effort often had come about in cooperation with the media and, according to the investigators, often after the public and rape crisis centers had informed the media of their desire for confidentiality of the victim.

Most investigators viewed sexual assault investigations as heavily dependent on the victim and appeared to be searching for training that would help them glean information from the victim. Many of the investigators with the smaller departments noted the difficulties of finding cost-effective training. Although the state training academy had offered training in the area of sexual assault, the training was not being offered at the time of the study.

Fewer than 50 percent of the departments maintained specialized sexual assault investigative units (47 percent), provided in-house victim advocates (18 percent), had developed written procedures specifically for the investigation of sexual assault (44 percent), trained patrol officers procedures for sexual assault complaints (32 percent), or had criteria specifically for the selection of sexual assault investigators (0 percent).

Not only did less than half of the departments surveyed have a specialized sex crime unit, many of the departments had only one or two investigators to follow up on all their cases. Investigators from those departments without a specialized unit told the researchers that the small number of sexual assaults did not warrant a specialized unit. As noted earlier, forming a specialized sexual assault unit sends a message to the community that the department was serious about investigating sexual assault and encouraged victims to report assaults (Epstein and Langenbahn 1994).

Several departments in communities that surrounded a university or major college campus did appear to have established a specialized unit or investigator, although the towns and departments were relatively small and their sexual assault rates low. The rape crisis centers had active relationships with those departments with specialized investigators and units. The law enforcement department procedures, in these cases, typically included a call to the rape crisis center as soon as a rape complaint was verified.

Lack of in-house victim advocates could be attributed to a number of factors: the lack of resources, the presence of a district attorney victim advocate, the use of rape crisis advocates. A service provided to victims in North Carolina and discussed by Epstein and Langenbahn (1994) is the presence of victim advocates within the offices of the District Attorney in every jurisdiction. In spite of such a widely available benefit, investigators in this study rarely mentioned the victim advocates in the District Attorney's offices. In fact, some investigators even seemed unaware of their existence. Most investigators saw the role of the District Attorney's victim advocates primarily in the court setting. These advocates often prepared the victim for court by providing information about the court proceedings and emotional support surrounding the victim's anxiety about testifying.

Most of the investigators discussed the importance of the rape crisis volunteers in carrying out advocate responsibilities. The rape crisis volunteer had a distinct liaison role between the law enforcement investigator and the victim of sexual assault. A majority of the investigators discussed the need for clear roles for both rape crisis volunteers and law enforcement; the police investigate and the rape crisis volunteers support the victim. A majority of departments allowed the rape crisis volunteer to meet the victim at the hospital, but some departments' investigators suggested the rape crisis counseling service to the victim only after the initial investigation and interview were complete.

Very few departments had procedures written specifically for sexual assault cases. Instead sexual assault cases were typically investigated with the same procedures used to investigate other major or personal crimes. With the exception of one city, departments that did have separate procedures for investigating sexual assault cases worked closely with other departments within their counties to develop similar procedures, at least in the area of sexual assault.

Although few departments had unique written procedures for sexual assault cases, most investigators were articulate in describing the investigative procedures they used. With few exceptions, the departments' procedures were similar, including in-depth interviews that began when the victim had had an opportunity to wash and rest. Investigators in general understood that the victim often needed to be interviewed several times to collect sufficient information. All those with written procedures also included rape crisis advocates early, allowing them to be present at the hospital when the victim was first examined.

The definition of rape continued to center on consent versus use of force (Krahe' 1991). In the American legal system, there is always a question about the veracity of the victim's claim of rape that is not present for other types of crime (Ullman 1996; Robin 1977). Various factors operate against the rape victim, particularly certain victims within the legal system. "Victims who violate societal expectations regarding appropriate female sexuality and behavior are more likely to be treated unfairly by the legal process" (LaFree 1980, 845). For example, investigators from a number of the larger departments described rapes reported by known prostitutes as "breach of contract." The investigators stated that prostitutes who were not paid for their services would report the incident as a rape. These officers implied that prostitutes could not be raped, therefore their complaints would not be classified as such. Another example was that of victims who were drinking alcohol at the time of the offense. Although most investigators agreed that an intoxicated victim could still be raped, many district attorneys would not prosecute a defendant in such a case. Consequently officers would not pursue the case. Because of the issues of consent and consequently false reporting, polygraphing continued to be used when deception was suspected. Marsh, Geist, and Caplan (1982), in their Michigan study, found the polygraph to be used more frequently in sexual assault cases than in the investigation of other serious crimes. Although Epstein and Langenbahn did not discuss the use of the polygraph in their report, the current study found that twenty-two of the thirty-four departments regularly polygraph suspects. Many departments polygraphed the suspect first and polygraphed the victim only when the report of the assault was very questionable. Investigators in other departments reported that they could uncover the truth just by the incongruities in the victim's statement; they believed that good investigations would uncover truth and deception without the use of polygraph examinations. Law enforcement officials in this study did not appear to fit the Feminist view that criminal justice officials believe that women in general lie about having been victimized.

The major lack of training in sexual assault was for patrol officers. Only nine departments had provided training for patrol officers. This training often was provided by rape crisis centers. A number of departments had developed a team teaching approach to sexual assault. Rape crisis volunteers teach patrol officers and new investigators about the trauma of the rape victim and services the rape crisis center provides. Law enforcement officers in turn teach rape crisis volunteers about the role of law enforcement. As Epstein and Langenbahn noted, "Such interactions improve collaboration . . . rape crisis centers and criminal justice agencies may discover common agendas"(1994, 47). Schmitt and Martin (1999) also identified training as a major example of "unobtrusive mobilization" by rape crisis centers.

Assignments to sexual assault investigations appeared to be based upon specific criteria in only two departments. In these two cases, the supervisors of the investigative divisions found it useful to choose sexual assault investigators based on interviewing skills and sensitivity toward the needs of the victim. Two additional departments actively recruited female officers. Epstein and Langenbahn noted that the departments they studied also actively recruited females. The premise was that female sexual assault victims would feel more comfortable talking to a female investigator rather than to a male investigator. In general, officers were promoted through the department's normal procedures and were then assigned to sexual assault cases. Volunteering was used in one department, and in some departments sexual assault was considered an early assignment that new investigators moved through to other areas.

Agency Variables

Logistic regression was used to estimate the probability that a department had implemented each of the thirteen reforms based on the five agency variables listed in Table 10.1. Separate models were developed with each reform constituting the dependent variable and the five agency variables composing the independent variables. These independent variables were (1) the type of department (municipal or sheriff), (2) total municipal or county population, (3) number of sex crimes reported per 10,000 citizens, (4) total number of crimes reported, and (5) number of sworn personnel. None of the agency variables was significantly related to the thirteen reforms.

Law Enforcement Departments' Interaction with Rape Crisis Centers

Each law enforcement department's interaction with its local rape crisis center was evaluated on the following criteria: (1) the point at which the law enforcement department allowed the rape crisis center volunteers to be involved with the victim in the investigation, (2) the use of third-party reports from rape crisis centers, and (3) the use of cross-training between rape crisis centers and the law enforcement departments.

Table 10.3 displays the number and percent of responses for each criteria. With 79 percent of the departments, rape crisis volunteers intervened early (e.g., met the victim at the hospital) and provided information about sexual assaults reported anonymously to them to 73.5 percent of the departments. However, only 38 percent of the law enforcement departments cross-trained with rape crisis volunteers.

Pearson's chi-square was used to test the comparison of Epstein and Langenbahn's procedures to the three criteria of the rape crisis centers' relationships with the law enforcement departments (Table 10.4). Written procedures and specialized units were significantly related to intervention. Those departments with procedures written specifically for sexual assault cases or those with investigators who were specially trained to handle sexual assault victims and cases were more likely to allow rape crisis advocates to intervene early. Approximately half the departments had written procedures or a specialized investigator/unit, but 85 percent of the departments allowed rape crisis advocates to intervene early. All departments with written procedures and/or a specialized investigator/unit allowed advocates to intervene early.

Table 10.3 Law Enforcement Departments' Interaction with Rape Crisis Centers		Total	Percentage
Point of Intervention	Early	27	79.4%
	Late	7	20.6
3rd Party	Yes	25	73.5
	No	9	26.5
Cross Training	Yes	13	38.2
	No	21	61.8

Table 10.4 Comparison of Law Enforcement Procedures with Criteria of the Rape Crisis Centers' Relationships with the Law Enforcement Departments

Procedures	Rape Crisis Center Relationship Criteria										
	Point of Intervention				Third Party Reporting				Cross-Training			
	Early		Late		Yes		No		Yes		No	
	N	%	N	%	N	%	N	%	N	%	N	%
Specialized Unit												
Yes	15	100%	0*	0%	10	66%	5	33%	5	33%	10	66%
No	13	72	5	28	14	78	4	22	8	44	10	56
In-house Victim Advocate												
Yes	7	100	0	0	5	71	2	29	3	43	4	57
No	21	81	5	19	2	22	7	78	10	38	16	62
Reporting												
Blind Reports												
Yes	24	83	5	17	23	79	6*	21	12	41	17	59
No	4	100	0	0	1	25	3	75	1	25	3	75
Interviewing												
Written Procedures												
Yes	16	100	0**	0	11	69	5	21	7	44	9	56
No	12	71	5	29	13	76	4	24	6	35	11	65
Multiple Interviews												
Yes	26	87	4	13	21	70	9	30	12	40	18	60
No	2	66	1	33	3	100	0	0	1	33	2	66
Polygraph												
Yes	12	92	1	8	11	85	2	15	7	54	6	46
No	16	80	4	20	13	65	7	35	6	30	14	70
Training												
Interviewing												
Yes	21	81	5	19	20	77	6	23	10	38	16	62
No	7	100	0	0	4	57	3	43	4	57	3	43
Collecting Evidence												
Yes	25	86	4	14	23	79	6	21	12	41	17	59
No	3	75	1	25	1	25	3	75	1	25	3	75
Coordinating Agencies												
Yes	23	82	5	18	21	75	7	25	12	43	16	57
No	5	100	0	0	3	60	2	40	1	20	4	80
Patrol Trained												
Yes	9	90	1	10	5	50	5*	50	6	60	4	40
No	19	83	4	17	19	83	4	17	7	30	16	70

* $p < .05$ ** $p < .01$

In addition patrol officer training and blind-report acceptance were significantly related to receipt of third-party reports. Those departments that received third-party reports from the rape crisis center were less likely to have trained patrol officers, but were also more likely to accept blind reports. Only ten departments trained patrol officers (30 percent). Fifty-eight percent of the departments did not train officers, but did receive third-party reports. Those departments that received third-party reports were also more likely to accept blind reports. Only one department received third-party reports but did not accept blind reports.

Summary

Law enforcement departments in North Carolina appeared to prescribe some of Epstein and Langenbahn's procedures. The majority of those departments studied accepted and received third-party and blind reports, obtained multiple interviews from victims, maintained victims' confidentiality, and provided sexual assault training to investigators; however, few had a specialized unit for sexual assault or selection criteria for such an investigator or unit. Few had victim advocates, written procedures, or trained patrol officers who usually arrived at the rape scene first.

Agency profile variables did not appear to be significantly related to the implementation of Epstein and Langenbahn's effective procedures. An effective relationship with rape crisis advocates did appear to be correlated with the existence of written procedures, a specialized investigator/unit, and the use of blind reports.

DISCUSSION

Although personnel from all the departments studied appeared to be conscious of the need to treat sexual assault victims with sensitivity and provide them with emotional support, the provision of related procedures varied greatly. The rape crisis center advocates might influence the priority placed on the investigation of sexual assault cases by law enforcement departments and the treatment of victims by law enforcement and medical personnel.

The current research supports Schmitt and Martin's (1999) findings on the benefit of institutionalization of rape crisis centers in performing functions for other institutions such as law enforcement agencies so as to indoctrinate their members in the understanding of rape victims and of the crime of rape. Active women's groups in North Carolina increased law enforcement departments' interest in sexual assault and its treatment of rape victims. High-profile feminist groups helped elect district attorneys in one county in the study when the candidates for the office promised to prosecute more sexual assaults. Unlike some counties where citizens often refused to believe that a sexual assault occurred, law enforcement officials in this county included in their definition of rape attacks on women who were intoxicated and assaults occurring on a date or in high-risk areas. Although the number of sexual assault complaints to several departments was low, departments with active relationships with the rape crisis centers in their communities were more likely to have specific investigators assigned to handle sexual assaults. Few departments attempted to budget an in-house advocate for victims, but many reported their reliance on the rape crisis volunteers to support the victim throughout the criminal justice process and beyond. In many cases, police officers or sheriff's deputies served on the boards of rape crisis centers, and training for law enforcement personnel was conducted by rape crisis volunteers. In fact, law enforcement officials in some areas were active in helping to establish the local rape crisis centers.

Developing written procedures specifically for the investigation of sexual assaults did not appear to be particularly important to the agencies interviewed. Most investigators felt that the general investigative procedures were adequate, although during the interviews, they articulated a number of steps that would be specific to sexual assault and its victim. Because these specific steps were not part of written procedures, there was a danger that these steps might not be passed to new investigators.

Sexual assault in these nine counties continued to focus on the issue of consent and the victim's behavior, supporting the feminist contention that victims of sexual assault are not accorded the same law enforcement attention as are other crime victims (Atkins 1996). As Krahe' (1991) found, if the victim had been drinking and was situated in a dangerous location, many departments were not willing to invest numerous resources to investigate the reported sexual assault complaint, and many courts were not willing to prosecute such cases. A number of departments not influenced by rape crisis centers had narrowed the definition of sexual assault to include only victims who had physical evidence of a sexual attack. The use of the polygraph was a common practice for many of the departments examined in the current study. Although many departments made it a practice to polygraph the suspect first, others polygraphed the victim first, especially if the victim's story seemed inconsistent with other facts of the case or with the suspect's story.

The process utilized in selecting sexual assault investigators did not resemble the process recommended by Epstein and Langenbahn. With two exceptions, none of the investigators interviewed mentioned such criteria as well-developed interpersonal skills, good interviewing skills, or sensitivity toward victims. Rather, good patrol officers were promoted to investigations and arbitrarily were selected to investigate sex offenses. Epstein and Langenbahn record the active recruitment of women by the departments that they identified as highly successful in investigating sex offenses. Several investigators in the current study did note their selection of female officers to investigate sex offenses. Another investigator expressed the desire to recruit a female investigator.

The law enforcement departments in the nine counties studied had implemented many of the reforms advocated by Epstein and Langenbahn; however, this implementation varied greatly from department to department. The evidence indicated that the implementation of some of these reforms was influenced by the departments' interaction with the rape crisis centers in their counties.

As noted by LaFree (1989) in his study of the Indianapolis Police, investigation priorities were influenced by community groups. The type of sexual assault case investigated and prosecuted in a county directly reflects the opinions and attitudes of the community whose citizens composed the juries. A district attorney was not likely to try a case that he or she believed would be lost. In turn, law enforcement was not likely to expend large amounts of resources investigating cases that were not likely to be prosecuted.

CONCLUSION

A number of law enforcement reforms described by Epstein and Langenbahn would require department administrators to give sexual assault victims and the investigation of their assaults a priority higher than what currently exists.

Research focusing on specific procedures of investigation and criteria for effectiveness appears to be sparse in the area of sexual assault investigation and support of the rape victim. Epstein and Langenbahn have pioneered a search for excellence in sexual assault investigation that needs to be expanded in future research efforts.

Law enforcement departments often measure the success of their investigative activities by the number of cases that they are able to close. With sexual assault cases, this means of evaluation does not include the victim's needs, and more specifically, often omits victims whose assaults do not meet the definition of sexual assault established by the law enforcement department. As a human service agency, law enforcement departments need to explore new ways of measuring their abilities to meet victims' needs.

References

Atkins, L.A. 1996. *Legal processing of rape cases: Integrating Black's Theory with a feminist perspective of rape*. Paper presented at the 1996 Annual Meeting of the American Society of Criminology, Louisville, KY.

Berger, R., P. Searles, and W. Neuman. 1988. The dimensions of rape reform legislation. *Law and Society Review*, 22: 329–57.

Bourque, L.B. 1989. *Defining Rape*. Durham, NC: Duke University Press.

Byington, D., P. Martin, D. DiNitto, and M.S. Maxwell. 1991. Organizational affiliation and effectiveness: The case of rape crisis centers. *Administration in Social Work* 15: 83–103.

Caringella-Macdonald, S. 1988. Marxist and feminist interpretations on the aftermath of rape reform. *Contemporary Crises* 12: 125–244.

Epstein, J., and S. Langenbahn. 1994. *The Criminal Justice and Community Response to Rape*. Contract No. OJP-89–C-009. Washington, DC: National Institute of Justice.

Frazier, P., and B. Haney. 1996. Sexual assault cases in the legal system: Police, prosecutor, and victim perspectives. *Law and Human Behavior* 20: 607–628.

Frohmann, L. 1991. Discrediting victims' allegations of sexual assault: Prosecutorial accounts of case rejections. *Social Problems* 38: 213–26.

Harvey, M. 1985. *Exemplary Rape Crisis Programs: Site Analysis and Case Studies.* Washington, DC: National Center for the Prevention and Control of Rape.

Horney, J., and C. Spohn. 1991. Rape law reform and instrumental change in six jurisdictions. *Law and Society Review* 25: 117–53.

Kerstetter, W., and B. Van Winkle. 1990. Who decides? A study of the complainant's decision to prosecute in rape cases. *Criminal Justice and Behavior* 17: 268–83.

Koss, M., and M. Harvey. 1991. *The Rape Victim: Clinical and Community Interventions*, 2nd ed. Newbury Park, CA: Sage.

Krahe', B. 1991. Police officers' definitions of rape: A prototype study. *Journal of Community & Applied Social Psychology* 1: 223–44.

LaFree, G.D. 1980. Variables affecting guilty pleas and convictions in rape cases: Toward a social theory of rape processing. *Social Forces* 58: 833–50.

———. 1989. *Rape and Criminal Justice: The Social Construction of Sexual Assault*. Belmont, CA: Wadsworth Publishing Co.

Largen, Mary Ann. 1988. Rape law reform: An analysis. In *Rape and Sexual Assault, II*, pp. 271–92, edited by Ann W. Burgess. New York: Garland Publishing, Inc.

Marsh, T.W., A. Geist, and N. Caplan. 1982. *Rape and the Limits of Law Reform*. Boston: Auburn House.

Martin, P., D. DiNitto, D. Byington, and S. Maxwell, 1992. Organizational and community transformation: The case of a rape crisis center. *Administration in Social Work* 16: 123–45.

Robin, G. 1977. Forcible rape: Institutionalized sexism in the criminal justice system. *Crime and Delinquency* 23: 136–53.

Schmitt, F., and P. Martin. 1999. Unobtrusive mobilization by an institutionalized rape crisiscenter. *Gender and Society*. 13: 364–84.

Searles, P. and R. Berger. 1987. The current status of Rape reform legislation: An examination of state statutes. *Women's Rights Law Reporter* 10: 25–43.

State of North Carolina Uniform Crime Report, 1994. North Carolina Division of Criminal Information, 78–117.

Ullman, S. 1996. Do Social reactions to sexual assault victims vary by support providers. *Violence and Victims* 11: 143–57.

11

Policing Sexual Violence: A Case Study of *Jane Doe v. the Metropolitan Toronto Police*

James F. Hodgson

INTRODUCTION: POLICING SEXUAL VIOLENCE

Public police institutions, as expressions and representatives of dominant cultural ideologies and practices, are sexist in nature. Typically and traditionally, the state apparatus has not treated gender issues and gender crimes with an equitable and appropriate level of importance, until such time as public or political pressure or litigation induce policy and procedural change. Moreover, it is important to recognize that although policies and procedures may have been altered within police institutions, many of the prevailing ideologies, norms, values, and beliefs continue to be produced and reproduced by and within the occupational subculture. Often the policies and procedures amount to little more than "impression management," masking the public face of the institution while the internal operations, for the most part, go unchanged and unchallenged.

Police investigations of sexual violence are often riddled with the facade of assessing the believability of victims of sexual assault. Again the historic perspective as articulated by the police is that the victim cannot be trusted to be telling the truth. There is no other crime, property or personal, that the police will continuously question the authenticity of the victim's complaint. There is no other crime in which the police will spend so much time trying to assess the credibility or the chasteness of the victim. The police often respond to physical injury to the victim, or the lack thereof, as signs of consent. The police continue to investigate this crime as a crime of sex as opposed to a crime of violence. The police often operate within a criterion of victim believability in that a victim who has received significant physical injury is perceived as to have not consented to the sexual assault. The police often use this criterion to mold, or stereotype to assess, the believability of victims' complaints. The police also use other factors to assess believability such as the victim's appearance, that is, dressing in a provocative manner; the victim's age; marital status; occupation; alcohol use; the victim's "mental state" before and after the assault; the victim's sexual history and practices; the location of the attack; and time of first report. These criteria are utilized by the police to assess "founded" and "unfounded" cases of sexual assault. These criteria set up a model of "women who cannot be raped," in that victims who do not meet the believability criteria as set out by the police often cannot be and often are not classified by the police as victims (Gregory and Less 1999; Clark and Lewis 1977; Holmstrom and Burgess 1983; Burt 1991).

This chapter provides an opportunity to assess systemic discriminatory process and practice as operationalized within the framework of police response to sexual violence. A case study approach is utilized within this chapter to demonstrate practical applications of police investigative strategies in regards to sexual violence in which a systemic discriminatory response becomes most evident. This case study incorporates civil litigation that was heard in the Ontario Court of Justice in 1997. The litigation asserted that instead of being warned, women in imminent danger of being raped at knifepoint were deliberately used as bait, without their knowledge or consent, in a misguided attempt to apprehend a serial rapist. The litigation maintained that the police investigation was ill-conceived and actionable within the civil courts as the police owed a duty of care to the plaintiff and other women within the narrow and readily identifiable group of women who were at risk. The litigation asserted that it was not only foreseeable, it was in fact foreseen by the police that the rapist would attack a member of the small group to which the plaintiff, Ms. Jane Doe belonged (Ontario Court of Justice 1996a).

Moreover, the litigation alleged that the police prevented themselves from conducting a competent investigation because of their stereotypical views about women. The stereotypical beliefs that the investigators held, and that training and supervision in the police force did nothing to alleviate, according to the litigation, included the views that women were prone to irrational hysteria and prone to lying about having been raped. The litigation supports that the result of the acts and omissions of the police, which were informed and guided by these stereotypical views, is that Ms. Doe suffered systemic discrimination. Jane Doe's position was that the investigations of the sexual attacks were hopelessly tainted from the onset because of the discriminatory views and assumptions the various investigating officers held about women. Aside from issues of the competence of individual officers, the litigation suggested that systemic discrimination within the police force made it highly likely that any investigation conducted by any member of the force would have been subject to the same or similar errors (Ontario Court of Justice 1996a, 1996b, 1997a, 1997b).

METHODOLOGY

The methodology utilized within this chapter includes a case study approach which assesses a case as heard before the Ontario Court of Justice in the fall of 1997. The incidents that stimulated this civil litigation occurred in 1985 and 1986; however, the plaintiff had to move the case through many different Appeal Court levels to be awarded the right to bring litigation against the police for systemic discriminatory issues. The plaintiff in this case used the pseudonym "Jane Doe" to protect her identity and to highlight the continued presence of societal attitudes in regards to women who have been sexually assaulted. Subsequently, this methodology includes intensive interviews with Jane Doe, content analysis of plaintiff and defense pretrial conference memorandums, plaintiff and defense written submissions, plaintiff and defense reply submissions, court transcripts, other significant court documents, police reports, and my preparation and participation as an expert witness in this litigation.

In preparing my expert report, which addressed issues regarding sexual violence and the police response, I spent well over fifty hours engaged in intensive interviews with Jane Doe. This courageous woman was able to articulate issues and concepts that relate to systemic discrimination and sexual violence well beyond anyone that I've ever interviewed. The data as offered by Jane Doe informs much of this chapter and brings to life court documents that otherwise are devoid of expression or emotion. Jane Doe as a survivor of sexual violence was able to confront the criminal justice system, expose its systemic discriminatory policies and practices, and subsequently generate reforms to the police response to sexual violence. Jane Doe stood alone to confront the criminal justice apparatus and make it more accountable to survivors of sexual violence. Jane Doe is indeed a true hero who, against all odds, was able to expose the systemic discriminatory process that she, and many other women before her, had been exposed to and victimized by.

The content review of court documents includes the review of many written submissions as composed by the plaintiff and defense counsels, court transcripts, expert reports, police reports, police memo books, police correspondence, court transcripts, and the court decision as written by Her Honor Madam Justice MacFarland. These court documents are utilized throughout this chapter to facilitate a practical application of police investigative strategies and policies that foster systemic sexual violence discriminatory practices. The utilization of these numerous court documents allows the systemic discriminatory policies and practices to be exposed as they are analyzed within the context of internal and external police activity and actions. These numerous court documents facilitate this case study to inform this chapter in obtaining access and disclosure of the policies and practices of a police institution that harbored systemic discriminatory responses to sexual violence.

A CASE STUDY OF *JANE DOE V. THE METROPOLITAN TORONTO POLICE*

Shortly before dawn on August 24, 1986, Jane Doe was awakened in her apartment by an unknown intruder who had scaled the outside of the apartment building in which she lived, and then entered her apartment from the balcony. He blindfolded Ms. Doe, sexually assaulted her in a variety of ways, and raped her at knifepoint. The attack lasted over an hour (Ontario Court of Justice 1996a). Before Ms. Doe was attacked, detectives employed by the Metropolitan Toronto Police Force had concluded that a serial rapist was at large in Toronto, periodically raping women who lived in Jane Doe's immediate neighborhood, in similar circumstances to those of Ms. Doe. In the eight months preceding the attack on Ms. Doe, the same perpetrator had attacked four other single women living within 500 meters of the intersection of Church and Wellesley Streets in the City of Toronto. The attacks were highly similar in nature. The police had linked the four rapes together before the attack on Ms. Doe, and anticipated that further attacks would occur (Ontario Court of Justice 1996a, 1996b).

Having concluded that four similar attacks had taken place at the hands of the same suspect, and having every reason to believe that he would attack again, the police contemplated issuing a warning specifically directed to women in the community most likely to be raped. However, after having contemplated and debated the point, the police elected not to issue the warning. It was asserted in the litigation that followed that the Metropolitan Toronto Police deliberately elected not to issue any sort of warning to potential targets, even though the narrow group to which they belonged had been correctly identified. This decision not to warn women was made in hopes, to quote a subsequent police memo, that the rapist would strike again and be apprehended entering or "leaving" his next victim's apartment (Ontario Court of Justice 1996a, 1996b, 1997a).

THE SEXUAL ASSUALTS: A HALO OF DOUBT

The chronologies of events in this case study are as follows. On December 31, 1985, victim "A" was raped at knifepoint in her apartment. On January 10, 1986, victim "B" was raped at knifepoint in her apartment. June 25, 1986, victim "C" was raped at knifepoint in her apartment. On July 25, 1986, victim "D" was raped at knifepoint in her apartment. Subsequently, August 24, 1986, "Jane

Doe" was raped at knifepoint in her apartment. All these rapes occurred geographically within a five-block area. Two of the sexual attacks occurred in the same apartment building. The attacker, later identified as Paul Callow, utilized an extremely similar *modus operandi* in all of the attacks, including very similar profiles of all the victims (Ontario Court of Justice 1996a).

Victim "A"

After victim "A" was attacked, she notified the police. The police arrived on the scene and immediately began to discredit the information that the victim was giving them. Victim "A" reported from the onset that the rapist had come in from the balcony. The police discounted this by suggesting that the "only practical way" onto victim A's balcony was by way of the adjoining apartment. Although the victim highlighted that a garbage bin beneath her balcony made it easy to scale the outside of the building, the police continued to discredit her information and insisted that she knew her attacker. Moreover, the police became obsessed with the condition of the victim's apartment as noted in a police supplementary report (Ontario Court of Justice 1996b, 15), which detailed that:

The apartment when entered was found to be quite filthy and in disarray. Upon examination of the bedroom where the attack took place, the following was observed. There were multicolored nylons tied to the bedposts of her four poster bed. There were pornographic sexual aids located on the night table next to her bed, including Vaseline. In her dresser drawer another sexual aid was located. Next to this was an erotic movie entitled "Bizarre Sexual Devices." At the foot of her bed was found a full size "bullwhip."

The police took numerous detailed photographs of the "pornographic sexual devices," but did not take a clear photograph of the garbage bin outside the building which the rapist used to scale the outside of the building. The police reports never mention the garbage bin that made it easy to get to victim A's balcony from the ground floor (Ontario Court of Justice 1996a, 1996b, 1997c).

From the outset, the investigators seemed captured by the stereotype that promiscuous or sexually active women ask for what might happen to them. Of course, there is nothing wrong in detailed observations about the scene of a crime. However, the pejorative tone of the report and the fixation on the victim's sexual practices, to the exclusion of, for example, noting how easy or hard it would be to scale the side of the building when the victim has said the rapist entered by the balcony, demonstrated how preconceived and irrelevant notions can hamper effective policing.

Victim A had valuable information to share with the police. However, she is the one source of information that was ignored. Instead of determining from her that it was "easy" to scale the outside of the building and believing her when she explained that she did not know the man, the police took her for either a manipulative liar, or a "dizzy" unreliable person, or both. According to victim A, the police continued with their insistence that she knew the rapist, despite her information to them that this was not the case. The police apparently never considered the absurdity of their insistence that a woman could not be counted upon to accurately state whether or not her attacker was known to her. The police insisted with their absurd position, notwithstanding what victim A was telling them, that victim A's boyfriend had attacked her. Given that the investigators refused to believe what victim A was telling them, and their distracting fascination with her sexual practices, as well as the absence of supervision that might have put the investigation back on the right track, it is not surprising that the investigation of this attack withered to nothing before being abandoned. The police created dead ends for themselves by marginalizing the one person with the most direct knowledge of what had occurred (Ontario Court of Justice 1996a, 1996b, 1996c; Hodgson 1997).

Victim "B"

The attitudes and beliefs that had been brought to the investigation of victim A, together with the absence of basic analytic skills and effective supervision, also characterized the investigation of the reports of sexual violence made by victim "B." Victim B was raped ten days after victim A. After being attacked, victim B called the police. The police attended the scene at 1:30 a.m. on January 10, 1986, and immediately began to question the victim's credibility. By 4:30 a.m., on the same day, the police documented in a supplementary report that there was "some doubt about the credibility of the victim's story" (Ontario Court of Justice 1996b, 14). The police note in their reports that the "superintendent . . . has revealed several fictitious complaints [regarding victim B's apartment] in the past and feels that the victim is a little unstable" (Ontario Court of Justice 1996b, 14). The superintendent's information was apparently more credible than that of victim B, although the superintendent also informed the police that he had been employed as the superintendent for less than a month at that time (Ontario Court of Justice 1996a, 1997b).

The police were also troubled because of what they observed at the scene of the crime. On "the bed was an undisturbed bowl of potato chips which she was eating before the rape [which] remained undisturbed in the double bed after the rape" (Ontario Court of Justice 1996b, 16). The implication is that a sufficiently chaste woman who was not consenting to intercourse would have put up more of a fight and "disturbed" the bowl of potato chips. The investigating police officers do not appear to have considered that Callow was holding an eight-inch knife against victim B's face, which he had already used to cut her chin at the outset of the attack. In contrast to victim A's "filthy" apartment, victim B's apartment was too neat. It was "immaculate and looked undisturbed. With the exception of the victim's blood, there is no evidence that anything happened in the apartment—no sign of forced entry," leading the police to conclude that victim B's "story" was not credible (Ontario Court of Justice 1996b, 16). Among the other observations that assisted the investigating officers in determining whether or not victim B had invented the rape are items such as "she has little furniture in [her] apartment" and "her living habits are very neat. She appears to be a loner or recluse" (Ontario Court of Justice 1996b, 16).

What victim B reported to the police was true. These faulty conclusions on the part of the police are clear evidence of a systemic predisposition to assume that women are lying about sexual assault. There is no other crime against the person where the police so routinely, thoroughly, and explicitly question whether the crime occurred in the first place and attempt to discredit the complaint. Although victim B (i.e., the woman) was not credible, the superintendent and the ex-boyfriend (i.e., the men) were able to provide a number of pieces of useful information. Contrary to victim B's statement that she "has ONE boyfriend," the superintendent "knows that she has two boyfriends with whom she spends the night with" (Ontario Court of Justice 1996, 16). The boyfriend was also found to be credible, notwithstanding his apparent animus against victim B, and his information was used to justify the conclusion that the rape was "fictitious." It was duly noted that victim B had given the boyfriend a venereal disease, and that after the boyfriend and victim B had broken up, the boyfriend had seen her with another man. He also explained to the police that "she probably made the story up [about being raped] as she would do so to get attention" (Ontario Court of Justice 1996b, 16). He offered to assist the investigation by providing the name of a friend of victim B so that the police could obtain further background information about her. It is not clear whether he was assisting with the investigation of the alleged rape, or the investigation leading up to the public mischief charges being laid against victim B (Ontario 1996a, 1996b, 1997a; Hodgson, 1997).

The police conclusions about the investigation, together with their detailed reasons for believing that the report was "fictitious," are emphasized on the information that victim B saw several men and had passed on a sexually transmitted disease, which "must go to show her possible sexual activities." It is important to emphasize that the three different officers who arrived at similar conclusions in the victim B investigation were different from the officers involved in the victim A investigation. Similarly, they reported to different supervisors. The problem is systemic, and cannot be blamed on a "few bad apples." The attitudes are institutional, which is evidence, if nothing else, of the failure of training or ongoing supervision to prevent or correct the attitudes and assumptions that characterized the investigation of the victim A and victim B rapes (Ontario Court of Justice 1996a; Hodgson, 1997).

Victim "C"

If the investigations of the rapes of victim A and victim B are remarkable because of the degree to which stereotypical views held by the various public officers who were carrying out their public duties impeded basic investigative skills, the investigation of victim C's rape is remarkable for its incompleteness. One of the same police detectives who was involved in the investigation of victim B's rape, which had occurred earlier that same year in another unit of the very same apartment building, did not link the two offenses together. It is unclear if his failure to link the offenses is because he also disbelieved victim C, or if he thought it a mere coincidence that he should be asked to investigate two such similar attacks. Very little was done in the investigation, until after Callow was apprehended (Ontario Court of Justice 1996a, 1996b; Hodgson, 1997).

Victim "D"

When victim D's rape was reported to the police, it became the fourth of Callow's rapes being simultaneously investigated by the police. By this point, the detectives were apparently prepared to believe that the women were not reporting "fictitious" rapes, and they finally managed to link the sexual attacks. It is important to note that the link was not established because there was an effective structure in place to detect crimes that were common to the same serial predator. However, because of informal discussions within the office, and because four of the rapes were fortuitously being investigated in the same police division, the link happened to emerge (Ontario Court of Justice 1996a).

A SERIAL RAPIST AT LARGE: THE "DRAWSTRING METHOD"

Once the police finally concluded that a serial rapist was at large and having finally identified at least some of the components of his *modus operandi*, the police immediately recognized the need to warn women in the area who were in danger of being attacked when he struck again. In his memo of July 29, one of the detectives wrote the following:

The writer feels that building superintendents should be contacted and that they advise "trusted tenants," *especially single women* [emphasis added] to be aware of the occurrences and advise police of any person they feel may be suspect (Ontario Court of Justice 1996b, 18).

At some as yet undetermined point after July 29, 1986, the proposal that a warning should be given to "trusted tenants, especially single women" was dropped. After Jane Doe was raped, the police did conduct a door-to-door canvass in the apartment buildings where they believed the rapist was likely to strike. The purpose of the canvass was not to warn women of the risk, but to gather information to be used in the investigation. Officers were instructed to canvass certain specified buildings in the area, to "obtain names and addresses of single women and note their hair colour." The "officers [were] not to mention anything about sexual assaults which have occurred in the area but to advise the people contacted that this is a crime prevention programme" (Ontario Court of Justice 1996b, 18). In other words, material information was deliberately withheld from the women to whom the police were speaking during their canvass. The police compiled a list of apartment buildings in the area where they felt Callow was likely to strike, to be used in the door-to-door canvass to gather information (Ontario Court of Justice 1996a, 1996b, 1997a).

Several days after Jane Doe was raped, a detective was interviewing her about her attack. He mentioned to her that the police suspected she had been attacked by a serial rapist, which led Ms. Doe to ask why she had not been warned about the fact that he was at large. The detective replied that the police had decided not to issue a warning because "women might become hysterical" (Ontario Court of Justice 1996a, 32). The canvas was followed by a thirty-police-officer stakeout of the area, organized to take place between September 20, 1986, and September 30, 1986. Groups of apartment buildings that had been identified as "climbable" were to be "staked out" by non-uniformed officers "in the event that there was an attack" (Ontario Court of Justice 1996a, 32). This investigative procedure was later described as the "drawstring method."

ANALYSIS OF THE POLICE INVESTIGATION

Sexist Systemic Discrimination

The women attacked by serial rapist Callow received police services that harboured and expressed sexist systemic discrimination. This sexist systemic discrimination manifested itself as a sexist ideology in regards to the police response and investigation, and in regards to the subsequent decisions made about protecting the community and apprehending the offender. This sexist ideology is evident when one reads the original reports of the first police officers at the scene of the reported sexual assaults. For example, the tone and innuendo of the reports in identifying various sex toys, or sex videos, all serve to bring the victim's credibility into question. The interviewing of ex-boyfriends, boyfriends, and apartment superintendents yields information that is given more credibility than the victim's statements. Police officers provided their own commentary and speculation as to what "more likely happened" to the victims, or what would motivate their "false reports." These are all good examples of the sexist ideology and expression that ran through this sexual assault investigation. If these victims were reporting a nonsexual assault, the police would most likely take the reports as genuine at first instance and would not try to discredit their claims as false (Ontario Court of Justice 1996a, 1996b, 1997a, 1997b; Hodgson 1997).

Professionalism and Training

The investigative elements of the Callow case are typical examples of responses by police institutions and officers that demonstrate a lack of professionalism and proper training. The efforts by the police to disqualify or dismiss victims of sexual assaults as unreliable, unbelievable, or outright liars are all examples of systemic discrimination. From the original officers on the scene of these sexual assaults to the investigating detectives, there are similar attempts to disqualify the victims' experiences, which can be seen in many of the reports made by the officers and detectives. There is little doubt that these sexist ideological influences and inferences seriously hampered and prohibited the police from originally detecting the patterns of sexual assaults that were emerging in the area. The police were spending so much of their time and efforts trying to disqualify the victims, they failed to place the appropriate emphasis on trying to locate and apprehend the offender (Ontario Court of Justice 1996a, 1997b; Hodgson, 1997).

Creditability of Victims

This sexism is again highlighted when the police finally came to the conclusion that there was a serial rapist operating in the area. When the police realized that there was indeed a serial rapist operating in the area, they immediately afforded the victims credibility and validation of their experiences as survivors of sexual assault. It is important to note that these women as individual complainants of sexual assaults were not creditable in the eyes of the police, but become somewhat creditable to the police only after several women reported similar experiences. Individual complaints of sexual assault appear to need significant corroboration before their reports become valid or are taken seriously (Hodgson 1997).

Sexist Ideology and Systemic Discrimination

Sexist ideology, as expressed and asserted within the systemic discriminatory framework, prevented the police from realizing within a more astute time frame that a serial rapist was at large, victimizing members of the community. Furthermore, the systemic discrimination prohibited, negated, and influenced the perspective of the investigation, such that the sexual assaults were not viewed as the serious, debilitative, destructive, and degradative crimes that they were. If the police had moved their focus from "blaming the victim" or "devaluating the victim" to focusing on the offender, they may have indeed seen the typologies being presented earlier. This in turn could have led to the appropriate investigative emphases and direction putting forward an investigative plan that would have afforded the public the necessary information and protection. The appropriate level of professionalism on behalf of the police would have determined the existence of this serial rapist much earlier in the investigation (Hodgson 1997).

Resource Allocation and Sexual Violence

Furthermore, if the appropriate departmental, fiscal, and resource priorities existed for sexual assault crimes, they would have developed a much larger, professional, efficient, and effective specialized sexual assault investigative unit. The enhanced level of professionalism would have traveled far in meeting the needs of survivors of sexual assault. Of course the "serious crimes" such as the frauds, auto thefts, holdups, morals' offenses, and homicides were all sent to the respective specialized units such as the Fraud Squad, Auto Squad, Holdup Squad, Morality Bureau, and the Homicide Squad (Hodgson 1997).

To Warn or Not to Warn the Public?

Many of the decisions made in this case are extremely questionable, but none more so than the decisions made in the final chapters of this investigation. Specifically, the decision not to inform the public, or at least the potential targets, of the fact that their personal safety was in extreme danger is an essential and fundamental error in judgment by the investigating officers. The actions of the investigators demonstrate an inability or failure on their part to distinguish between an extreme crime, such as a sexual assault, and the effect it has on the victims, from crimes such as theft or vandalism. There is no apparent thought given to the consequences that a victim will almost certainly suffer as a survivor of sexual assault. The "serious" nature of sexual assault and how it alters, transforms, and in many cases devastates the victim would compel most individuals who have control or are charged with administering public safety to realize and act on the basis that they cannot risk any further victimization. The risk and consequences to the victims are so extreme that to think or act any differently is not only unprofessional but evidence of a wanton and reckless disregard for the lives and safety of others (Hodgson 1997).

Public Safety

Keep in mind that the risk to potential victims is not centered around random street violence with no pattern or typology in existence. The victims in this case are being attacked in their homes. The point of entry appears to be from the balcony. Therefore, victims are very much in a position of control over their own environment. Armed with the appropriate information, the potential victims could have taken measures to protect themselves. For example, potential victims could have secured their balcony windows and doors as a reasonable measure in ensuring personal safety. The point is that ensuring the safety of the public in this case was extremely manageable and achievable if the Metropolitan Toronto Police Department really wanted to protect this vulnerable part of the community. If the job of the police is to try to ensure that the public is safe, the police should be protecting the public from crimes that are as devastating as sexual assault. Public safety should not be an afterthought but obviously a priority that maintains a minimum level of professional competence. Failing to inform the public, or at least the potential targets of the danger they were facing, demonstrates a complete disregard for public safety (Hodgson 1997).

Public Participation in Crime Solving

The investigative choice not to release information about the serial rapist and the attendant safety risk in the community is further brought into question when one assesses the role of the public in "clearing cases." The public, being the eyes and ears for the police, has traditionally and continues to provide police with information and "tips" that have a direct effect on the ability of the police to solve criminal cases. Without public assistance and support, the police are not only restricted, but are, for the most part, out of the crime-solving business. It is not accidental that we see an increased use of community-based policing, crime stoppers, neighborhood watch, and other programs that are developed to entice and elicit community involvement in reporting criminal activity to the police. The choice made by the police in this case not to release this information to the public did not allow potential victims to protect themselves and furthermore did not allow the community to assist the police in their investigation. Most crimes that are "cleared" by the police are the result of information received from non police sources. The decision not to engage and inform the public regarding a serial rapist at large in the community seriously restricted and hampered the police in their ability to apprehend the offender. This decision not to release information to the public seriously reduced the number of investigative eyes and ears and therefore deprived the investigating officers of potentially valuable sources of information (Hodgson 1997).

The Drawstring Method—Faulty Assumptions

The drawstring method was predicated on two faulty assumptions. First, in order for the method to work and the fleeing rapist to be apprehended, it would be necessary for the victim to call the police immediately after the attack, failing which, the police would not know that the rape that they had been waiting for had been committed. The second flaw in the plan relates to the fact that one of the detectives had (correctly) theorized that the rapist lived in the neighborhood. A person living in the area would notice the increased police presence during the stakeout. Even if the drawstring method were otherwise sound, it is evident that giving a warning would have made the method more effective. Heightened awareness on the part of residents would lead to suspicious prowlers being reported to the police officers conducting the stakeout and would have made women who had been raped aware of the need to contact the police immediately. If women had been warned, they could have taken steps to protect themselves (such as double-checking windows or hiding their knives), and even if the rapist had got close to entering their apartments, they would have had more time to call the police. They could have made sure that they went to bed with a telephone close to their bed. The ultimate error was in believing that the issuance of a warning would in any way jeopardize the effectiveness of police surveillance in the area (Hodgson 1997).

The notion of professionalism by itself demands that *at no time* should the police be empowered legislatively, morally, or ethically to put potential victims of serious crimes at risk, in order to increase the likelihood of apprehending a suspect. At no time should the idea of subjecting individuals to increased risks of becoming victims of serious crimes even be perceived as an investigative option. If one compares this case scenario to a serial homicidal offender, the investigators would have informed the public without delay that a serial homicidal offender was at large in their community. Without question, professional ethics dictates that the first priority of the police is the protection of life. The protection of life is and needs to be the priority in all matters involving public policing (Hodgson 1997).

Obviously apprehending this serial rapist was necessary to protect the public, but not at the risk of increasing the level of immediate danger to the public. The police would have informed the public about a serial homicidal offender at large so that the public could take precautions and further assist the police in their investigation. If the investigative officers really understood the impact of sexual assault on victims, they would have been more likely to conclude that the risk to victims, as in homicides, is extreme. The investigative officers would have to put the safety of potential victims and the protection of life first, and would have informed the public, instead of withholding information for reasons that are of dubious rational value (Hodgson 1997).

Displacement and Criminal Activity

The question, of course, that is raised is whether, by warning the public, the police may have caused the rapist to flee. The answer to this question is that the rapist may, indeed, have fled the area. However, there is no real method of assessing that possibility. Again, if one's priority is protecting the public, the apprehension of the rapist becomes a secondary matter. Furthermore, by informing the public, the community is most likely to assist in solving the case by providing information that may contribute to the investigation. By informing the public, the police would have greatly increased their chances of solving the case. Keep in mind that the police had the option of utilizing a restricted method of informing the public, such as notifying only potential victims so that at the very least these community members could have taken the appropriate precautions and measures to ensure their own safety. This method of protecting the public would have reduced the potential public information base and would also have reduced the likelihood of the serial rapist finding out that the police were investigating his activities (Hodgson 1997).

The fear of the offender fleeing the area in response to a public warning does not survive scrutiny. Presumably, the concern is that the rapist might realize that the police were investigating his crimes if there were a public warning. Is the suggestion that the serial rapist actually believes that none of his victims notified the police after they had been sexually assaulted? It is almost certain that some of the victims did not notify the police. However, the serial rapist must already be keenly aware that some of his victims did notify the police. Therefore the serial rapist is already aware that the police are investigating his activities. Interestingly enough, the police knew that the serial rapist had not left the area knowing that the police were investigating his crimes (Hodgson 1997).

Protection of Life

Even if the rapist had changed his area of operation or ceased raping in response to a police warning to the public, the police would have at least satisfied what should have been their first goal and priority at the time, protection of life. This change in location or cessation of activity by the rapist might have reduced chances of his apprehension or it might have increased it depending on the circumstances. Forcing the rapist to change his behavior may have allowed for increased levels of investigative opportunities. The process of the police making the rapist change his behavior would have given some control back to the police and therefore would have allowed the police to invoke other investigative strategies. The rapist may or may not have moved to another location or ceased offending if a public warning was issued. The answer to that question is unknown. The investigators could not control the actions of the offender, but they did have direct control and influences over the protection of the public. The risk to the public was real and controllable. The risk of the offender fleeing was not real or controllable. Professional police practice dictates that the protection of law abiding constituents is a priority. Apparently this priority got lost in the investigative process. The investigators were offering a direct focus on the offender and took great risk with the community that they were sworn to protect. One cannot help but ask, "If the investigating officer's family members were within the serial rapist's danger zone, would the officers have informed their family members as to the pending danger?" (Hodgson 1997).

Police Surveillance and Apprehension

What makes the investigative choices of the police officers even more problematic is their attempt to conduct visual surveillance in the serial rapist's activity zone. The logistical challenges present in this area of Toronto make effective surveillance extremely unlikely. Generally, there is pedestrian and vehicular traffic in this area twenty-four hours a day. Specifically, the area houses large apartment buildings that have many mature trees and bushes that restrict visual inspection of the backs of the many apartment buildings. This setting makes it unlikely that police officers would be able to apprehend a suspect before he entered an apartment balcony or an apartment itself (Hodgson 1997).

Therefore, were the investigators hoping to apprehend the offender after he attacked his victim and was leaving the area? This concept of letting a person become a victim of sexual assault in order to facilitate apprehension of a suspect is troublesome to say the least. Even so, the likelihood of the victim notifying the police right after the offense took place does not necessarily represent reality. Again, many of the survivors of the sexual assaults in this case called others or made sure that their personal safety was reestablished before they notified the police. Therefore, the likelihood of the police catching the offender after the criminal act was completed is most unlikely given these circumstances and the area in which the serial rapist was operating (Hodgson 1997).

The intended result of the visual surveillance was to employ the investigative tactic labeled the "drawstring method." The drawstring method is more than surprisingly naive; it is patently ridiculous and unprofessional, given the risk factors and the physical environment in which the serial rapist was operating. The risks associated with this surveillance method were great, whereas the chance of apprehending the serial rapist by this process was minimal. Again, one must recognize that a serial rapist is a repeat offender who usually successfully eludes police detection. The subject of the surveillance would be keenly aware of his environment and furthermore would be a master of detecting surveillance in his area and would likely excel in deception. This option of choosing surveillance over informing the public, as a method of apprehending the offender was a tactical, professional, and ethical blunder that resulted in further levels of victimization in the community (Hodgson 1997).

THE ONTARIO COURT OF JUSTICE SPEAKS: CASE DECISION

On July 3, 1998, Madam Justice Jean MacFarland of the Ontario Court of Justice released her decision regarding this litigation. Justice MacFarland ruled that the Metropolitan Toronto Police Force was indeed "utterly negligent" in the way it handled the sexual assaults as reported in this case study. The Justice handed down a scathing indictment of the police force and its officers for failing to warn women about the serial rapist that was at large in the community. Moreover the Justice ruled that Jane Doe's Charter rights had been violated by the police as the police operated within a system that was fueled by systemic sexist discrimination that was inclusive across the police force and obviously generated significant misunderstanding on how the crime of rape affects women. The justice (MacFarland 1998, 25) noted that "to me it is indicative that the Metro Toronto Police Force as a whole did not understand the fundamental concept that sexual assault is not about sex, it is about violence and anger against women." The justice (MacFarland 1998, 36) continued in noting that "when all the circumstances are taken and considered together, it certainly suggests to me that women were being used, without their knowledge or consent, as 'bait' to attract a predator." The justice further ruled that the police department was engaging in "impression management" rather than any indication of real genuine commitment for change in their response to sexual violence in the community. The Justice concluded that the conduct of the police force and its officers, in this investigation and the resulting failure to warn women in the community about the serial rapist, was motivated and informed by a pattern of systemic discrimination that adhered to rape myths as well as sexist stereotypical reasoning about rape, about women, and about women who have been raped.

CONCLUSION

This case study facilitated the disclosure of the systemic discriminatory process and practices as operationalized by the Metropolitan Toronto Police in their response to sexual violence. The case study reveals the consequences when police institutions are informed and guided by "rape myths" and stereotypical views about women. The police investigation of these sexual assaults, as outlined in this case study, were hopelessly tainted from the onset because of the discriminatory views and assumptions that the various investigating officers held about women and sexual violence. These police investigations were compromised as a result of the police officers' obsession of assessing the believability of the survivors of sexual violence. Many of the police investigators embraced the traditional historical values and attitudes about sexual violence. Subsequently, Jane Doe received police services that were discriminatory and unprofessional. The discriminatory and unprofessional actions of the police generated a sexist ideology that tainted the police response and investigation and affected subsequent police decisions regarding protecting the community and apprehending the offender.

REFERENCES

Brownmiller, Susan. 1975. *Against Our Will: Men, Women, and Rape.* New York: Bantam.

Burt, Martha, 1991. Rape Myths and Acquaintance Rape. In *Acquaintance Rape: The Hidden Crime*, edited by Andrea Parrot and Laurie Bechhofer. New York: John Wiley and Sons.

Clark, Lorenne, and Debra Lewis. 1977. *Rape: The Price of Coercive Sexuality.* Toronto: The Women's Press.

Gregory, Jeanne, and Sue Lees. 1999. *Policing Sexual Violence.* London: Routledge.

Hodgson, James F. 1997. *Expert Report—Anticipated Evidence Re: Jane Doe v. Metro Toronto Police.* Toronto: Ontario Court of Justice Document.

Holmstrom, Linda, and Ann Burgess. 1983. *The Victim of Rape: Institutional Reactions.* New Brunswick, NJ: Transaction Books.

MacFarland, Madam Justice. 1998. *Jane Doe and Board of Commissioners of Police et al. Decision.* Toronto: Ontario Court of Justice.

Ontario Court of Justice. 1996a. *Jane Doe and Board of Commissioners of Police et. al.: Plaintiff's Pretrial Conference Memorandum—Volume 1.* Toronto: Court Document.

———. 1996b. *Jane Doe and Board of Commissioners of Police et al.: Plaintiff's Pretrial Conference Memorandum—Volume 2—Documents.* Toronto: Court Document.

———. 1997a. *Jane Doe and Board of Commissioners of Police et al.: Plaintiff's Written Submissions.* Toronto: Court Document.

———. 1997b. *Jane Doe and Board of Commissioners of Police et al.: Plaintiff's Written Reply Submissions.* Toronto: Court Document.

12

Assessing the Role of Sexual Assault Programs in Communities

Elizabethann O'Sullivan

INTRODUCTION

Sexual assault programs do more than counsel victims of rape. They document sexual violence in the community, keep it on the public agenda, and work toward lasting social change. Focusing exclusively on a program's client services may give an inaccurate picture of its effectiveness. More than one agency may provide crisis counseling, victim advocacy, in-service training, or community education; furthermore, many victims never report an assault or contact a rape crisis center. Drawing on a study of sixteen North Carolina sexual assault programs, this article presents a strategy to establish a program's role in its community. It details how a program can use information on its (1) definitions of sexual assault, (2) client mix (client demographics and type of incident), (3) interagency relations, and (4) community education to monitor, improve, and evaluate its impact on its community. The same information can be gathered from other community agencies to identify gaps and overlaps in community services.

THE COMMUNITY IMPACT OF SEXUAL ASSAULT PROGRAMS

Sexual assault programs document sexual violence in the community, monitor how criminal justice agencies and hospitals handle sexual assault cases and treat victims, and collaborate with others to develop and deliver effective survivor services. Through their presence, they identify and promote needed changes in policies and procedures and work together with other agencies and organizations to eliminate sexual violence. To form an accurate picture of the value of sexual assault programs requires documenting what they do in their communities. Some researchers imply that anti-rape programs have abandoned the goal of "eliminating sexual violence against women" (Collins and Whalen 1989; Matthews 1994; Gornick and Meyer 1998). This judgment seems harsh and ignores the importance of centers keeping sexual assault on the public agenda and achieving lasting social change. Through their presence, centers can bring about change by carrying out activities that:

1. Broaden and enrich prevailing community knowledge, understandings, and beliefs, and

2. Create new linkages with the outside world so that prevailing beliefs are regularly challenged and reexamined (Koss and Harvey 1987, 59).

In addition, as professionals from throughout a community meet and work, they may develop greater trust, learn from each other, evaluate new information and ideas, and develop innovative approaches for dealing with sexual violence (see Child and Faulkner 1998). It takes time for change to occur. Sexual assault programs should play a key role in developing and disseminating new knowledge as the definitions of sexual violence, its causes, effects, and prevention strategies continue to evolve (Donat and D'Emillio 1992).

Sexual assault programs observe agency practices allowing staff and volunteers to identify and reinforce sensitive and effective behaviors and to note troubling practices or ignored policies. A hospital, criminal justice agency, or school system may adopt a protocol for handling sexual assault cases, but staff may not follow it. In-service training or community education efforts are ineffective if they are not regularly delivered and reinforced. New employees may be ignorant of sexual assault statutes, victim reactions and needs, and available services (see Campbell and Johnson 1997). Trainees may abandon recommended behaviors that are neither valued nor promoted within the agency.

A single sexual assault program cannot meet all of a victim's needs nor the needs of all victims. More than one agency may provide crisis counseling, victim advocacy, in-service training, or community education. Furthermore, some populations may be more receptive to services, training, and presentations tailored to their specific concerns. Effectively addressing the needs of all members of a community—including gays; males; specific ethnic, racial, religious, and age groups—may be beyond what a given program can do well. Sharing responsibility with other organizations may be efficient, allow victims to maintain their autonomy in seeking and consuming services, and motivate cooperating organizations to focus on specific needs.

Client services should not be ignored. They consume a major portion of a program's resources, and the question "How well are we doing at meeting victim needs?" is compelling. Nevertheless, focusing exclusively on client services may give an inaccurate picture of a program's effectiveness. First, sexual assaults often go unreported, even to a rape crisis center. According to the 1998 Crime Victimization Survey (Rennison 1999), only 32 percent of sexual assaults were reported to the police. In a survey of college women, Koss (1988) found that 58 percent of the rape victims told someone about the assault, and 4 percent contacted a rape crisis center. A study conducted in Los Angeles at the same time found 3 percent of sexually assaulted women contacted a rape crisis center (Sorenson and Siegel 1998, 219). Second, obtaining representative and accurate client data presents challenges (Stelmachers 1980). Low response rates may be expected (Blomberg 1989; Carrow 1980). Accurately assessing the effectiveness of a relatively brief intervention is hindered when (1) control groups cannot be organized, and (2) external forces may mask any impact. The behavior of one agency or actor can distort recollections about the behavior and helpfulness of others.

This chapter presents a strategy for developing an accurate picture of a sexual assault program's role in its community. The strategy is relatively easy to implement and allows a program to regularly assess its strengths and weakness and to document the community's response to rape. The information can form the foundation for program evaluations, strategic planning, and research on community responses to sexual assault.

This chapter originated in a study comparing North Carolina's independent rape crisis centers with other sexual assault programs (O'sullivan and Carlton 2001). The literature review suggested that rape crisis centers could be described as social service agencies. This designation seemed misleading, insofar as the centers continued to seek social and policy change (Byington 1991; Gornick, Burt, and Pittman 1985; Koss and Harvey 1987, ch. 4; Matthews 1994, ch. 9). Sixteen centers were studied; eight independent rape crisis centers, five multi-service centers, and three combined sexual assault and domestic violence programs. Staff interviews and state-maintained data provided information on definitions of rape, client characteristics, and relationships with hospitals and criminal justice agencies. The programs did not clearly vary in whom they served and how; however, the independent centers were most likely to act as advocates for victims and conduct activities intended to eliminate sexual violence and change attitudes.

In collecting and analyzing the information, its value became clear. Finding a distinct difference among programs was pleasing. More satisfying was recognizing the importance of community networks centered on sexual assault. These networks help meet the immediate needs of individual victims and keep sexual assault, its prevention, and survivor concerns from being ignored. The endurance of the networks underscores that rape prevention and treatment are community problems beyond simple, quick solutions. As sexual assault programs carry out their activities, relationships with community organizations form, and informal or formal networks may emerge. The relationships may be as simple as supporting a client or as complex as carrying out a joint project.

This chapter identifies the elements that establish a rape crisis center's role in the community and implies how each element can be interpreted. To avoid ambiguity, all sexual assault programs, whether they are autonomous or not, are identified as "rape crisis centers." Similarly, because of variations in organizational structure, the term "center staff" does not exclude volunteers and board members. To illustrate the value of the information, major findings from the North Carolina study are included. The chapter goes on to suggest how the information can be used to assess, improve, and track a center's impact on the community; to document a community's response to sexual assault; and to support research on the outcomes of specific community-focused activities.

ELEMENTS NEEDED TO ASSESS IMPACT ON A COMMUNITY

Defining Sexual Assault and Client Mix

A key feature of a rape crisis center is its definition of sexual assault. Centers identify what constitutes sexual assault, its causes, and appropriate responses to sexual violence. Their understanding of sexual assault should help them answer the questions: Who are our clients? How can we best meet their needs? What strategies will lead to the elimination of sexual violence? They communicate their observations in public forums and in meetings with service providers and public officials. Bourque (1992, ch. 14), in *Defining Rape*, documents the lack of consensus about what constitutes rape. The lack of consensus may lead women to brush off unwanted sexual acts, their friends and families to excuse sexual coercion, and police, prosecutors, and jurors to discount assaults lacking clear signs of physical force and physical resistance. Identifying a center's definition is critical to assessing whom it serves and whom it misses and whether its education efforts could change attitudes and behaviors. Furthermore, the investigators may uncover evolving definitions of sexual assault.

The practices of rape crisis centers encourage them to regularly reevaluate how they define sexual assault. The centers usually do not have formal intake procedures. They do not document a person's eligibility for services, nor determine if a prosecutable sexual offense occurred. Consequently, they hear from men and women who have been criminally assaulted by acquaintances, dates, partners, or strangers; from the caretakers of sexually abused children; from survivors of childhood sexual abuse; and from sexually harassed females. They counsel victims indirectly through their families, friends, school counselors, employers, and social services staff. They talk with the families and friends of survivors about their own feelings and fears. As they hear victims' stories, staff and volunteer advocates may alter their definition of sexual assault. They may expand the types of acts they consider as rape, speculate on the causes and effects of sexual violence, and develop theories of effective prevention strategies.

Cultural reactions to sexual assault also enter into definitions. Members of different groups, albeit a group based on ethnic or racial identity, sexual orientation, religion, disability, or age, may vary in how they define sexual assault, their reaction to sexual violence, whom they confide in, and how they evaluate services offered. Research on how specific groups define and respond to sexual assault is limited. Empirical studies have been conducted in single geographic locations, involve samples drawn from few ethnic groups, and ask different questions; the findings are mixed and not generalizable. Clues exist that groups vary in what their members consider a sexual assault (Bourque 1992; Fischer 1987; Williams and Holmes 1981), whom survivors confide in (Sorenson and Siegel 1998), and how they view their treatment (Williams and Holmes 1981). Programs that work directly or indirectly with members of special populations will probably develop hypotheses and implement activities tailored to their specific community.

A center's definition of sexual assault cannot be separated from its client mix. How a program defines sexual assault may be inferred from the types of clients it works with; conversely, clients may lead a program to refine its definition of a sexual assault. Both the nature of the assault and client characteristics, such as age, racial or ethnic group, need to be considered. Data on the type of incidence indicates if a program hears from the full range of people affected by sexual violence. It should hear from survivors' parents, partners, and friends, as well as adult women who were assaulted by a date or acquaintance. It should handle occasional cases of sexual harassment, sexual assault perpetrated on an adult male, and sexual assault committed by a female. Its teenaged clients should include survivors of incest and young women raped by acquaintances or boyfriends.

If no teenagers call, if most clients are coping with domestic violence, or if clients come from one major ethnic, racial, or cultural group, one may reasonably assume that the center itself does not fully meet community needs. Perhaps potential clients are unaware of the center or cannot access it (Attkisson and Broskowski 1978; Gutierrez 1992). A center's name may not suggest that it deals with sexual assault, its publications may not indicate what constitutes sexual assault, or its publicity may not reach all segments of the community. A center may be accessible only to people fluent in English or able to communicate by telephone. Potential clients may reject a center with little diversity in its staff and volunteers.

A center's definition of sexual assault may be ascertained by reviewing its publications. Staff interviews offer more valuable and expansive information. Descriptions of a center's clients and services detail client needs and how the center attempts to meet them. Observations about clients from "special" populations document staff insights about important cultural variations in beliefs about sexual assault and appropriate responses. To study the client mix, data can be compiled on each client's demographic characteristics (age group, racial or ethnic group, gender, and other relevant characteristics), type of incident, and services used.

What is the value of this information? First, learning a program's definitions of sexual assault picks up variations among centers and how they respond to their client population. Staff interviewed in North Carolina differed in their definitions of sexual assault. Staff at combined domestic violence and sexual assault programs did not seem to distinguish between domestic violence and rape. For example, one director observed, "Many times sexual assault victims are also domestic violence victims are also victims of childhood sexual abuse. We always find an overlapping of all three of them. It's rare not to find it." Some centers focused on the sexual abuse of children. Others saw sexual assault as forming a continuum of sexual violations ranging from forcible intercourse to sexual harassment.

Comments on cultural concerns showed that the staff recognized that client needs and reactions varied. Directors critiqued their ability to work with unique victims, such as disabled persons and Spanish speakers. They puzzled over why they rarely heard from Asians or Asian Americans. Staff questioned the appropriateness of sharing their strongly held beliefs with individual victims. One staff member concluded that she should not question the beliefs of religious women who felt that they had to forgive the assailant. To challenge these women was saying, "Hey listen you are wrong, and we are not listening to you either." When a center could not help a specific victim—for example, because of language difficulties—staff identified and contacted appropriate agencies.

Second, specifying the definition allows center staff to deliberate whether it communicates its understanding of sexual assault to the police, emergency room personnel, staff from other agencies, and the public. A center may discover that it is accepting others' definitions of sexual assault. If so, members may debate ways to effectively communicate and disseminate its knowledge of sexual assault. Breaking a definition into its components may suggest ways to systematically increase the public's knowledge of sexual violence, address its causes and prevention, and communicate how to help family or friends who are assaulted.

Third, knowledge of the center's client mix suggests what part of the community it is reaching and what part it is missing. Type of incident and client characteristics may be linked with service utilization to identify patterns that may improve program services and the understanding of different clients' needs. If a center does not hear from different types of victims, the reasons should be explored. Other community programs may work with the "missing" victims—for example, children. Alternatively, the center's services may be unknown, unacceptable, or inaccessible. Potential clients may assume that center's services are not intended for them or offer them nothing of value.

The North Carolina data was largely uninformative. Incidence data was not included in the database. The correlation between the percentage of nonwhite clients and the county's nonwhite population was so high, ($r^2 = .80$), that the accuracy of a center's racial data was suspect. The most striking finding was that combined domestic violence and sexual programs heard from relatively few teenagers. The finding suggested that domestic violence dominated these programs' identity to the extent that they did not serve other victims of sexual violence.

Interagency Cooperation

A rape crisis center benefits from contact with other agencies. A community with strong interagency networks best meets the needs of sexual assault victims. First, the networks operate as a referral system. With referrals from law enforcement, hospitals, schools, social services, and mental health agencies, a rape crisis center reaches clients that it might otherwise miss. Centers supplement their services by referring clients for follow-up services or information. Second, networks educate participants. Police officers, nurses, rape crisis center volunteers, and others may acquire knowledge that they later use to offer accurate information and effective support in the course of their private lives. Third, if rape crisis center advocates—that is, staff or volunteers—stay with victims at the hospital, they can monitor how rape victims are treated. The advocates are also observed. Ideally, these encounters lead the actors to appreciate each other's skills and consider ways of improving their performance. Fourth, interagency cooperation can result in joint undertakings leading to innovative strategies to prevent sexual assault and to provide stronger support services.

To gather information on a center's agency relationships, staff members can be asked to describe their relationships with the police, hospitals, and prosecutor's office. They should be asked about in-service training, referrals, and advocacy, and any joint activities. The answers establish a center's capacity to advocate against sexual violence and to inform and support persons affected by it. Relationships between a center and criminal justice agencies and hospitals are probably most common and most important. Among the North Carolina centers, cooperative arrangements ranged from handing out printed materials to requesting an advocate whenever a victim arrived at the hospital. Various interpretations can be drawn from the nature of the relationships. Obvious cooperative arrangements can legitimize a center (Koss and Harvey 1987, 63–64) and help victims easily access available services. Few requests do not necessarily denote ineffectiveness. Police and hospital personnel who seldom see advocates cannot assess if an advocate can make their jobs easier or case outcomes better. If new patrol officers or emergency room personnel do not receive an orientation to sexual assault, lack of referrals may reflect ignorance. The North Carolina centers with few advocates received few referrals, which may have been due to limited outreach or inconsistent availability. Centers that work closely with community agencies risk co-optation—that is, an agency's agenda becomes a center's agenda. For example, if a large proportion of clients file police reports, one may wonder if clients are being manipulated or if the center only hears from people with strong, prosecutable cases. Nevertheless, without relatively frequent contact, transferable knowledge, effective working relationships, new programs or approaches seem unlikely to occur.

Because relatively few sexual assaults are reported, other relationships may serve to inform and support reticent victims. School-center collaborations, reported in the North Carolina interviews, can play such a role. The collaborations included drafting a sexual assault protocol for a school district, having center staff hold office hours in middle schools and high schools, and developing and implementing rape prevention curriculum components. At the time of the interviews, centers were planning to contact immigrant groups to discuss their concerns about sexual violence.

To hear about interagency relationships is to learn how a center fits into its community and the community's capacity to respond to sexual assault. In conjunction with the client mix data the interviews, should disclose if community resources serve the full-range of men and women affected by sexual assault and document a center's involvement in the design and delivery of services.

Community Education

Centers may carry out community education to publicize their existence; reach sexual assault survivors, their families, and friends; prevent sexual assault; create ties with diverse communities, influence people whose lives may be affected by sexual assault, including future jurors; increase awareness of sexual assault as a community problem; educate citizens about how public institutions—for example, the criminal justice system—handle sexual assault. A center may promote a broad definition of sexual assault and confront existing attitudes about sexual violence, or it may do much less. It may only speak to community groups that request a speaker, or it may offer regular training to law enforcement and medical personnel, be part of a school district's curriculum, and seek out opportunities to present education programs to targeted audiences.

A center's message does not have to filter through an organization. A center may avoid a culture that defines sexual assault primarily as a criminal justice issue or as a mental health issue. A center can go beyond narrow definitions of the cause of sexual assault and examine how the power structure and gender relations contribute to sexual violence. A center does not have to compete with other agency units for resources nor argue that rape prevention education is consistent with its mission.

To learn about community education, staff can be asked to describe the center's community education program. They should be asked specifically about its objectives, the content of their presentation(s), where they make presentations, the frequency of their presentations, evidence of their effectiveness. In addition they should be asked about their participation in in-service training programs. The answers should establish whether a rape crisis center plays a central role in its community—that is, gathering, organizing, and disseminating information on sexual assault. The answers will also identify innovative approaches to community education that other programs may adapt.

ASSESSING, TRACKING, AND IMPROVING COMMUNITY IMPACT

Center staff can collect information on a center's definitions of sexual assault, its client mix, interorganizational relations, and community education (see Figure 12.1); write a report; and debate about how well the center is doing and how it can improve. The report tells a center's story. The descriptions of each element suggest the center's capacity to "broaden and enrich prevailing community knowledge, understandings, and beliefs and create new linkages with the outside world so that prevailing beliefs are regularly challenged." The data suggest the extent of a center's impact. Armed with this information, center staff can lay out a strategy to improve its impact. Nevertheless, having a report does not mean that it will have an impact. Staff, volunteers, and board members need to meet and critically review the report, discuss what it suggests about the center's effectiveness, and decide what actions they should take (see Preskill and Torres 1999, ch. 3–4). The reviewers may debate the following:

- How well is the center doing at reaching its goals?
- What is the center's impact on the community in respect to client services, interagency relations, and community education?
- What are the center's strengths and weaknesses? What factors seem to contribute to these strengths and weakness? Is additional information needed to confirm the strengths and weaknesses or their causes?
- What should the center do during the next year to improve its services or impact on the community?

The staff should consider producing the report annually and tracking changes. The client mix, referrals from agencies, requests for advocates, number of in-service and community education programs can be monitored from

Figure 12.1 Elements to Include in Community-Focused Evaluation of Rape Crisis Centers.

Definition of Sexual Assault, including its causes and appropriate responses.

- **Purpose:** Establishes what a center is trying to do; implies why it hears from some populations and not others; suggests the effectiveness of its education efforts.

- **Data:** Gives qualitative information on what constitutes sexual assault, its causes, and appropriate responses (including rape prevention). Data obtained through a review of a center's publications and staff interviews.

- **Analysis:** Organizes information to determine the consistency between the center's definition, its client mix, and its in-service training and education programs.

Client Mix

- **Purpose:** Establishes whom a center hears from and from whom it does not; identifies variations in service utilization that may suggest a need to investigate the service's accessibility, availability, or acceptability.

- **Data:** For each client record: type of assault, demographics (age, ethnic or racial identity, gender), and services used.

- **Analysis:** Organizes information to include (1) frequencies for types of assaults, client characteristics, and services; (2) relationship between (a) types of assaults reported ad client characteristics, (b) types of assaults reported and services utilized, (c) client characteristics and services utilized.

Interagency Cooperation

- **Purposes:** Establishes extent of center's community coverage—that is, receiving and making appropriate referrals and exchanges of information; provides opportunities to observe, monitor, and learn from other agencies; encourages creation of innovative projects; implies center's legitimacy.

- **Data:** For each referral or request related to sexual assault, records nature of the referral or request and the agency involved; for in-service training, records the agency(ies) involved, the content of the presentation, the number of trainees and their job responsibilities, how trainees evaluate the training; identifies existing protocols and evidence that they are used; describes interagency undertakings and their outcomes.

- **Analysis:** Organizes information to indicate (1) frequencies of requests for advocates, referrals, or information by agency; (2) frequencies of center referrals or requests for information by agency; (3) content of in-service training and data on trainees and their evaluation of the training; (4) interagency activities, the participants, and the outcomes.

Community Education

- **Purpose:** Establishes what a center is doing to affect community knowledge, attitudes, and behaviors.

- **Data:** Identifies objectives of the community education program and content of presentations; for each presentation, records type of presentation, sponsor, size of audience, audience feedback.

- **Analysis:** Organizes information to determine consistency between community education objectives, program content; provides frequencies on types of presentations; relationship between type of presentation and audience size, audience feedback; relationship between sponsor and audience feedback.

year to year. Over time the center will develop a picture of demands for its services and whether program changes affect the level of demand. The annual report should track plans made the year before: What is the current status of each plan? If a plan has been implemented, how well does the implementation process work? What outcomes have been achieved thus far? Each year the stakeholders should meet, assess what has changed during the year, and decide what should be done in the coming year.

A logical next step is to get a complete picture of a community's capacity to respond to sexual assault. A center or advocacy group may start by identifying the agencies serving "missing" client populations or conducting "missing" activities. If possible, each agency's definition of sexual assault should be determined. How much more information to collect depends on the purpose of the expanded study and the available resources. The most expansive effort would adapt Figure 12.1 and conduct separate studies of selected community organizations, including criminal justice agencies and hospitals. A report may be written with separate case studies for each agency and summary sections (1) describing links between agencies, (2) identifying gaps and redundancies in community services, and (3) determining if existing services are comprehensive and integrated. Readers may infer if a rape crisis center has a vital role in a community's anti-rape response and identify opportunities to improve its response. Furthermore, readers may identify ways to improve services in their own agency or community.

The reports can also facilitate strategic planning. Advocacy groups or centers may use the information to set priorities. Advocacy groups may identify and endorse "model programs" or "model communities." They may find gaps in services and develop and promote a policy recommendation. A center may use the information to debate whether its impact will be greater if it adds, expands, alters, or drops an activity. To decide requires knowledge of the center's strengths and weaknesses and information on the availability and extent of alternative services (Allison and Kaye 1997). A center's strengths and weaknesses can be inferred from the original report. An expanded report should contain information on alternative services. Centers may expand or add a service that is consistent with their strengths and not available locally. If an alternate service is noticeably stronger, the center may drop its service and rely on the other agency. Nevertheless, a center may rely on another agency only if they share a compatible definition of sexual assault.

Knowing that a community has the capacity to respond effectively to sexual assault does not confirm that it does respond effectively. Neither the descriptions nor the data indicate that clients were helped, that trainees were competent and empathetic, or that audiences understood and could use what they learned. To demonstrate effectiveness, staff can undertake a program evaluation. At the meeting to review the original report, participants may decide whether and when to conduct an evaluation. An evaluation should only be done if it can answer questions that staff need answered, and if the staff plans to use the answers to make program changes (Wholey 1994).

Although conducting an evaluation may require the assistance of a social scientist, the staff determines its design. Staff may find that the process of designing evaluation encourages them to think about what they are doing, how they are doing it, and why. Consider in-service training. Staff members may want evidence that their training is worthwhile. They may start by describing the components of each activity (Scheirer 1994). They may specify the characteristics of intended trainees, recruitment and selection methods, characteristics of trainers, and training materials and activities. For each component, reviewers might ask, "Why is this component important to program success?" Staff may indicate the outcomes they expect for an activity. Before measuring the outcomes of inservice training, the staff should agree whether they expect it to affect trainees' definitions of sexual assault, knowledge of agency protocols, or ability to conduct empathetic interviews. As part of the discussions, staff may reflect on the components and make sure that materials and training activities are consistent with the desired outcomes.

Program evaluations focus on activities and outcomes; yet unanticipated and valuable impacts of rape crisis centers occur apart from planned activities. Interagency cooperation may be critical to a center's influence and community change. Staff representing different organizations may influence each other, encourage changes in organizational practices, undertake joint projects, and create innovative approaches to victim services and rape prevention. The relationships identified in a report can be examined in depth, yielding information on the factors that facilitate or impede cooperation and the effects of cooperation on the participants and their agencies. An important outcome is the one least directly traceable to a rape crisis center—that is, a public that does not judge sexual assault victims, that recognizes and works against the social forces that cause sexual violence, and that knows how to support friends and family affected by sexual assault. Researchers may determine whether community members are aware of sexual assault, its causes, and its consequences and whether their awareness varies by center or community characteristics.

CONCLUSIONS

The purpose of this chapter is to restore the reputation of rape crisis centers as community change agents. Examining centers' definitions of rape, interagency relations, and community education efforts should counter the perception that they are just another social service agency. Nevertheless, similar to other social service agencies, rape crisis centers need to demonstrate that their efforts yield results. The results of specific activities can be measured and counted. Marked social or policy changes are neither easily attained nor easily measured. A way around this limitation is to focus on a center's role in its community. A center should be judged on the basis of its ability to develop and disseminate new knowledge about sexual assault, to monitor agency practices, and to facilitate interagency relations. Strong relationships with community agencies should establish sexual assault as a community issue, not just the concern of a single agency. Reviewing what a center does in its community is in itself valuable; it forces center staff, volunteers, and board members to focus on what the center is doing and whether its influence affects an entire community or just a small group within it.

REFERENCES

Allison, M., and J. Kaye. 1997. *Strategic Planning for Nonprofit Organizations: A Practical Guide and Workbook*. New York: John Wiley and Sons.

Attkisson, C.C., and A. Broskowski. 1978. Evaluation and the emerging human service concept. In *Evaluation of Human Services*, edited by C.C. Attkisson, et al. New York: Academic Press.

Blomberg, T.G. 1989. An assessment of victim service needs. *Evaluation Review* 13: 598–627.

Bourque, S. 1992. *Defining Rape*. Durham: Duke University Press.

Byington, D.B. 1991. Organizational affiliation and effectiveness: The case of rape crisis centers. *Administration in Social Work* 15: 83–103.

Campbell, R. and C.R. Johnson. 1997. Police officers perceptions of rape: Is there consistency between state law and individual beliefs? *Journal of Interpersonal Violence* 12: 255–274.

Carrow, D.M. 1980. *Rape: Guidelines for a Community Response*. Washington, DC: U.S. Department of Justice, Law Enforcement Assistance Administration.

Child, J., and D. Faulkner. 1998. *Strategies of Co-operation: Managing Alliances, Networks, and Joint Ventures*. New York: Oxford University Press.

Collins, B.G., and M.B. Whalen. 1989. The rape crisis movement: Radical or reformist? *Social Work:* 61–63.

Donat, P.L.N., and J. D'Emillio. 1992. A feminist redefinition of rape and sexual assault: Historical foundations and change. *Journal of Social Issues* 48: 9–22.

Fischer, G.J. 1987. Hispanic and majority student attitudes toward forcible date rape as a function of differences in attitudes toward women. *Sex Roles* 17: 93–101.

Gornick, J., M.R. Burt, and K.J. Pittman. 1985. Structure and activities of rape crisis centers in the early 1980s. *Crime and Delinquency* 31: 247–268.

Gornick, J., and D.S. Meyer. 1998. Changing political opportunity: The anti-rape movement. *Journal of Policy History* 10: 367–398.

Gutierrez, L.M. 1992. Empowering ethnic minorities in the twenty-first century: The role of human service organizations. In *Human Services as Complex Organizations*, pp. 320–338, edited by Y. Hassenfeld. Newbury Park: Sage Publications.

Koss, M.P. 1988. Hidden rape: Sexual aggresson and victimization in a national sample of students in higher education. In *Rape and Sexual Assault II*, edited by A.W. Burgess. New York: Garland Publishing.

Koss, M. and M. Harvey. 1987. *The Rape Victim: Clinical and Community Approaches to Treatment*. Lexington: The Stephen Green Press.

Matthews, N. A. 1994. *Confronting Rape: The Feminist Anti-Rape Movement and the State*. New York: Routledge.

O'Sullivan, E. and A. Carlton. Forthcoming 2001. Victim services, community outreach, and contemporary rape crisis centers: A comparison of independent and multi-service centers. *Journal of Interpersonal Violence*.

Preskill, H., and R.T. Torres. 1999. *Evaluative Inquiry for Learning in Organizations*. Thousand Oaks, CA: Sage Publications.

Rennison, C.M. 1999. *Criminal victimization 1998: Changes 1997–98 with Trends 1993–98*. U.S. Department of Justice, Office of Justice Programs, NCJ 176353.

Scheirer, M.A. 1994. Designing and using process evaluation. In *Handbook of Practical Program Evaluation*, pp. 40–68, edited by J.S. Wholey, H.P. Hatry, and K.E. Newcomer. San Francisco: Jossey-Bass Publishers.

Sorenson, S.B., and J.M. Siegel. 1998. Gender, ethnicity, and sexual assault: Findings from a Los Angeles Study. *Journal of Social Issues* 48: 93–104. Reprinted in *Confronting Rape and Sexual Assault*, edited by M.E. Odem and J. Clay-Warner, pp. 211–222. Wilmington: Scholarly Resources, Inc. Worlds of Women #3.

Stelmachers, Z.T. 1980. Evaluations of victim services: Is enough being done? *Evaluation and Change* Special Issue: 127–130.

Wholey, J.S. 1994. Assessing the feasibility and likely usefulness of evaluation. In *Handbook of Practical Program Evaluation*, pp. 15–39, edited by J.S. Wholey, H.P. Hatry, and K.E. Newcomer. San Francisco: Jossey-Bass Publishers.

Williams, J.E. and K.A. Holmes. 1981. *The Second Assault*. Westport, CT: Greenwood Press.

13

Megan's Law in California: The CD-ROM and the Changing Nature of Crime Control

Suzette Cote

INTRODUCTION

In the 1990s, state legislatures and the federal government enacted legislation directed at protecting the wider community from one of society's most hated criminals—the sex offender. These crime policies that deal with habitual, violent sex offenders reflect an increased use of risk management techniques and actuarial principles to assess levels of risk, dangerousness, and future harm that these offenders pose to specific vulnerable groups and to society in general. The manner in which sex offenders are classified invokes notions of risk. Current legislative practices and trends suggest that risk has become the primary organizing principle of crime control strategies today, as evidenced by various sex crimes and the vehement reactions by the public to them. In other words, the shift that has occurred in penal law and in the criminal justice system involves classifying these types of individuals not based on what they have done but what they might do.

California's law concerning sex offenders provides an effective example of the manner in which women and other vulnerable groups within communities have taken control over some of the risks that these dangerous sex offenders pose to them. In September 1996, the California Legislature passed Assembly Bill No. 1562, sponsored by former Attorney General Daniel Lundgren and then signed into law by former Governor Pete Wilson (California Department of Justice [DOJ] 1998). California's Megan's Law enables law enforcement to notify law-abiding citizens of "serious" or "high-risk" sex offenders who reside in, are employed in, or frequent communities throughout California (California DOJ 1998).

In addition, the law requires the California Department of Justice to develop a CD-ROM containing information about "serious" and "high-risk" sex offenders (California DOJ). Access to the CD-ROM is available by the public at all sheriff's departments and many police departments, as well as through the California DOJ. California's Megan's Law also developed and expanded a 900 Line, which provides information to the public regarding offenders who have been convicted of sex crimes against adults and children (California DOJ 1998). California represents a unique example of this penological transformation primarily because it is the only state in the nation to report the use of a CD-ROM that makes this information available to the public.

This chapter examines the nature of this philosophical and pragmatic shift within the criminal justice system and its policies by looking specifically at the current technologies used in the implementation of Megan's Law in California. After a brief discussion of the background of Megan's Law, I describe the general shift in crime control policies from open to hidden forms of social control in terms of a theoretical analysis of the changing dimensions of time, space, trust, and empowerment within modern communities. Second, I focus exclusively on California's Megan's Law, by discussing the history of sex offender registration and notification in California and the development, nature, and use of the CD-ROM and 900 Line as tools for dissemination. I conclude this analysis by contending that California's law commences an important legislative transformation toward the increased use of technology within and by members of communities in the effort to combat increased levels of risk among dangerous offenders.

BACKGROUND OF MEGAN'S LAW

Although this past decade has witnessed a flurry of legislative activity concerning sex offenders, laws mandating registration of sex offenders have been on the books for more than five decades. California created the nation's first sex offender registry in 1947 (Pearson and Cooper 1998). In October 1994, the New Jersey legislature enacted the first Megan's Law in reaction to the sexual assault and murder of seven-year-old Megan Kanka, for whom the law was named. Megan's death came at the hands of a twice convicted sex offender, who received the death penalty in a May 1997 trial. Within two years, all jurisdictions within the United States had enacted some version of Megan's Law (Cote 2000).

In 1994, Congress enacted the Jacob Wetterling Crimes Against Children and Sexually Violent Offenders Act as an element of that year's omnibus Violent Crime Control and Law Enforcement Act (Pub. L. 103–322, 42 U.S.C. § 14071[1994]).

Since its inception, the Jacob Wetterling Act has been amended several times. The first amendment in 1996 involved the creation of a national Megan's Law, which requires states to allow public access to sex offender registry information (Pub. L. 104–145, 42 U.S.C. § 14071(d) [1996]).[1] Megan's Law mandates that convicted sex offenders register with their local law enforcement agencies just prior to parole, probation, or release from prison.

Forty-four states have notification provisions in effect that authorize local law enforcement agencies to notify the general public, vulnerable groups and individuals, and/or to provide access to registration information. This legislation received an overwhelmingly supportive response by the public, legislatures, and the judiciary as well. Despite numerous legal challenges to the sexual predator laws and Megan's Laws, a vast majority of the provisions of the statutes have been upheld as constitutional (Cote 2000).

The widespread availability of this information to the public suggests that the California Legislature and other state legislatures are more concerned than ever with protecting vulnerable populations from the risks that sex offenders pose. The notification methods employed by California and a variety of states are significant in several ways. Primarily, the methods used today by law enforcement agencies reflect the importance of technology at this stage of late modernity.[2] Second, the increased reliance on technology to disclose information to the public promotes notions of empowerment and trust throughout the communities. Not only do communities have general access to this information, but also they have access to it quickly over a broad geographical area. Consequently, current technologies allow law enforcement agencies to displace the notion of geographic place in relation to time and space. In other words, it is not necessarily exactly *where* the information gets placed but *how* it gets disseminated and *whom* it reaches that become important today.

THEORETICAL SCOPE OF THE PROBLEM: THE SHIFT TO HIDDEN CONTROLS

The language of the sex offender laws suggests that state legislatures aim to manage risk through the control over time, space, and knowledge with the primary objective of protecting the community of potential victims. These issues of time, space, and knowledge within the context of risk, trust, and empowerment play an important part in an evolving area of criminal and penal law as it applies to sex offenders (Giddens 1991). More specifically, they reflect the manner in which social control strategies have shifted from open to hidden systems of control and the way in which these controls have been dispersed through the individual sex offender and the community of potential victims.

The contemporary sex offender laws contain several common characteristics that distinguish themselves from sex offender legislation enacted earlier this century and indicate a recent shift toward risk management policies. These factors embody the themes of risk, trust, and empowerment that form Anthony Giddens' (1991) theory of modernity. The following points highlight the most significant characteristics of Megan's Law as they currently exist:

1. The primary intent behind the laws involves protecting a community of potential victims. The scope of the laws' intent reveals not only ideological changes in the criminal justice system, but changes in the public's attitude toward this new breed of sex offender.

2. All of the laws construct the sex offender as a subject possessing numerous factors of risk. Expert committees later use these risk factors to make determinations regarding risk level assessments and classifications, which are used mainly for the purpose of assigning the released sex offender to an appropriate risk level for notification purposes.

3. The laws do not aim to change sex offenders through the use of traditional disciplinary tools. Rather, the laws manage sex offenders through the control of time, space, and knowledge via discourse. In addition, the Megan's Laws transform common assumptions about "space." By empowering victims with information, some sex offenders are managed within and by the "space" of knowledge itself (Cote 2000).

According to Giddens (1991), notions of time and space concern the manner in which mechanisms of social control have become hidden, or altered in their relationship to a specific place or domain of discipline. In a pre-modern era, the elements of time and space were connected to a specific place and a singular point in time. In contrast, modern social organizations and relationships presume a "lifting out of time and space" where the control over certain individuals does not necessarily have to be solely connected to a particular place or institution. In other words, this *displacement* of time and space through hidden forms of social control, such as electronic monitoring and video surveillance, refer to what Giddens calls "disembedding mechanisms."

These forms of technology have the effect of removing notions of place and distance and replacing it with invisible, yet powerful, forms of social control. As Giddens (1991) maintains "[m]odern social organisation presumes the precise coordination of the actions of many human beings physically absent from one another; the 'when' of these actions is directly connected to the 'where,' but not, as in pre-modern epochs, via the mediation of place" (Giddens 1991, 17). This notion of disembedding mechanisms relates directly to the issue of risk: risk, or the control of risk, does not have to be grounded in a particular place. Rather, risks consist of a variety of complex factors that flow throughout societies and across boundaries.

The notion of "lifting out of time and space" refers to the additional factors of trust and empowerment in Giddens' (1991) theory. Like risk, trust and empowerment also involve the issue of control and the manner in which control is dispersed throughout the community and address the concerns and interests of the wider community rather than the individual offender.

Time and Space

"Their stock and trade is anonymity. [The registration and notification requirement] takes their anonymity away" (Faulkner 1997, page 2, article 1).

These laws represent this shift in control strategies on two different levels. The first level concerns the issue of time and space. The notion that certain forms of control have become hidden suggests that traditional notions of the way in which we conceptualize and define time and space have changed. In pre-modern societies, time and space were linked through identification of place (Giddens 1991). In terms of social control, this place consisted of a prison, a mental institution, or a jail. Correctional officials ordered space via classification and assignment into a particular wing of the prison. A judge and then later correctional officials ordered time not only by the length of one's sentence but by how long a person could spend doing certain activities, such as showering, eating, and participating in recreational activities.

Although the ordering of time and space within the prison continues to flourish today, hidden forms of control—inside and outside of the prison—*dis-place* these notions of time and space in terms of their relationship to place. In other words, the control of criminal offenders does not have to be solely oriented to a particular place such as the prison. Today's modern crime control strategies can monitor, manage, regulate, and calculate from afar. For example, with the use of electronic monitors, law enforcement and parole officers can monitor the behaviors and movements of parolees from their agencies. Video surveillance cameras transmit images of inmates in various wings spread out over the grounds of a prison, allowing correctional officers to monitor all the inmates' behavior at the same time, from one or two control stations. These disembedding mechanisms—"the lifting out of social relations"—have removed the notion of place and distance from the equation altogether via "the tremendous acceleration in time-space distanciation which modernity introduces" (Giddens 1991, 28).

The registration and notification laws provide an excellent example of this disembedding process and the shift towards hidden systems of crime control. By requiring sex offenders to register with their local law enforcement agencies and provide these agencies with identification information, the police can monitor, or manage, these offenders from their departments without having to go directly to a sex offender's home unless necessary. Furthermore, the notification laws disperse the locus of control throughout the community, thereby further dismantling the wall that defines the *space* of control. By removing the active use of technological surveillance devices, the sex offenders become controlled by knowledge and discourse. In other words, although no one is directly watching them or tracking them through the use of an electronic device, they are monitored by the dissemination of information into the wider community.

Therefore, controlling risk through the dissemination of knowledge removes the need for the focus of control to be on the sex offender. Indirectly, the sex offender remains the center of these controls; all the disseminated information concerns the sex offender. But, what has changed is not only the nature of the control—control through the spread of discourse, or knowledge—but the central focus of that control—risk.

Trust and Empowerment

"The main message behind [the creation of an online sex offender registration database] is power"[3] (Faulkner 1997, page 2, article 1).

This dispersal of knowledge into the community comprises the second level of this shift in crime control strategies. More specifically, notification—the dispersal of sex offender information—concerns two important issues of control: trust and empowerment. Like risk, these issues do not concern the sex offender. Rather, with modern crime control policies, these issues have become of primary importance to the wider community.

The notion of trust concerns a community putting its faith in crime control policies and systems of justice; trust requires believing that these policies will work and will protect them from harm. This type of trust extends beyond merely reflecting on policies of the past and then determining whether a certain policy will be effective in the present or the future. Confidence of this kind in policymaking and in politicians is not enough to define a trust interrelationship. Instead, trust involves the community placing its faith in particular crime control policies and legal systems and having the belief that these policies will be effective in preventing crime and protecting them from harm.

The need to trust policymakers and criminal justice officials becomes more significant when we consider that the public does not truly know how the experts make their decisions regarding sex offender notification risk levels, guidelines, and who's committed or released. The public may have the information—the end result of the decision-making process—but the nature of the process still remains (intentionally) elusive to most of the general public. Therefore, they possess that driving need to trust that the experts will "do the right thing" and protect them from these risks.

Criminal justice officials gain the trust of the public through the process of empowerment. In a sense, trust and empowerment work together in a relationship of reciprocity: Through empowerment, the public can trust the criminal justice officials, and by gaining the public's trust, criminal justice officials can allow their cryptic walls to break down and then empower the community with knowledge. To illustrate, by providing the public sex offender information either directly or by making it available for access at a law enforcement agency, criminal justice officials empower community members and give them a sense of control over the risks that threaten their safety, well-being, and sense of order.

In this way, the notification process works to counteract the effects of high modernity on society. These "effects of high modernity" are frequently reflected in the moral panic that surrounded the violent sex crimes of the 1990s. With increased risks, an elevated level of awareness of these risks due to the media and other forms of technology, and the hidden nature of social control systems, the public frequently feels as though they have no control over their own lives and the risks they confront on a daily basis. A lack of understanding regarding expert systems and the presence of risks create a ripe environment for social anxieties. With access to sex offender information, the public regains that control that had been lost through the accumulation of risks. By having access to sex offender information through the notification process, individuals in risk-threatened communities become empowered and regain some control that had been lost due to an increasingly high presence of risk.

In contrast to those who believe that human agents passively accept the circumstances that are shaped for them by larger social institutions, a majority of people do react against social conditions that impact their daily lives and render them feeling helpless and out of control. The sex offender notification process suggests that the public may be taking control of some of the risks they confront daily and may be able to break down that once impenetrable wall of bureaucratic institutions to gain that control. As Giddens (1991) aptly notes, "[m]odern social life impoverishes individual action, yet furthers the appropriation of new possibilities; it is alienating, yet at the same time, characteristically, human beings react against social circumstances which they find oppressive" (Giddens 1991, 176).

In terms of modern crime control strategies, expert systems may be less visible than they have been in the past. Yet, the gap between public and professional discourse regarding sex offenders is slowly narrowing as a result of these notification laws. By becoming empowered with and through knowledge, the public can make a more knowledgeable assessment of the problem violent sex offenders, penetrate that barrier of institutional expertise, and adjust their lives accordingly. For instance, as I discuss next, the California Attorney General's office provides the public with open access to information about sex offenders. Consequently, risk management no longer becomes solely the job of criminal justice officials; risk management entails a community-wide effort because risk disperses itself throughout the community.

MEGAN'S LAW IN CALIFORNIA

California has made extensive use of Internet technology and other electronic media resources both within and outside the jurisdiction of law enforcement agencies. In general, the local law enforcement agency remains the primary facilitator and distributor of information about registered sex offenders. In terms of access to information, the California DOJ operates a 900 Number that members of the public can call to inquire whether a named individual is listed. The department also provides a CD-ROM or other electronic medium containing basic identifying information about the sex offender including, but not limited to, the offender's name, physical description, and criminal history (*California Penal Code*, sec. 290 [1999]).

900 Line—The Sex Offender Identification Line (SOIL)

California made impressive strides in terms of its use of technology in the dissemination process. On July 3, 1995, California established the nation's very first telephone service for sex offender identification purposes. The Child Molester Identification Line, as it was known at the time, used a fee-based 900 line and provided information to adults regarding convicted child molesters. Following the passage of the national version of Megan's Law in December 1996, California renamed the 900 line the Sex Offender Identification Line (SOIL) to illustrate the expanded inclusion of sex offenders who have committed sex crimes against adults (California DOJ 1998).

Interested adults may contact the SOIL at 1–900–463–0400 (California DOJ 1998). The service charges the caller a $10 fee, and the caller is allowed to inquire about up to two individuals (Office of the Attorney General n.d.). The state mandates the following:

- Callers must be at least 18 years of age.
- Callers must provide their name, the county from which they are calling, the reason for the inquiry, and the number of people at risk;
- Callers must provide the name of the individual on whom the caller is checking;
- Callers must provide the individual's exact street address; or exact date of birth; or California driver's license, personal identification number, or Social Security number.
- If the caller only knows the subject's name, s/he will need to provide a description of the subject, including at least five of the following characteristics: eye color, hair color, height, weight, race, and/or scars, marks, or tattoos (Office of the Attorney General, n.d.; California DOJ 1998; Pearson and Cooper 1998).

Specially trained Department of Justice employees use this information to search the SOIL database. A SOIL "hit" happens when the information given by the caller matches information about a person listed in the SOIL database. Once a "hit" has been made, the DOJ employee informs the caller of the subject's status as either a "high-risk" or "serious" convicted sex offender (California DOJ 1998).

Organizations, businesses, and individuals wishing to check on six or more persons, such as volunteers or employees, may submit a Mail-In Request Form with a $4 processing fee (California DOJ 1998; Office of the Attorney General n.d.). The form must include the name of the organization or individual, telephone number, a contact person, number of people at risk, and information concerning the individual to be checked. The service provides the information within one week of the request. The service will accept calls to the 900 line and mail-in requests from California residents only (California DOJ 1998).

The California DOJ, Bureau of Criminal Information and Analysis (BCIA) maintains the SOIL. According to the National Criminal Justice Association's (NCJA) *Policy and Practice* report, California officials have expressed satisfaction with the effectiveness of the SOIL (Pearson and Cooper 1998).[4] As of April 1998, the SOIL had received 13,319 telephoned inquiries since it became active in July 1995 (Pearson and Cooper 1998). According to Randy Rossi, assistant chief of the BCIA at the time of the report,[5] there has been "'virtually no vigilante activity,' with fewer than 10 acts of vigilantism out of approximately 60,000 fax, mail, and telephone disclosures since 1995" (Pearson and Cooper 1998, 3).

The BCIA also has the responsibility of analyzing the relationships between the callers to the serious sex offenders about whom they search for information. According to the NCJA *Policy and Practice* report, data compiled by the BCIA's Investigative Services Program (ISP) show that during the SOIL's second year of operation, persons looking for information had the following relationships to the serious sex offenders about whom they inquired (Pearson and Cooper 1998).

- 25 percent were neighbors, tenant, or landlords.
- 22 percent were friends or acquaintances.
- 20 percent were employers or employees.
- 19 percent were family members.
- 9 percent were victims or victims' family members.
- 5 percent were affiliated with faith institutions or had miscellaneous relationships that did not fall into the above categories.

Overall, the SOIL has been "very well received" by the public, and the demand for mailed requests actually exceeds that of telephone inquiries. For instance, in April 1998, a total of 2,300 inquiries were made—400 by telephone and 1,900 by mail (Pearson and Cooper 1998).

California's Registered Sex Offenders: Megan's Law CD-ROM

Currently, California is the only state in the nation to distribute CD-ROMs to state and local law enforcement agencies in order to enable interested citizens to look at information about convicted sex offenders in their communities (Pearson and Cooper 1998; Adams 1999).[6] The use of CD-ROMs may give state and local law enforcement agencies more control over sex offender registry information by establishing safeguards in order to discourage illegal or inappropriate distribution. Both California and Tennessee have taken steps toward this end by restricting who may access information. To ensure that appropriate access and dissemination ensues, the states have done the following:

- Requiring the state to provide quarterly updates on the CD-ROM to designated state and local law enforcement agencies;
- Encouraging law enforcement agencies to limit the disclosure of CD-ROM information to those individuals who can express a purpose or a need for the information, are in possession of a state driver's license or identification card, are over age 18,[7] and are willing to sign a statement indicating they understand that the purpose of releasing the information is to enhance public safety and it is unlawful to use the information to engage in illegal discrimination or harassment of registered offenders;
- Maintaining confidentiality of information about the victim;
- Restricting to law enforcement agencies the records of citizens requesting to view the CD-ROM (Pearson and Cooper 1998).

On July 1, 1997, the California DOJ released the CD-ROM, which provides the following information about registered convicted sex offenders in California:

- Registrant's name and aliases, if any
- Photograph, if available
- Gender
- Physical description
- Registered sex offenses
- County of residence and Zip code (Pearson and Cooper 1998)

As of October 1, 1997, 64,580 offenders were defined as "serious" sex offenders; of these, 1,640 were designated as "high risk" (California DOJ 1998, 22). The April 1998 version of the CD-ROM contains information on approximately 65,700 registered sex offenders in the state (Pearson and Cooper 1998). The 1997 report stated that there were 213 Megan's Law CD-ROM public viewing sites under the supervision of 145 local law enforcement agencies. More than 24,000 had viewed the CD-ROM during the first year of implementation, with approximately 12 percent of those who viewed the CD-ROM recognizing individuals listed on the CD-ROM (California DOJ 1998).

A variety of factors led to California's decision to develop and use CD-ROM technology for notification purposes (Pearson and Cooper 1998).[8] A primary factor suggests that the CD-ROM provides the state more control over the information that is eventually disseminated. According to then-Attorney General Dan Lundgren's office, the CD-ROM satisfies the legislative intent behind Megan's Law by providing information to local citizens who could be at risk (Pearson and Cooper 1998). Making the information broadly available over the Internet increases the opportunity for misuse by making it globally available. Furthermore, policymakers and the DOJ expressed concern over the fact that additional public media, who have the responsibility of disseminating information, may be tampered with by computer hackers. To combat this potential problem before it even occurred, the state opted for the CD-ROM because it is an appropriate and easy way to allow public access to the registry information.

Policymakers and the DOJ also expressed concern with the cost of developing and implementing the CD-ROM. The DOJ and other state agencies have worked closely with local law enforcement officials to ensure that they are able to use it properly. Although the law requires the DOJ to update the CD-ROM on a quarterly basis, the CD-ROM has been updated six (6) times as of April 1998 (Pearson and Cooper 1998).[9] In addition, the California Commission on Peace Officer Standards and Training (CPOST) has made training and a videocassette available to local law enforcement agencies to guide their use of the CD-ROM and implementation of Megan's Law provisions.

Although numerous opponents of this technology expressed concern over the accuracy of the information contained on the CD-ROM, the DOJ has taken steps to ensure that only the most accurate and appropriate information is included on the CD-ROM. For example, opponents asserted that since California began its sex offender registry in 1947, individuals convicted of consensual sodomy that do not warrant registration today might be included on the CD-ROM. However, several years ago, DOJ officials reviewed the registry records and deleted the files of deceased offenders and those offenders convicted of crimes that no longer mandate registration (Pearson and Cooper 1998).[10]

Independent Web Sites

Several organizations have established their own Web sites independent of local law enforcement. For example, as a result of Polly Klaas' disappearance and murder in Petaluma, California, in October 1993, the girl's father, Marc Klaas, established the Klaas Foundation for Children, which is dedicated to the memory of Polly Klaas. The Foundation's purpose is to inform parents, children, and communities about how to prevent crimes against children. In general, the Foundation strives to promote nationwide parental awareness and child safety information, to provide communities with proactive steps for creating safer neighborhoods, and to educate the public on the necessity for establishing uniform laws to punish and monitor criminals who target children.[11]

Another Web site in California, www.sexoffenders.net, which is maintained by the organization CrimeFight USA, provides information about the sex offenders' names, Zip codes, and criminal histories that can be found on the CD-ROM. The organization accesses the CD-ROM by visiting local policing agencies and copying the information (Pearson and Cooper 1998). The Web site includes the names, crimes, and birth dates of sex offenders only if they are listed as "high risk." Other information includes how many sex offenders live in each city and the number of those considered serious ("Megan's Law Taken On-Line" 2000).

When the Web site was launched in August 1997, the American Civil Liberties Union and the Attorney General's Office initially opposed the decision to publish the information about sex offenders. The Attorney General's Office contended that sex offenders may use the site to network with each other. The ACLU worried about the privacy issue of releasing names and potential inaccuracies of the data being disseminated. Child advocacy groups also had mixed feelings about that Web site. Marc Klaas, president of the Klaas Foundation for Children, stated that although he did not have a problem with the site, he added that people concerned about vigilantism might be troubled by it ("Megan's Law Taken On-Line" 2000).

Despite its initial opposition to the Web site, in November 1997, then-state Attorney General Dan Lundgren concluded that the Web site did not violate the state Penal Code. He added that the site's organizers could legally collect and disseminate the information as well as garner volunteer assistance with the distribution of the information (Pearson and Cooper 1998).

"CYBER"-SPACE: THE FUTURE OF CRIME CONTROL

Use of the Internet, or cyberspace, takes the issue of sexual assault and sexual abuse prevention to a higher level in which the locus of control is truly dispersed throughout an alternative medium of space. Traditional modes of registration and notification remain in place; the visibility of these strategies makes known the communal effort toward order and control. *Place* may only gain importance for the purposes of specifying where meetings should be held and where press releases, newspapers, and other mailings should be sent. The sex offender knows that he or she is being controlled because of this open forum of notification.

However, the new technologies of late modernity displace the notion of place and replace it with pure discourse. The growth in Internet technology, CD-ROMs, and other electronic media in California and around the country contain no semblance of a definitive "place," or even "space" for that matter. Both criminal justice officials and the public need to take an accounting of these various changes in crime control strategies as examples of risk management.

Primarily, these novel "technologies" of control signal a change not only in the focus of crime control but the manner in which it is carried out.

Advantages and Disadvantages of Technology

Contemporary notification methods mainly emphasize the hidden nature of crime control strategies. For instance, agencies in at least sixteen states have posted information from their sex offender registries on the World Wide Web (WWW) (NCJA 1999).[12] There are a variety of advantages and disadvantages to placing sex offender registry information on the Internet. Table 13.1 describes some of the advantages and disadvantages of the use of technology in states' notification strategies (Pearson and Cooper 1998).

Many states contend that one important reason for disseminating sex offender information via the Web is "to control its unofficial distribution and to deter citizens from distributing information on their own" (NCJA 1999, 12). For example, in New York, the establishment of the parents' group Web site has apparently collided with the precautions undertaken by the notification requirements of Megan's Law (Warner 2000). However, many state officials recognize that, despite the efforts to control unofficial dissemination of registration information, concerned members of the community will take it upon themselves to disclose this information out of what they feel is necessity.

Table 13.1 Advantages and Disadvantages of Technology in States' Notification Strategies		
Technology	**Advantages**	**Disadvantages**
800/900 Lines	Accessible from any phone.	May require the public to pay a fee to use the service.
	Easy to use.	Does not provide photos or a "wildcard" search option-- a search of the database using incomplete search terms or missing data.
	Precise subject information needed from caller to prevent false identification.	Need for precise information from caller may prevent him/her from learning about an offender in the community.
World Wide Web/Internet Pages	Broad information dissemination.	Access available beyond affected community; concern regarding hackers contaminating the data.
CD-ROMs	Control over who views the information is maintained by local law enforcement.	Citizen must take the initiative to go to a local law enforcement agency to view the information.
	Updating records is relatively inexpensive.	May be unable to update information as frequently as other media.

Due to these technological advances, crime control strategies have the capability of shifting toward risk management because the technologies themselves are really knowledge banks of identifiers called *information*. But this information remains powerless without the public's action upon it. The existence of the information has the capability of providing the public with power to take control over this risk, but they do not become truly *empowered* by it until they use it. Therefore, the risk management process does not become fully complete, nor successful, until the communities, in conjunction with their local law enforcement agencies, make use of these crime control strategies.

Criticisms of Technology

Despite overwhelming support from law enforcement agencies and the public, the legislation and the widespread use of technology have been met with some criticism. Main concerns include the global nature of information posted on the Web, the potential for data corruption, increased "networking" or pornography trading by sex offenders, and potential liability for state and local officials, if they unwittingly provide inaccurate information via technological mechanisms (Pearson and Cooper 1998).

Public access to sex offender information under California's legislative scheme has two major implications concerning the confidentiality accorded to sex offenders and the public's sense of safety. First, the degree of sex offenders' privacy actually increases as a result of the use of the access-driven legislation in California (Burns 1999). Since the public will have to make the effort, and likely pay a small fee, to access the sex offender registry information, one author suggests that "fewer people will make that effort to request the information than would see it if it were broadcast publicly" (Burns 1999). Because the risk of widespread dissemination is limited, the risk to invasions of privacy becomes minimized.

A counterargument suggests that independent Web sites may undermine these privacy concerns, because many have the legal capability of publishing a sex offender's personal information. However, citizens who access registry information will be punished if they violate the statute's confidentiality provisions. California's statute mandates that all citizens who access the registry must sign a statement stating that they understand the intended uses of the information that they will receive [*Penal Code*, sec. 290.4(a)(4)(A) (1996)]. The statute provides for stiff penalties, including imprisonment and/or a fine up to $1,000 should anyone violate its confidentiality provisions [*Penal Code*, secs. 290.4 (b)(2) and (c) (1996)]. Therefore, although the availability and accessibility of sex offender registry information has the potential to empower those California citizens and their communities should they utilize it, the law does provide some protection for those individuals subject to it.

But how safe will this technology really make the public feel? Some critics argue that community notification, especially through 900 lines and the CD-ROM, fosters a false sense of security within communities. Kim English, Director of Research at the Colorado Division of Criminal Justice, expressed concern that the notification lists may actually make people drop their guard. She stated in an interview on the MSNBC Web page that "[people] get this feeling that you go on the Web and get a list of people and addresses and you'll be safe. But research shows the scary people are the ones more likely to be in your family" (Sommerfield 2000). English added that many sex offenders remain unregistered, and those are the identities with which the public needs to be concerned. In contrast, many citizens have reacted more vigilantly with respect to crimes against women and children. The registry acts primarily as a tool that parents can use to empower themselves, gain trust in their local law enforcement agencies, and protect their families (Sommerfield 2000).

CONCLUSION

The sex offender laws of today embrace what is quickly becoming a hidden and dispersed dimension of crime control. Not only are the methodologies by which offenders are being managed becoming hidden and dispersed throughout the community. The sex offenders themselves are also becoming hidden and dispersed within the registries as bits and pieces of information about the risks and dangers they pose to communities. In this sense, the fact that many of these managerial techniques remain hidden within the context of information yet fairly open to the public clearly illustrates the state of high modernity that our society has entered. When faced with uncertainties and risks in our day-to-day living, we must implement strategies that parallel them.

An interesting facet about the nature of these contemporary sex offender statutes is that they are not really new. California's early registration law emphasized some of the same principles and goals emphasized by today's laws. The difference is the central organizing principle around which the statutory scheme functions. To deal with the risks that sex offenders pose to the public, especially its children, communities must "fight" with risk-oriented strategies of management on a large scale. Based on the level of popular and judicial support given to these sex offender laws, it is likely that this legislative trend against sexual assault and sexual abuse will continue.

NOTES

1. An additional change occurred when Congress enacted the Pam Lychner Sexual Offender Tracking and Identification Act (42 U.S.C. § 14072 [1996]). This act authorizes stricter registration requirements for the most serious and habitual sex offenders and requires the Federal Bureau of Investigation (FBI) to establish a National

Sex Offender Registry (NSOR) to enable law enforcement agencies and criminal justice officials to track sex offenders across state lines.

2. According to Giddens, characteristics of modernity include capitalism, institutions of surveillance, nation-states, and the rise of the large organization that has become more self-reflexive. *Late* modernity refers to the increased rate and speed of social change and extreme dynamism and discontinuity in terms of time-space relations (Giddens 1991).

3. Patty Wetterling made this statement. Her eleven-year-old son was abducted in 1989 in Minnesota. Mrs. Wetterling pushed for federal legislation in 1994 requiring states to maintain a registry of sex offenders. States that failed to have one in effect by 1999 were to lose federal funds.

4. Despite this satisfaction, a call to the SOIL will not allow the public to view photographs of sex offenders and does not allow a search of the database using incomplete search terms or missing data, such as "Smit*" to search for Smith or Smits (Pearson and Cooper 1998).

5. At the time of this writing, I am not sure if Randy Rossi still holds that position at the California DOJ. He is quoted in the NCJA Policy and Practice report.

6. Tennessee's law will require the TBI to create a similar system. However, the state must wait until the federal appeals court has made a decision before the TBI can implement community notification procedures.

7. The California legislature recently made several changes to Megan's Law. Under AB 1320, signed by Governor Gray Davis on September 26, 2000, children accompanied by a parent or guardian will be able to view the CD-ROM. The bill, which was sponsored by Attorney General Bill Lockyer, also extends the expiration date of Megan's Law to January 1, 2004 (Bee Capitol Bureau 2000).

8. Much of the information on the implementation of the CD-ROM was provided to NCJA by Mike Van Winkle, public information officer with the DOJ at the time of the report.

9. The changes reflect updates, new offender information, and additional corrections made to the registry database itself.

10. The DOJ also stated that the state has not received specific complaints regarding the inclusion of incorrect information on the CD-ROM. The NCJA report stated that a concerned citizen had a common name that happened to be the same name as that of an offender whose name was included on the CD-ROM. As it turned out, the file contained enough identifying information so that viewers could determine that the concerned person and the offender were, in fact, two different people.

11. For example, the KlaasKids National Child Safety Awareness Project allows the KlaasKids Foundation to provide services and information designed to protect America's children. The KlaasKids Foundation aims to raise awareness about this important issue and provide a bio-document containing fingerprints, photographs, and child safety information to families. See http://www.sentrykids.com/; KlaasKids Foundation, The Polly Klaas Story, http://www.klaaskids.org/pg-stry.html; http://www.klaaskids.org/pg-calendar.html. The Foundation also created its own Web page, http://www.klaaskids.org/, which has enabled this organization to disseminate its message and information nationwide. It also provides Internet text links to other

Web pages dealing with missing and exploited children, children's rights issues, and legislation. One Web page features a presentation of Megan's Law in all fifty states. See http://www.klaaskids.org/pg-legmeg.html

12. The states include Alabama, Alaska, Connecticut, Delaware, Florida, Georgia, Indiana, Iowa, Kansas, Michigan, North Carolina, South Carolina, Texas, Utah, Virginia, and West Virginia.

References

Adams, D.B. 1999. *Summary of state sex offender registry dissemination procedures.* Report prepared for Bureau of Justice Statistics, U.S. Deptartment of Justice: Washington DC: U.S. Government Printing Office.

Bee Capitol Bureau. 2000. Megan's law extended. *Sacramento Bee,* September 27, sec. A, p. 4.

Burns, M. 1999. Do sexual predators have the right to privacy? Confidentiality provisions for registered sex offenders in California and Massachusetts. [article on-line]. Accessed May 9, 2000. Available from http://www.cs.cmu.edu /~burnsm/SOR.html. Internet.

California. *Penal Code.* 1999.

California Department of Justice. 1998. *California's Megan's Law—the First Year: Lifting the Shroud of Secrecy.* Office of the Attorney General.

Cote, S. 2000. Modernity, risk, and contemporary crime control strategies as risk management: an analysis of sex offender statutes and the shift toward a risk society. Ph.D. dissertation, State University of New York at Buffalo. Ann Arbor, Mich.: UMI, 2000. 99-58253.

Faulkner, N. 1997. Sex offender notification law protects children [article on-line]. Accessed February 2, 1999. Available from http://www.prevent-abuse-now.com/news2.htm. Internet.

Giddens, A. 1991. *Modernity and Self-Identity: Self and Society in the Late Modern Age.* Stanford: Stanford University Press.

Jacob Wetterling crimes against children and sexually violent registration act. 1994. Pub. L. 103–322, 42 U.S.C. § 14071. 1994.

Megan's law, Pub. L. 104-145, 42 U.S.C. § 14071(d). 1996.

"Megan's law" taken online [article on-line]. Accessed May 9, 2000. Available from http//news.cnet.com/news//0-1005-200-321359.html. Internet.

National Criminal Justice Association. 1999. *Sex Offender Registration and Notification: Problem Avoidance and Barriers to Implementation and Sex Offender Registration and Notification Costs Survey Results.* Washington, DC: U.S. Department of Justice.

Office of the Attorney General. Megan's law in California: How to obtain information by telephone [report on-line]. Accessed May 9, 2000. Available from http://caag.state.ca.us/megan/phoneinfo.htm. Internet.

Pearson, L., and S. Cooper. 1998. Sex offender registries and community notification: States' use of technology for public safety. *Policy and Practice,* 1–8. Washington, DC: National Crime and Justice Association.

Sommerfield, J. Are online registries unfair? Web sites listing sex offenders accompanied by controversy [article on-line]. Accessed May 9, 2000. Available from
http://msnbc.com/news/298815.asp. Internet.

Warner, G. Click of mouse will display full list of sex offenders. 2000. *The Buffalo
News*, May 6, sec. B, p.1.

14

Revisiting Megan's Law and Sex Offender Registration: Prevention or Problem

Robert E. Freeman-Longo

INTRODUCTION: AN OVERVIEW OF REGISTRATION AND NOTIFICATION LAWS

Public notification of sex offender release has been in place as a national policy since 1996. In 1994, the Jacob Wetterling Crimes Against Children and Sexually Violent Offender Registration Act was enacted. The Jacob Wetterling Act required all states to establish stringent registration programs for sex offenders by September 1997, including the identification and registration of lifelong sexual predators. The Jacob Wetterling Act is a national law that is designed to protect children and was named after Jacob Wetterling, an eleven-year-old boy who was kidnapped in October 1989. Jacob is still missing. Megan's Law, the first amendment to the Jacob Wetterling Crimes Against Children and Sexually Violent Offenders Act, was passed in October 1996. Megan's Law mandated all states to develop notification protocols that allow public access to information about sex offenders in the community. Megan's Law was named after Megan Kanka, a seven-year-old girl who was raped and murdered by a twice convicted child molester in her New Jersey neighborhood.

Sensationalized cases, such as the rape and murder of seven-year-old Megan Kanka of Hamilton, New Jersey, have shocked and angered our society. The public is rightfully outraged at the nation's level of crime, particularly sexual crimes. Unfortunately, the public response is often more emotional than logical. During the 1990s, many legislative actions regarding sex offenders appeared to result from emotional public response to violent crime rather than from research showing that these laws will make any difference in correcting the problem and reducing crime. The laws sound and feel good when they are passed, but they may give citizens a false sense of security. Public notification of sex offender release, Megan's Law, is one example of "feel-good legislation" that has led to harmful conditions rather than the betterment or safety of society.

The first law to address the registration of sex offenders was passed in California in 1947. In 1990, the State of Washington passed its Community Protection Act that had a provision for notifying the public about sex offenders (National Criminal Justice Association). Presently, all fifty states have sex offender registration laws[1] (twenty-seven states require some or all juveniles adjudicated for sex offenses to register[2]); and all fifty states have sex offender public notification laws.[3] Most of the states that register juveniles also do some kind of notification in certain situations.[4] Additionally, sixteen states now have laws providing for the indefinite civil commitment of sex offenders to state mental institutions[5] (S. Matson, personal communication, January 26, 2000).

Revisiting Megan's Law and Sex Offender Registration

Portions of the Jacob Wetterling Act, including Megan's Law, are examples of legislation that was passed quickly, without securing public opinion through polls or community meetings. Necessary, detailed research was not conducted into the cost involved, the resources necessary to implement the laws, and the potential impact on law-abiding citizens. Professionals working with and treating sexual abusers and the national organizations that focus on sexual aggression (i.e., The Association for the Treatment of Sexual Abusers, The National Adolescent Perpetrator Network, The American Professional Society on the Abuse of Children) were not contacted or asked for input into these laws.

Since the passage of the Jacob Wetterling Act and Megan's Law, there have been many instances of violence toward sexual abusers and innocent persons. Some states have posted registration lists and notification materials on compact disks (CDs) and the Internet. Numerous problems have occurred, including, among others, innocent families being harassed, victims of sexual abuse being identified, and private residences of law-abiding citizens being posted on registries and the Internet as the residences of sex offenders. Some states have applied these laws retroactively, resulting in persons charged with indecent exposure for urinating publicly being labeled as sex offenders. Other states have applied registration and notification laws to youth, labeling children as sex offenders for life. The list of problems does not stop here.

This chapter builds on the author's previous work that addresses the potential impact of public notification on the greater community, including citizens, families, victims, and offenders (Freeman-Longo 1996a, 1996b). This chapter includes problems and case examples with sex offender registration laws in addition to Megan's Law since the two laws are now part of the Jacob Wetterling Act and are so closely linked. Case examples from the news media and professional contacts, and information from colleagues are used to illustrate the reality of the impact of Megan's Law and sex offender registration laws four years after they were passed. To acquire as many case examples and articles as possible from different regions of the United States, a request for information regarding Megan's Law and sex offender registration on a professional list-serve run by The Association for the Treatment of Sexual Abusers (ATSA) was posed on this Internet site. An Internet list-serve run by The Center for Sex Offender Management (CSOM) also was used to post requests for case examples. Further, word of mouth among professional friends and colleagues and requests of organizations such as Cure-Sort proved very helpful in providing case examples and newspaper articles addressing both laws. Many more case examples and news articles were submitted than could be realistically incorporated into this chapter. Those cited are representative of the cases and issues associated with the implementation of these laws. The following is the original list of concerns and impact issues that might result from public notification of sex offender release with brief explanations of each point. While not an exhaustive list, it provides some of the more pressing points to consider regarding this law. The numbering of each point does not indicate relative importance, but rather is used for ease of reference.

The Problems with Megan's Law and Sex Offender Registration

Origins of Public Notification. Initially, public notification laws were proposed in response to the public's reactions to horrific crimes. Often, these crimes have been rape-murders, or extremely violent assaults on victims. Contrary to public belief, the vast majority of sexual offenses do not involve murder or violent assault of the victim. In fact, rape-murders and sadistic assaults account for less than 3 percent of all committed sex offenses. Unfortunately, Megan's Law and sex offender registration laws have been used even in cases involving incest and have resulted in families and victims being identified and harassed. In a recent article, as a result of a class action suit, a federal judge has ordered New Jersey to rework its Megan's Law and threatened to shut down the notification process if prosecutors cannot put tighter controls on who receives information (Associated Press 2000). Judge Irenas noted that New Jersey has failed to implement consistent standards of how notifications were conducted.

Lack of Supporting Data Determining the Efficacy of Public Notification. At the time this chapter was written, states with public notification laws had not yet offered scientific evidence to support the efficacy of such laws in promoting community protection and safety. Washington, which passed a public notification law in 1990, preceding Megan's Law, is the only state that has researched the efficacy of its public notification law. The State of Washington found no reduction in sex crimes against children; however, a benefit was the level of community education regarding sex crimes (Matson and Lieb 1996). At this writing, there are no other published studies that demonstrate the efficacy of Megan's Law.

Cost. Public notification requires continuous monitoring by public service agencies (police, courts, and probation and parole agencies) to ensure offender compliance. All states have had to finance the costs of this mandated law (which did not come with funding for implementation). States face losing federal funding if they do not implement the law, but they do not have the resources necessary to implement it properly. Many states report that the registered addresses are not updated, and in many cases, incorrect addresses have been given. Many states post these on the Internet, listing innocent people's addresses as those of convicted sex offenders. Additional and unexpected costs also have been associated with these laws (such as the following examples), further taxing social and criminal justice agencies (Sex offender notification laws . . . 1997).

In Antelope Valley, California, the state had to pay a sex offender's rent because convicted sex offenders cannot live within thirty-five miles of the victim's residence or employment. California law requires that convicted sex offenders live within the county of their last known residence. However, in one case, a convicted child molester had to move (at the request of the victim's family) to a different county than the one in which he originally resided to meet the provisions of the penal code requiring him to live at least thirty-five miles away from the victim's residence. Upon release, the paroled offender had no place to live and no means to move to a new home in a different county. Without the state paying his rent, he would have been homeless and in violation of his parole. The funds came from a portion of California's general fund for state corrections (Matros 1998; Fox News).

Some states, including Virginia, have reported that the initial cost of setting up registration and notification has been as high as $200,000. Additional costs are an ongoing fiscal challenge, such as those for law enforcement agencies and other agencies in the criminal justice system responsible for maintaining and updating the registries and conducting notification. Despite these costs, most states acknowledge that the registries are not accurate, and 25 percent or more of names and addresses may be incorrect.

Subsequent Violence. Public notification may lead to further violence. Some states already have experienced vigilante activities. The violence is not limited to convicted and registered/notified sex offenders. In many cases, innocent people, mistaken for sex offenders, have been assaulted or had their property damaged.

Among the most notorious cases of violence and vigilantism resulting from Megan's Law was the burning down of a sex offender's house in the State of Washington. Another that occurred in New Jersey involved the mistaken identity of a man who was thought to be a sex offender. His house was broken into, and he was severely beaten, resulting in the need for hospitalization.

Confidentiality. The American Psychiatric Association's *Diagnostic and Statistical Manual of Mental Disorders-IV* classifies the sexual abuse of children under a diagnostic category known as pedophilia. Public notification laws require that this mental health/medical diagnosis be made public, whereas many other harmful conditions and behaviors remain private.

The use of confidentiality waivers is commonplace in working with sex offenders. Unfortunately, when the details of their lives and crimes are posted on public registries and divulged through notification, it is not only the offenders' confidentiality that is violated. Through the misuse and abuse of these laws, the names and addresses of families and, in some cases, the victims of sexual abuse are revealed.

Constitutional Rights. The constitutionality of registration and public notification laws and an individual's right to privacy have undergone considerable debate. State registries on the Internet have increased the problem around these issues. It is no longer a community that knows about a specific offender, his address, and the particulars about his crime, but the entire world—anyone with access to the Internet—can have access to this information.

Federal laws regarding sex offender registries, public notification, and now those laws that address sexual predators and civil commitment also have been under legal scrutiny.

There have been, and continue to be, legal challenges to registration and notification laws in several states. However, predator laws are now beginning to come under fire. On January 10, 2000, the Supreme Court "refused to revive Pennsylvania's law requiring that some sex offenders be designated as 'sexually violent predators' subject to lifetime registration and public notice of their address." The law was struck down and labeled as "constitutionally repugnant" (Asseo 2000).

Beyond Punishment. Legal scholars and others have looked at public notification as a form of punishment. There are several examples of how professionals and others have used this law beyond the way it was designed. For example, in some cases, law enforcement personnel have organized neighborhoods to exclude sex offenders from housing. In addition, law enforcement officers and others have released inaccurate information about registered sex offenders and/or those subject to notification laws (P. Dennis, personal communication, December 13, 1999). When these laws harm sex offenders and others, such as families and other community members, beyond the intent of the law, how can one not consider the impact as cruel, unusual, and excessive punishment?

One convicted offender in South Dakota (where there is no law on the books about notification to the community) purchased property four miles outside the city limits, not knowing that the city police chief lived three doors away. The chief went door to door notifying neighbors, which was beyond his authority, and used his position to find out the original criminal charges, which he also disclosed to the neighborhood (Anonymous, personal communication, January 21, 2000).

In extreme cases, being subject to registration and notification laws has resulted in the unnecessary end of life. For example, in Santa Rosa, California, a convicted sex offender, forced to comply with Megan's Law, was found hanging from a tree in his yard, an apparent suicide (Purdum 1998).

Primary Prevention. The best way to stop sexual abuse is to prevent it before it begins. Public notification laws are tertiary prevention efforts at best, and the antithesis of prevention at their worst. When laws result in a decrease in reporting of a particular crime, increased plea-bargaining, and causing harm to innocent people, they cannot be seen as preventive. The arguments used over and over again in favor of sex offender registration and public notification laws has been that if they save one child, they are worth it. But is any law worth harming others, especially innocent persons, for the sake of one?

Most public health officials believe that primary prevention is much less costly and more effective than tertiary prevention. Treating sex offenders is primary prevention, especially when treatment is successful and the abuser no longer reoffends. In New Jersey, one of the side effects from Megan's Law is a reluctance to prosecute juveniles for sex offenses, thus subjecting them to life-long registration. The "diverted" juvenile sex offenders are not getting treatment (Brieling 1998).

False Sense of Security. Public notification is an easy solution to the highly emotional issue of sexual offending. The very nature of the law leads one to believe that by knowing where sex offenders live, one will feel safer. Safety is more than knowing. Some people feel more anxious knowing they now live near a convicted sex offender. Others cannot sell their homes when they want to move and known sex offenders are residing in nearby housing.

In St. Louis, Missouri, more than 700 registered sex offenders, or approximately 46 percent, do not live at the addresses posted on the sex offender registry, and many sex offenders (approximately 285 sex offenders released from prison as of May 1999) never get put on the list (Dunklin 1999). With this and similar situations, can one truly feel more safe? Misinformation can be more damaging than no information.

Terrorizing of the Community. As sex offender registration and public notification laws begin to identify an increasing number of offenders, these laws will create increasing levels of panic and possibly may begin to terrorize communities. One can only feel so safe knowing that there are sex offenders moving into and living in one's neighborhood and community. In some cases there are concentrations of sex offenders living in certain neighborhoods. As numbers increase and citizens become more concerned, more drastic measures to address the issue may result.

In one neighborhood, a residential program for juvenile sexual abusers has been operating for more than ten years. As a result of sex offender registration and notification laws, citizens banned together to have the program moved, despite prior knowledge of its existence in their neighborhood (R. Louks, personal communication, January 20, 2000). Fear of what may happen in the future, versus looking at the absence of incidents in the past, created panic among local residents.

Impact on Victims. Public notification affects more than just offenders. When left to individual state discretion, many states have carried these laws to the extreme.

In Virginia, these laws have had an impact on victims and the families of convicted sex offenders. In one case, the wife and family (including the daughter who was also the victim) were harassed when the registry went on the Internet and their address was posted, even though the offender was sentenced to prison where he will remain incarcerated for some time. Despite the offender being in prison, his family's address was posted on the Internet as the address of a convicted sex offender (O'Brien 1999).

Impact on Others. The impact of public notification goes well beyond the offender and, in some cases, even beyond the victim. Highly publicized cases have demonstrated a severe and negative impact on the victim's family and the offender's family. In other instances, innocent persons, incorrectly identified as sex offenders, have been harassed and assaulted.

In Dallas, Texas, a man mistaken as a child molester was beaten, and four of his front teeth were knocked out by four men as they shouted, "Child molester" (Lydia 1999).

In Virginia, an innocent man targeted by a detective, intent on nailing him for a sex crime, was falsely charged with indecent exposure, was arrested, had his home scoured in his absence, and had his computer and some family photos removed from his home (Jackman 1999).

A civil liberties group wants Michigan State Police to notify citizens if their addresses are placed on the sex offender list on the Internet. Recently, it was discovered that as many as 25 percent of registry addresses were incorrect, which has resulted in citizens having their addresses improperly included on the registry (Webster 1999).

Plea-bargains. Sexual offense cases are often weak in evidence, resulting in plea bargains to lesser offenses. With the coming of sex offender registration and community notification laws, persons charged with sex offenses now have a greater motive to avoid prosecution and to plea-bargain their crimes to lesser, nonsexual crimes. In some cases, social workers and child protection workers are reluctant to report cases involving juvenile sexual abusers to authorities out of concern that these young persons will be subjected to sex offender registration and community notification laws (Freeman-Longo and Blanchard 1998). In these cases many are quietly and privately referring these young persons to sex offender treatment specialists to get them treatment without the negative consequences of the law.

Risk Determination. New Jersey and other states have established levels of public notification based on a determination of the dangerousness of the particular offender in question. There is no consistent tool being used to determine risk, and in many states, risk is not determined by trained professionals or by the use of researched and reliable risk scales. In other cases, risk assessments are misused or misinterpreted to make individuals look more dangerous than they are.

In Washington State, one professional reports several incidents. When sex offenders move into Thurston County, Washington, the Sheriff's Department uses psychosexual evaluations to increase their risk levels, resulting in higher levels of notification under Megan's Law, despite no new crimes and lower risk levels previously determined under Megan's Law. According to the clinicians working with these men, law enforcement is undermining the supervision of the clients who are developmentally delayed sex offenders. Law enforcement is organizing neighborhoods, and in some cases, residents have tried to buy houses to keep sex offenders out of neighborhoods. In the case of one homeless client living in hotels, law enforcement went to each hotel threatening to notify the community, using the hotel's address, unless the hotel kicked out the client (Dennis 1999).

External versus Internal Control. Getting tough on crime, the death penalty, and "three strikes" sentencing options stem from emotional responses to serious societal problems and crime. Such "get tough laws on crime have not always proven to be effective and, in some cases, have made managing crime worse" (Freeman-Longo and Blanchard 1998). Registration and public notification of sex offender release laws appear to be headed down a similar path.

Adversarial Role / Ethical Dilemma. It often happens that professionals who treat sex offenders do not receive professional respect from their colleagues who do not treat, or are opposed to treating, such offenders. Additionally, professionals in other disciplines often see little value in the work done by those who treat sexual abusers. Many of the case examples provided in this chapter have been from professional colleagues who treat sexual abusers. They have provided numerous personal accounts of how their work with other agencies and other professionals has been damaged due to their treating sex offenders.

In one case, a well-established mental health clinic in Webster, New York, opened a sex offender clinic. Word got out, and a nonsex-offending patient threatened to go to the media to suggest that women and children were not safe at the clinic (M. McGrath, personal communication, September 9, 1999).

Undermining Treatment. The majority of sex offender treatment specialists identify similar problem areas for sex offender clients, including (but not limited to) poor anger management skills, fear, lack of trust, low self-esteem, feelings of rejection, inadequate social skills, lack of empathy, isolation from others, and poor communication skills. These skills need to be improved, and that happens when sex offenders have good community support systems and close ties in the community.

Recently, Megan's Law resulted in zoning laws being changed in Colorado. The revised law prohibits more than one sex offender from living in the same residence. This, in turn, led to a residential group home for adolescent sex offenders being required to move from the location it had occupied for more than ten years (Abbott 2000).

One clinician treating sexual abusers in Michigan states, "Many of the adult clients—adult sex offenders—have stated that they are afraid of the 'witch-hunt' that is occurring. At first (about 5 years ago), I passed it off as displacement and projection. . . . When I hear about the registration and notification laws, and the new punitive laws being passed, I wonder if sex offender therapy will even achieve its ultimate goal" (Rosenberg 2000).

Misplaced Responsibility. Public notification places responsibility for community safety and appropriate individual conduct on the community instead of the offender. Treatment is most effective when offenders are required to take total responsibility for their behavior.

Several examples in this chapter illustrate that these laws are having an impact on sex-offender treatment, and in some cases, they are resulting in sex offenders not getting treatment at all. In the absence of treatment, sex offenders will never learn to take responsibility for their behavior and stop the abuse. Unfortunately, sex offender registration and notification laws are impacting quality sex-offender treatment in many states, continuing to put the responsibility for personal safety on potential victims, existing victims, and society—where the responsibility has been all along. These laws have not demonstrated their ability to prevent sex crimes or make communities safer, and it is not likely they will if the first five years have not been able to demonstrate such.

Limiting of the Offender's Ability to Function in the Community. Sex offenders need to learn appropriate skills that assist them in functioning appropriately and safely in the community. In the absence of these skills, they do not function well and are at greater risk of reoffending. Threats, harassment, and fear of reprisal by citizens keep the offender in a state of stress and anxiety and, thus, more likely to reoffend. To function in the community, the offender has to feel a part of the community like anyone else. Sex offender registration and public notification laws compromise the sex offender's ability to do so in a healthy and safe way.

One man who was released from prison in California and was doing well for three years was subjected to Megan's Law when it was implemented in California. He experienced the loss of three jobs and was run out of town twice. After flyers were distributed, the news media showed up at his door, and he was put on television. He knew of two other cases in California where sex offenders also were affected by these laws; one had his car bombed, and the other committed suicide (Anonymous, personal communication).

In Fallon, Nevada, a woman was the recipient of death threats as a result of her husband's arrest for committing a sexual offense and the publication of his crime. Her home was also broken into and extensively damaged, and some of her property was stolen (Garcia 1999). Her husband was in the news for failing to reregister with police in California as a sex offender.

In Milwaukee, Wisconsin, a judge ordered the Department of Health and Family Services to assist an offender, who was being released, to find housing. The Department of Health and Family Services claimed that it was not able to find a place for him to live and was consequently under the threat of a $1,000 per day fine for contempt of court if housing was not found (B. West, personal communication, February 1, 2000).

In Kentucky, a convicted sex offender released from prison had his picture placed in the local newspaper, and he was labeled a high-risk sex offender. He lost his job and housing and ended up living in his car (Breed 1999).

In Lake Oswego, Oregon, a group of residents in a neighborhood were pooling funds to send a registered sex offender to college, preferably out of state or in a different part of the state, to move him out of their neighborhood (Hoppin 1999). In cases like this, I am constantly struck by the lack of concern for others and their neighborhoods or, in this case, the college they send him to. This is an example of the "not in my back yard" (NIMBY) syndrome.

Age of the Offender. Public notification laws often assume that the offender is an adult. With tougher laws, laws waiving youth to adult courts, the public sentiment toward all sex offenders, and the general failure to separate different types of sex offenders by age and risk, juveniles are now subject to sex offender registration and public notification laws in a growing number of states. This is being done without regard for the youths' maturity and developmental stage, or the potential long-term consequences on their lives.

In Michigan, adolescents are now listed on the Internet. In one case, an eleven-year-old was listed improperly, exposing his name to other adult sex offenders who might prey on him (R. Grooters, personal communication, January 24, 1999). In another example from Michigan (where juvenile sex offenders are registered), an eighteen-year-old male who engaged in a "senior prank" of "mooning" the school principal, was convicted of indecent exposure, had to register with the state for twenty-five years, and has his name, address, and crime publicly posted (Rosenberg 2000). In yet another Michigan case, one professional had two juvenile clients who were harassed at school by class-mates as a result of having their names and addresses posted on the Internet (R. Grooters, personal communication, October 22, 1999).

The state of Texas does registration of all sex offenders, children and juve-niles included. The youngest on the list is ten years old. The name and address of this ten-year-old are now posted on the registry for anyone to see (G. Davis, personal communication, November 2, 1999).

In another Texas case, foster parents asked to have two of their foster chil-dren removed from their home to avoid having their address listed on an Internet sex offender registry (G. Davis, personal communication, November 2, 1999). In still another Texas case, a young teen male asked a girl out on a first date. She initially accepted but then turned him down, as his name was on the Internet sex offender registry (G. Davis, personal communication, November 2, 1999).

In Oklahoma, a two-and-one-half-year-old child was placed on a state un-published internal registration system list for youth with sexual behavior prob-lems. The child was seen touching another child and kissing the child (M. Chaffin, personal communication, March 11, 2000).

In recent months, the public has become more aware of the Texas sex of-fender registry's existence through the media. As a result, juvenile probation officers are encountering an unexpected dilemma. In a recent case, a landlord, after looking at the Internet and finding a registered juvenile sex offender resid-ing in his apartment complex, went to the apartment and told the parent of the eleven-year-old boy that they had two days to move out. The probation officer then had to deal with a family that was being evicted, had nowhere to move to, and would be subject to dealing with the sex offender registry and community notification requirements elsewhere. At the same time, the probation officer had to effectively supervise the family with no stability (a moving target) while trying to ensure that treatment services continued (A.T. Aguirre, personal com-munication, March 11, 2000).

An eleven-year-old boy from an upper middle class family in Texas was ad-judicated delinquent for having sexual intercourse with his six-year-old sister. He was sent out of state to an inpatient treatment program for adolescent sex of-fenders. He successfully completed the treatment program, and the staff rec-ommended that he return home. However, the probation officer and the judge denied his return home and ordered his involvement in additional treatment. The boy then successfully completed an outpatient program for children ages six through twelve with sexual behavior problems. His parents drove sixteen hours each month to participate in the program. To meet requirements of the court, the boy wrote an apology letter and participated in a family session in which he apologized to his sister. Following overnight visits in his home, the boy was to be returned to the community. At that point, the judge requested a letter from the treatment provider that could be used to justify not placing the boy on the Texas sex offender registry. Registration would include the boy's name being published in the local newspaper and all schools being notified. After several drafts of carefully worded text by the provider, the judge accepted the letter and did not place the boy on the registry. One year later, the boy, his sister, and the family were functioning well with no further sexual or other behavior problems by the boy (B. Bonner, personal communication, March 11, 2000).

Mentally Ill Sex Offenders. A small percentage of offenders sexually abuse because they suffer from a biological anomaly or a mental illness. Despite this handicap, and the need to be sensitive to people with mental illnesses, once a mentally ill sex offender is registered or subject to notification, they are treated with the same level of disrespect and disregard as other sex offenders.

In Michigan, a forty-seven-year-old mentally ill sex offender was arrested and sentenced to more than five years in prison because he failed to register his name and address with the Sheriff's Department in Saginaw County within ten days of being released from prison after serving a sentence for a rape conviction. His previous address was at a homeless shelter (Tucker 1999). These circumstances only make it more difficult for these men to adjust to society.

Intelligence of the Offender. Many sexual abusers are developmentally disabled. Some are mildly retarded; others have severe learning disabilities. Like the mentally ill, they live in society with a handicap that makes their lives more difficult, and the need to adjust to society more stressful.

In Washington State, one program for developmentally disabled sex offenders has had very negative experiences with Megan's Law. Staff working in the program have received death threats and have been physically assaulted. Clients were harassed, and dead animals were left on the porch of the program (P. Dennis, personal communication, December 13, 1999).

Female Sexual Abusers. Female abusers are being identified in increasing numbers. As of the writing of this chapter, I have not received any cases or news stories regarding the impact of sex offender registration and Megan's Law on females who sexually abuse. In one case I was made aware of, the female sexual abuser was so distraught by the impact of these laws on her life that she requested that the therapist not forward any information about her case, even if made confidential. Given the absence of cases involving female sexual abusers, it may be possible that the public feels less threatened by females who sexually abuse.

Decrease in Reporting. Reports from New Jersey and Colorado indicate that there is a decrease in the reporting of juvenile sexual offenses and incest offenses by family members and victims who do not want to deal with the impact of public notification on their family.

Although reported, many sex crimes are not resulting in convictions, now, or the charges are reduced to nonsexual offenses through plea bargaining. In Michigan, many judges and prosecutors are having a difficult time obtaining convictions for juvenile sex offenders because many jury members do not want to live with the guilt of ostracizing a fifteen-year-old for the majority of his life. Moreover the actual prosecutors, judges, and referees are reluctant to convict these juveniles for the very same reason. They are placing a growing number of juveniles under advisement status. (If the juvenile sex offender completes treatment, the juvenile record is dismissed.) (Rosenberg 2000).

In Idaho, one professional noted that since enacting the juvenile registry law, actual juvenile sex offenses are down approximately 85 percent. Original charges are being reduced to unspecified "battery" charges in order to avoid the registry law (Meyers 1999).

Other Issues

Besides the issues already addressed, there have been additional negative effects on offenders and others that have been the direct result of sex offender registration and notification laws. Some were hard to foresee; others are simply a matter of technology and advancement. These are addressed briefly next.

Real Estate. Real estate does not sell when potential buyers learn that a sex offender lives in the neighborhood (Hoppin 1999). In New Jersey, it is not legal to advise prospective buyers that there is a registered sex offender in the neighborhood (K. Singer, personal communication, February 2, 2000). In contrast, in Cleveland, Ohio, one large real estate company is asking on the disclosure statement form (along with the leaky basement, radon, and roof questions) whether the sellers have ever been notified of a registered sex offender living in their neighborhood (Fazekas 2000).

In Detroit, a couple trying to sell their home had their address incorrectly included on a sex offender registry list. After reporting the error, the couple was informed by police that the police department could not remove the listing until they could track down the former owner of the house who bought their house three years earlier from a sex offender (Associated Press 1998).

Use of Technology. Today's world is full of technological advances that have advanced communications beyond dreams and expectations. CD-ROMs can store large amounts of data on a small plastic disk. The Internet makes it possible to put information in large quantities on the World Wide Web for access by anyone. These technologies also have the potential to spread harm as quickly as they spread knowledge and information.

A growing number of states are posting sex offender registries and notification announcements on the Internet. Many of these lists are not kept updated, as mentioned previously, and as many as 25 percent of the materials listed on them are incorrect (W. Bowers, personal communication, February 2, 2000).

Abuses of the Law. There is a saying that goes, "Laws were meant to be broken." Certainly we know that people take advantage of the law in many instances, and apparently sex offender registration and notification laws are no different.

Several states (Florida, Minnesota, and Washington) are considering laws that restrict residency options for sex offenders. In Minnesota, there is an effort to create a law that addresses the problem of sex offenders congregating in certain neighborhoods (usually poor inner-city neighborhoods). Several landlords now target sex offenders as potential renters, therefore creating clusters of sex offenders in particular neighborhoods (Hout 2000). In Washington, a proposed law would prohibit sex offenders from residing within a mile of their victims (O'Connell 2000).

A company that falsely identified itself as a state agency mailed postcards to all registered sex offenders asking for information correction. The card, being a postcard and therefore not sealed, let mailmen know addresses of registered sex offenders (G. Davis, personal communication, October 8, 1999).

In California, a sex offender moved to a small town, put all of his money into buying a plumbing business, and registered, as was required by law. Despite his being a low-risk offender (his offense was a very minor, one-time offense), and the fact that his registration was not intended for public notification, word got out after he registered that he was a convicted sex offender. As a result of the leak of information, he lost his business (C. Steen, personal communication, October 5, 1999).

CONCLUSION

There is no doubt that unexpected problems and blatant abuses of sex offender registration and notification laws have occurred. Many of these were foreseeable and could have been avoided with more planning, research, and forethought about potential problems. With the writing of this chapter, I hope that we will not take another five or six years to revise these laws. The laws need to be more uniform between states, less punitive and destructive to sex offenders, less destructive to the lives of innocent persons, and more preventive (even though prevention will only occur in a limited way with these laws). Until we look at them closely and research their potential effectiveness, laws designed to protect our citizens may instead do more damage than if they did not exist at all.

NOTES

1. Massachusetts is having difficulties in the courts with their public notification law. This is related to the severe retroactivity of the statute (1981) and the appeals process for risk determination.

2. Arizona, California, Colorado, Delaware, Florida, Idaho, Indiana, Iowa, Kansas, Kentucky, Louisiana, Massachusetts, Michigan, Minnesota, Mississippi, Montana, New Jersey, North Carolina, Oregon, Rhode Island, South Carolina, South Dakota, Texas, Utah, Virginia, Washington, and Wisconsin.

3. Technically, Vermont's program is not adequate (the legislature has not enacted a federally compliant version) and New Mexico has not yet started notifying. Massachusetts is having legal difficulties; see note 1.

4. California, Colorado, Idaho, Minnesota, Mississippi, Missouri, North Carolina, and South Dakota register juveniles, but do not perform notification on them. The remaining states in note 2 perform notification.

5. Arizona, California, Florida, Illinois, Iowa, Kansas, Massachusetts, Minnesota, Missouri, New Jersey, North Dakota, South Carolina, Texas, Virginia, Washington, and Wisconsin.

References

Abbott, K. 2000, February 14. Group homes in peril. *Denver Rocky Mountain News*, p. 5A.

Asseo, L. 2000, January 10. Court won't revive PA predator law. Associated Press.

Associated Press. 1998, November 27. Couple battling Net sex registry. *Lansing State Journal*, p. A8.

Associated Press. 2000, January 27. Judge: Megan's law must be rewritten. *The Rutland Daily Herald* (Trenton, NJ), p. 2.

Breed, A.G. 1999, September 1. Ky. Couple takes in sex offender. Associated Press.

Brieling, J. 1998, August 27. The Association for the Treatment of Sexual Abusers list-serve, public posting.

Dennis, P. 1999, October 2. The Association for the Treatment of Sexual Abusers list-serve, public posting.

Dunklin, R. 1999, May 2. About 700 sex offenders do not appear to live at the addresses listed on a St. Louis registry. Many sex offenders never make the list. *St. Louis Post Dispatch*.

Fazekas, D. 2000, February 2. The Association for the Treatment of Sexual Abusers list-serve, public posting.

Fox News. 1999, August 11. Massachusetts's Court: Sex offenders must get hearing. Http://foxnews.com/js_index.sml?content/news/national/ 0811/d_ap_0811_206.sml.

Freeman-Longo, R.E. 1996a. Feel good legislation: Prevention or calamity. *Child Abuse & Neglect* 20 (2): 95–101.

———. 1996b. Prevention or problem. *Sexual Abuse: A Journal of Research & Treatment*, 8 (2): 91–100.

Freeman-Longo, R.E., and G.T. Blanchard, 1998. *Sexual Abuse in America: Epidemic of the 21*st *century*. Brandon, VT: Safer Society Press.

Garcia, M. 1999, February 9. Woman says she's being harassed after husband's arrest published. *Lahontan Valley News/Fallon Eagle Standard*, p. 1.

Hoppin, E. 1999, October 19. Neighbors consider sending a registered sex offender to college to keep him out of Lake Oswego. *The Oregonian.*

Hout, S.J. 2000, January 31. The Association for the Treatment of Sexual Abusers list-serve, public posting.

Jackman, T. 1999, November 8. Wrong man's arrest leads to nightmare. *The Washington Post.*

Lydia, A. 1999, November 4. Is sex-offender registry accurate? New York: The Associated Press.

Matros, S. 1998, October 20. State to pay molester's rent. *Valley Press.*

Matson, S., and Lieb, R. 1996. Sex offender community notification: A review of laws in 32 states. Washington State Institute for Public Policy. Evergreen College, Olympia, WA.

Meyers, R. 1999, October 24. The Association for the Treatment of Sexual Abusers list-serve, public posting.

National Criminal Justice Association. 1998, Summer. Sex offender registries and community notification: States' use of technology for public safety. *Policy and Practice.* Washington, DC: Author.

O'Brien, K. 1999, July 11. Mom: Sex offender registry also hurts victims. *The Roanoke Times.*

O'Connell, M. 2000, January 31. The Association for the Treatment of Sexual Abusers list-serve, public posting.

Purdum, T.S. 1998, July 9. Death of sex offender tied to Megan's Law. *The New York Times.*

Rosenberg, M. 2000, February 2. The Association for the Treatment of Sexual Abusers list-serve, public posting.

Sex offender notification laws add to criminal justice system workloads. 1997, April 15. *Criminal Justice Newsletter* 28 (8): 3–5.

Tucker, D.Q. 1999, November 3. Unregistered sex offender goes to prison. *The Saginaw News.*

Washington's civil commitment law studied by other states and used as model to avoid. (2000, January). *Newsletter.* Bothell, WA: Whitestone Foundation, p. 1.

Webster, S. A. 1999, May 18. ACLU: Sex offense list error-filled: State, not individuals should verify names organization says. *The Detroit News.*

Index

About the Contributors

FRANCES P. BERNAT is an Associate Professor in Adminsitration of Justice at Arizona State University West. Dr. Bernat's research has been focused on criminal law, its policy and application. Her most recent research includes the study of crime and the fear of crime among elderly populations, the nature and extent of crime committed by youth, and the degree to which social service programs can reduce recidivism among youthful offenders. In 1998, Dr. Bernat received several awards, including the following: Governor's Spirit of Excellence Award from Governor Hull, State of Arizona; Innovations in American Government, Semi-Finalist Award, Ford Foundation and the John F. Kennedy School of Government at Harvard University in partnership with the Council of Excellence in Government. She has articles forthcoming in the *Encyclopedia of Criminology and Deviant Behavior*, the *Encyclopedia of Women and Crime*, the *Social Science Journal*, and *Journal of Criminal Justice Education*.

SUZETTE COTE is currently an Assistant Professor in the Division of Criminal Justice at California State University, Sacramento. Having recently completed her dissertation, *Modernity, Risk, and Contemporary Crime Control Strategies as Risk Management: An Analysis of Sex Offender Statutes and the Shift toward a Risk Society*, she is presently focusing her research interests in the areas of sex offender legislation, moral panics, and the effectiveness of the legislation as it has been implemented in California and nationwide. Other research interests and areas include gender, crime, and the media; juvenile justice; sociology of law; penology; and theoretical criminology.

CHARLES CRAWFORD is an Assistant Professor of Sociology at Western Michigan University. He has recently published in the areas of race and punishment, police use of force, suspect resistance at arrest, and the use of media in teaching. His current research involves the study of situational factors in police use of force, gender and sentencing, and media construction of crime events. Currently he teaches Sociology of Law Enforcement, Correctional Process at the undergraduate level, and Violence and Firearms in American Society at the graduate level, as well as conducting evaluation research for the Kalamazoo Department of Public Safety.

GIANNETTA DEL BOVE is a Research Associate in the Child Psychiatry Program at the Center for Addictions and Mental Health where she is conducting research on young offenders. She has recently graduated from the Master's program in Counseling Psychology at the University of Toronto. Her research interests include psychology and law, feminist theory, and child development.

MARGARET A. DENIKE is an Assistant Professor and Coordinator of Women's Studies at Nippising University in North Bay, Ontario, Canada. She is the former president of the National Association of Women and the Law (NAWL), a national nonprofit equality-seeking organization that engages in lobbying, legal education, and law reform. She sits on the Advisory Council to the Law Commission of Canada and is a member of the Equality Advisory Committee to the Court Challenges Program of Canada.

DAVID N. DIBARI holds degrees in both psychology and anthropology, and is currently working on his Master of Criminal Justice degree at the University of Colorado. He is employed in the law enforcement field where he works in the investigations division. His field of expertise is rape, sexual assault, child abuse, and domestic violence. He also volunteers for the victim assistance program at five different law enforcement agencies. He is co-author of "Is It Sex Yet? Theoretical and Practical Implications of the Debate Over Rapists' Motives," which appeared in the Spring 1999 Edition of *Jurimetrics Journal of Law, Science and Technology*.

ROBERT E. FREEMAN-LONGO is an independent consultant, educator, trainer, and author dedicated to sexual abuse prevention and treatment based in Vermont. Robert is co-founder and first President of the Association for the Treatment of Sexual Abusers and served as Director of the Safer Society Foundation, Inc. and the Safer Society Press from 1993 through 1998. In addition, Rob has published more than thirty articles and book chapters in the field of sexual abuse treatment.

JAMES F. HODGSON is an Associate Professor of Criminal Justice and the Criminal Justice Program Coordinator at Ferrum College. His current research interests are policing, juvenile delinquency, and social and criminal justice policies and practices. He is the author of *Games Pimps Play: Pimps, Players, and Wives-in-law: A Qualitative Analysis of Street Prostitution* and *The Criminal Justice System: Alternative Measures,* and has published articles on policing, juvenile delinquency, and social consciousness.

DEBRA S. KELLEY is an Associate Professor in the Department of Sociology and Anthropology at Longwood College. Her research interests are in the areas of violence against women, the practices of criminal justice agencies, and research methodology. Currently she is involved in several research projects including one on the role of victim witness advocates in criminal justice environments.

VIVIAN B. LORD is an Associate Professor of Criminal Justice at the University of North Carolina at Charlotte. Dr. Lord's areas of research interest include police selection and practices, law enforcement assisted suicide, and workplace violence.

ELIZABETHANN O'SULLIVAN, Associate Professor and Director, Graduate Public Administration Programs at North Carolina State University, helped found the D.C. Rape Crisis Center in 1972. Her current research focuses on program evaluation and interorganizational relations.

CRAIG T. PALMER is an Instructor of Anthropology at the University of Colorado at Colorado Springs. His research interests include human sexuality, religion, altruism, and ecology. He has done extensive fieldwork in Newfoundland.

GARY RASSEL is Associate Professor of Political Science and Coordinator of the Master of Public Adminstration Program at the University of North Carolina at Charlotte. Dr. Rassel's areas of research interest include state and local government administration, research methodology, public budgeting and finance, and welfare reform.

K. EDWARD RENNER is an Adjunct Research professor at Carleton University. He works as a consultant in the areas of sexual abuse and assault and evaluation research.

LANA STERMAC is a professor in the Counseling Psychology program at the University of Toronto and a research consultant at the Sexual Assault Care Centre of Sunnybrook and Women's College Health Sciences Center. Her research interests are in forensic psychology and psychology and law. She has written several articles in the area of sexual aggression, specifically on the victim-assailant relationship and on risk factors associated with adult re-victimization.

RANDY THORNHILL is Regents' Professor and Professor of Biology at the University of New Mexico. Over the last ten years, he has focused his research on the evolution of human sexuality. He is the co-author of the recent (2000) book, *A Natural History of Rape: Biological Bases of Sexual Coercion*, Cambridge, MA: MIT Press.

LIVY A. VISANO is Associate Professor of Sociology at York University. Livy Visano is the former Dean of Atkinson College at York University. He has numerous regional and province wide Awards for Outstanding Teaching. He has an extensive publication record, which includes *Teaching Controversy* (with L. Jakubowski) 1998 (forthcoming 2002); *Crime and Culture: Refining the Traditions* (1987); *This Idle Trade* (1992); *Canadian Penology: Advanced Perspectives and Research* (with K. McCormick) (1992); *Understanding Policing* (with K. McCormick) (1983): *Deviant Designations: Crime, Law and Deviance in Canada* (with T. Fleming) (reprinted 1987), and a dozen articles in refereed journals.